The New Asian Women

Women's Magazine and Spread of Mass Culture

The New Asian Women

Women's Magazine and Spread of Mass Culture

A K Yadav

MD Publications Pvt Ltd
New Delhi
www.mdppl.com

Published by :

MD Publications Pvt Ltd
"MD House", 11, Darya Ganj,
New Delhi-110 002
Phone : +91-11-45355555
E-mail : contact@mdppl.com
Website : www.mdppl.com

ISBN : 978-81-7533-294-2

Published and Printed by Mr. Pranav Gupta on behalf of **MD Publications Pvt Ltd** at Printext, New Delhi.

PREFACE

There is a large variety of magazines throughout Asia, ranging from regional types that cover local topics to international types that cover an entire country. But a magazine that covers a wide region beyond just a single city or country is something of a rarity. In the very early women's press, the contents were predominantly literature, with a lesser amount of personal advice. What distinguished women's magazines was the personal nature of the material. When general magazines diversified into women's magazines, they merely moved all of the personal or private queries into the Lady's section, while questions of science and philosophy remained in the general publication. Women continued to submit scientific and philosophical questions to the general issue, while personal questions submitted by men were printed in the ladies edition.

As stated, the roles of women's magazines, as educators, as virtual communities and as trade papers, are interrelated. The areas that magazines choose to educate their readers in, and the elements that define the trade of housewife are aspects of the community created and represented by magazines. While magazines have long been profit-making ventures, they would not have been possible without the complicity of the reader. They do not serve as clear examples of an ideology imposed upon women by an outside source. They also do not serve as a clear or simple indicator of women's ideas or history. Women did have other reading material, and these magazines cannot be said to represent every aspect of women's interests, however popular. Also, many of these magazines have had very influential editors, such as Sarah Hale or Edward Bok, and can also be viewed in part as the work of those individuals.

These publications do, however, serve as a wonderful window onto the culture of their times.

Another role women's magazines have played from the start is as a source of education, as well as an arena for debate and promotion of education for women. More importantly, one of the unique features of magazines, as mentioned above, is that they allow for two-way communication between readers and writers. Oftentimes, the distinction between reader and writer was blurred, as when readers sent in contributions, or when frequent contributors became editors. The reoccurring nature of magazines may have something to do with the emergence of this two-way communication.

I am very grateful to Mr. Pranav Gupta, Director of MD Publications Pvt Ltd, New Delhi, for his kind cooperation and support for this book.

A K Yadav

Contents

	Preface	*v*
1.	Trends of Asian Women in Melodramatic Constructions	1
2.	Women in India and Spread of Mass Culture	35
3.	Malaysia in the Front-Line State	103
4.	What's Different in the New Asia	131
5.	Women and Change: Understanding Social Roles	163
6.	Family Roles and their Modification	213
	Bibliography	241
	Index	245

1

Trends of Asian Women in Melodramatic Constructions

A structure belonging to modern Western culture can doubtless be seen in its historiography: intelligibility is established through a relation with the other; it moves (or 'progresses') by changing what it makes of its 'other' - the Indian, the past, the people, the mad, the child, the Third World. Through these variants that are all heteronomous - ethnology, history, psychiatry, pedagogy - unfolds a problematic form basing its mastery of expression upon what the other keeps silent, and guaranteeing the interpretative work of a science (a 'human' science) by the frontier that separates it from an area awaiting this work in order to be known. [There is] ... a circuit of productivity that draws its capital from others' deprivation while refusing to accept its own presence as endowed ... they choose to see in others' powerlessness an idealized image of themselves and refuse to hear the dissonance between the content and manner of their speech their own complicity with violence.

By naming the academic postures and constructions that surround the subaltern female (a highly heterogeneous and fractured entity) as melodramatic this chapter looks back at the academy, from the insides of the beast that is from the privileges of academia, through the eyes of someone who is at least partially inculcated in its language and habitus. Working through different academic moments, with genres loosely marking them out, the discussion will focus on academic representations of South Asian women, and at the ways in which the subjectivities of academics themselves are related to the subjecthoods we assign to others. In this sense, this chapter is a call for academics to pause in their scholarly tracks and to think about how their own investments are intimately linked to the very postures and productions they produce.

Looking at the historical scholarship on childhood, a discipline that she is a participant in, Carol Steedman notes 'the split between children and "the child" as a figure in academic construction. Locating this split in a transferential relationship, whereby we project our own fantasies of childhood, she asks scholars to 'make plainer to ourselves the arena of romanticism and post-romanticism within which we describe and theorise childhood' with the realization 'that as we watch, talk to, teach and write about children, we desire them, want something from them, which is our own lost childhood'. The body of the subaltern female - in the image of the hybrid metropolitan youth who dons saris and trainers, the sati on the funeral pyre of her husband, the sweatshop worker in the East End of London, the domestic cleaners in the homes, offices and airports of global cities and the 'dextrous' fingers on electronic circuits in free trade zones - is the text upon which a whole array of academic fantasies and anxieties are written.

The benevolence of charity, the calling for salvation, the guilt of class and racial privilege, the excitement of exotica as well as metropolitan hybridity, the longing for revolutionary change and the search for ethical love, all hover around the haloes of these objects (subjects?). Melodrama marks the place of this figure in popular, official and academic, including feminist, Western discourses. Looking at the long routes of academic wisdom alone, in relation to the figure of the South Asian woman it is possible to map at least four melodramatic moments, all of which bear traces of each other. A great many of these conceptualizations and compositions sway between the extremes of victimhood and heroinehood, pity and celebration, even though they are located in competing and diverse theoretical orientations.

Mapping is no doubt always an act of power; it determines what is visible and how it is visible. The voyeurism available to a panoramic view of the world can easily delight in the position of being a superior onlooker, situated on the outside of what one is looking at. The mapping in this chapter is not conducted from a lofty position that pokes fun at the dealings of those who are the subjects of its observation (academics). The view from which my observations are offered has its own positionality. Specific histories lie behind the cartography I chart. Certain observations throughout my academic life have brought me to the particular signature the writing of this chapter carries.

Too often South Asian women in the academy as students and scholars feel the force of relations and conceptions that objectify them within reified frameworks, that offer some sense of eschewed recognition while containing vestiges of personal violation (epistemic, symbolic and bodily) by looking at the some of the effects of the postures and constructions surrounding the academic study of South Asian women. Furthermore, I make a plea for scholars to think about their own investments in the subjects we study and the entities we create. We need to consider our own position in a much more difficult way than what has now become the customary laying out of the 'me' in the usual 'race', class and gender mantra.

Intellectuals are no doubt needed for setting the record straight, in so many respects. Yet at the same time, by raising the plight of the underdogs we can't hide behind the radicalness of our labour. Academics are not outside the power relations that they document. In bearing witness to the ills and joys of the world we also need to be alert to the subjects (as in people) to which we give life in the course of our pronouncements. I am not writing off the radical potential of intellectuals to generate powerful critiques that governments and other power brokers would rather do without. I fully sign up to Edward Said's assertion that the role of the intellectual 'has an edge to it, and cannot be played without a sense of being someone whose place it is publicly to raise embarrassing questions, to confront orthodoxy and dogma (rather than produce them)'.

The 'insiders, experts, coteries, professionals make public opinion "conformist" should be criticised by intellectuals'. Simultaneously we need to be alert to our own academic orthodoxies as these emerge in our midst, as we play the 'big' power wars. Embarrassing questions need to be put to our own 'experts' and 'coteries'. The question this chapter seeks to put on the academic table is, I repeat: How are the subjectivities of academics intimately mingled with the subjecthoods we assign to 'others'? What investments do academics have in the constructions we make and the postures we adopt in this very making? The story of the figure of the South Asian woman in academia has some telling clues for us.

WOMAN'S BURDEN

The first time a student of social theory has to meet the figure of a South Asian woman in academic texts is usually through Emile Durkheim's work on suicide. In textbooks and lecture halls the notion of fatalistic suicide is illustrated with reference to the ghostly figure of sati, the image of a widow burning on a funeral pyre in India. While flames and memories of barbaric, uncivilized Other Eastern cultures where women are held captive and ruthlessly oppressed are certainly ignited, there is, hardly ever, any discussion of how orientalism marks this specific anthropological gaze, which trollops and gallivants around the world, collecting facts and figures, and undertakes the noble task of comparative social analysis for the sake of discovering universal social rules of behaviour.

This of course is the high noon of anthropology. It is the classic moment where distinctions between the West and the Rest give rise to a method of epistemic jurisdiction encased in observations, measurements, categorizations, spectacles and cabinets of curiosity. The bodies of women from these 'Other' places have occupied a central place in the production of difference, between the barbaric and the civilized, the spiritual and the rational, the passive and the strong. All that is seen to be enticing as well as repulsive and in need of correction from these 'Other' places is projected on to these female figures.

Images of downtrodden sensuous women full of eastern promise need to be freed from the captivity of backward cultures by Western discourses run riot in the Western imagination. Representing the white man's as well as the white woman's burden, women from 'Other' places, including South Asian women, have offered a sense of mission to those who have looked to the East for a career, constituting for them a sense of identity as politicians, social reformers, travellers or indeed academics. The particular and interstitial ways in which this politics of salvation is repeated throughout different contexts is of course specific to both time and space. They can, and indeed often do, sit side by side with a politics of celebration. Political, economic, social and institutional locations are incredibly important for appreciating the local contexts out of which the specific idealization, romanticization, pathologization and celebration of the female subaltern arises.

The language of feminism and the liberation of women were used by colonialists, such as Cromer, to mark the boundary between the liberated West and the barbaric East, and thereby to produce a subject position for white colonial masculinity. The irony is that while the men in the Victorian establishment resisted the feminist cause in their own countries, they captured the language of feminism and colonialism and '... redirected it, in the service of colonialism, toward Other men and the cultures of Other men'.

Looking at this from the ghostly figure of the blazing sati, so often repeated in Western discourses, Spivak has famously noted that the abolition of sati and the series of laws that were enacted on behalf of Indian women by the British were a classic case of 'White men saving brown women from brown men', making way for what Rajan describes as a 'trope of chivalry', a rite of passage for young white men into amorous masculinity. The depiction of women who underwent the practice of sati in official accounts as victims or heroines, precluded the possibility of a 'female subjectivity that is shifting, contradictory, inconsistent', but enabled the proliferation of a 'rescue paradigm', which was often tinged by 'voyeuristic pleasure', especially if the sati was tragically considered to be young and beautiful.

It was not, however, only the knight in shining armour who set about saving women in India and other parts of the colonies under the masquerade of the 'rescue paradigm'; Western women, 'Imperial Ladies', also donned this cloak, albeit with a different affectation, to style, perhaps unconsciously, a subject position for themselves. The fashioning of Western women as enlightened agents who took on the mission of relieving the patriarchal plight of women in the colonies was pivotal to the yielding of political rights and agency by Western women.

They could use charitable postures to assert themselves as agents against the exclusionary political agendas of white masculinity in the face of conceptions of the liberal political 'individual' that did not include women. The exclusions in the body politic posed by the 'sexual contract' were undercut by a gendered 'racial contract'. Thus 'in the process of campaigning for women whom they considered to be more badly treated than themselves ... Western women could achieve a subject position for themselves, often at the expense of indigenous women's subject position and sense of agency'. Here we see the beginnings of the 'productive' power of limited representations of Indian women for men and women located in the West.

The image of the passive downtrodden South Asian woman is replicated in what can be identified as a second moment in which Area Studies meets the metropolis. This is the moment when anthropology comes home and watches people from the ex-colonies in the metropolitan industrial centers, in the form of an ethnography that goes searching for stories. Pitted against a tradition of social research that either (1) ignored the plight of these newly arrived immigrants or (2) documented some aspects of these lives with a view to assimilating these arrivals into the normatively defined British way of life, an 'insider' account, whose influence has unfortunately been long-lasting, emerged.

Based on neat managerial categories of ethnic difference, this posture sought to both understand and assist in the so-called cultural splits faced by South Asian women. Verity Khan's work is a classic case of a study that is itself caught in the 'caught in- between two cultures' paradigm that is so often used to describe the state of South Asian women who are torn between the freedom and liberation of Western values and backward, tradition-bound families. This version of the melodramatic missionary image of women from other places as victims of archaic patriarchal practices who are desperately in need of help was at the time and has been since reproduced by institutional discourses, including the state, schools and the media.

It is a posture that is particularly prone to rear its ugly head in discussions of highly determined issues, such as sati, which became 'a larger-than-life symbol of "Hindu" and "Indian" culture in a way which transcended the actual facts of this limited practice'. Arranged marriages and veiling occupy a similar place in postcolonial Britain. This framework also continues to be the principal means by which students are encouraged to make sense of the lives of South Asian women. Working out of Black feminism in Britain, and influenced by black feminists in the United States, articles in The Empire Strikes Back, the special issue of Feminist Review and the anthology Charting the Journey led the way in interrogating the ways in which South Asian women had up until then been made visible in academia.

These pioneering black feminist accounts paid particular attention to the imperial nature of Eurocentric feminist perspectives on families, sexuality and political activism. Pathological accounts of Asian families and stereotypes of passive Asian women who need 'help' were called into question. The 'culturalism of anthropological works' was criticized for taking cultural practices and traditions out of their specific social and historical circumstances and interpreting them, as the practice of sati had been in colonial India, as being timeless, static and uniformly applicable to all Asians. An overemphasis upon the 'ethnic' features of these women's lives meant that the place of structures of racism was overlooked in favour of accounts that sealed Asian families and their cultures in little ethnic social vacuums.

At the same time, a similar critique was directed at feminist studies of 'third world' women on an international scale, including the urban centers of the West. In a highly influential article Chandra Mohanty pointed out the 'latent ethnocentrism' within Western feminism, which had a tendency to: (1) produce/represent a monolithic category of the 'average third world woman' and (2) to measure and judge the lives of these Other women through a 'yardstick' which took the lives of middle-class women in the West as the norm, 'as the implicit referent'. Picking up on an academic genre that was becoming increasingly popular within feminism, as well as working-class histories, as it was seen to allow for the possibility of hearing perspectives and voices that had hitherto been ignored and silenced, black feminists interrogated the use of in-depth qualitative methods as a quick-fix for the racist thinking that percolated through existing epistemic frameworks.

The presumed 'goodness' of oral histories that sought to give a voice to black women and to reverse the so-called bad stereotypes and invisibility of black women in feminist frameworks with real and positive images was problematized for engaging in a process of objectification that all too easily disavowed relations of power. Carby asserted: 'In arguing that feminism take account of the lives, her stories and experiences of black women we are not advocating that teams of white feminists should descend upon Brixton, Southall, Bristol or Liverpool to take black women as objects of study in modes of resistance. We don't need that kind of intrusion....

Texts that sought to 'give voice' to Asian women were, perhaps unwittingly, feeding the historic Western 'need' to feel pain and intense sympathy for this figure. Commenting on Amrit Wilson's Finding a Voice, Pratibha Parmar noted that, while this book goes a long way in dispelling the notion that Asian women are 'helpless creatures', it lacks a political and economic framework, which makes it easier for the readers, including academics, social and community workers, to exclaim '"I had to put it down, half way through reading it, because it made me cry"'.

Parmar stressed the importance of taking account of how patriarchal, imperial, social and political economic factors came together in the lives of these women. She, like other black feminists, asserted that an analysis of the interactions of capitalism, racism and patriarchy as they were experienced by South Asian women needed to take precedence over an obsession with capturing the culture of these ethnic Others in packaged descriptions. Despite the force of the black feminist arguments, to this day students, especially Asian women who want to study the dynamics of gender in Asian communities, are more often than not asked to start off with descriptions, no doubt for the sake of the curiosity of their tutors, of what it means to be a Muslim or a Sikh, for instance. Thus the search for quick-fix guidebook-version accounts of other cultures is continually endorsed through academic practices and regimes.

And so is the urban anthropological fascination with collecting stories or reading stories by women of colour internationally. This academic practice is, as I shall show later, especially rife in our existing moment. Carby's critique seems to have fallen on deaf ears. While the methods for gaining contact with the other have changed, the quest to know the other has not gone away; it's just that the technological tools have shifted. For now, I will turn to a third moment, a moment that is somewhat preempted in Parmar's call for understanding the 'oppression' of South Asian women through attention to racist structures of capitalism and patriarchy. However, this relatively radical emphasis does not preclude tears, postures of pity, or a politics of salvation. In fact, even in the hard-nosed area of political economy, idealization marks the order of the day. These are some of the dormant effects of this scholarship. They have, however, remained largely underexplored.

Much of the feminist analysis that has looked at the economic location of South Asian women has emerged out of series of points of contestation over the place of race and gender within Marxist analyses of class. The studies have focused on the ailing industries the first generation of South Asian women were concentrated in as workers, especially textiles, and have been incredibly important for giving recognition to the labour of South Asian women. Despite this contribution, to borrow a phrase from Chow, these texts are however riddled with the anguish of undertaking the 'noble' task of returning the hitherto 'defiled' images of South Asian women to their 'sanctified' correct image of workers and fighters. And the problem is that 'defilement and sanctification belong to the same symbolic order', that of idealization.

As the daughters of the workers enter the academy as students of the humanities and the social sciences they are finding that while these studies grant recognition to the labour power of their mothers, aunts and sisters, at the same time the framework is skewed and limited. One of the major problematic effects of these texts is that the subject position of South Asian women is simply and overwhelmingly of producers; they are cogs, albeit important and hitherto ignored cogs, in the capitalist machinery. They are hardly ever recognized as consumers; as impure participants in the circuits of capitalism. Instead they are pitied for their work conditions and idealized for occupying the most oppressed position in the metropolis. They are especially loved when they strike - then they are the heroines who are fighting the system, with saris and banners in tow.

Here we see a different, although little recognized, version of the politics of salvation: the salvation and uplifting of the figure of the downtrodden South Asian sewing machinists bent over their machines, working in sweatshops or as home workers. Such constructions enable academics to occupy a subject position that: (1) undertakes the noble task of highlighting the awful plight of the subaltern female in the metropolis of Britain; and (2) hopes to engender social change through this enlightened task, as traces of social philanthropy lie quietly sealed in-between the pages of the research; and (3) by allying themselves with the subalterns in the West these authors create a subject position for themselves, amongst their gender- or race-resistant colleagues, that is seen to be more radical than that of the most radical of Marxists.

These academic texts, which are a variant of political economy directions in the area of Development Studies, and more recently of the escalating studies of globalization, can be seen to represent, albeit unconsciously, a version of the economically privileged person's burden in the international capitalist economy. Thus the 'mood of self-congratulation as saviours of marginality' can I argue also reside in constructions ostensibly concerned with the serious issue of capital and labour in a global economy. The force of the power lines of capitalism in the lives of subaltern women, at assembly lines and as domestics, sex workers and home workers, must indeed be underlined.

After all, as is pointed out by Spivak, notwithstanding the specificity of Spivak's definition of the subaltern female and the use of the term in a wider sense, 'it is the urban sub proletarian female who is the paradigmatic subject of the current configuration of the International Division of Labour'. It is however the ways in which this recognition is granted that is at issue in this chapter. Often it is assumed that one is doing the right thing by adopting analytical frameworks that look at race and gender in the international and globalized economy. This worthy cause is not without its gaps and fantasies. It is, like so many of the other gestures that have gone before it, well-intentioned; it can also project certain anxieties and idealizations on to the figure of the subaltern woman.

In an analysis of feminist texts in the area of development studies, Aihwa Ong notes that collections which attempt to look at 'women's position in the encounter between global capitalist forces and the everyday life of paid and unpaid work' give more consideration to the mechanisms of capitalism and patriarchy than to the lives of these women. She notes that 'capitalism is delineated as a historically conditioned, polymorphus system; it has more contradictions and personalities than the women and men who are ostensibly the subjects of the volume'. Working out of a position which had famously criticized the flattening out of complexity in the lives of third world women all around the globe, including the metropolis of the West, Mohanty's contribution to the debates on political economy offers a more nuanced perspective. Women are not simply viewed as innocent workers who are super exploited in the global economy; they are also acknowledged as being contradictory subjects who are themselves implicated as consumers, as well as producers, in the discourses and structures of the globe. Mohanty states:

> The challenges for feminists in this arena are a) understanding Third-World women workers as having objective interests in common as workers (they are thus agents and make choices as workers); and b) recognizing the contradictions and dislocations in women's own consciousness of themselves as workers, and thus of their needs and desires - which sometimes militate against organizing on the basis of their common interests (the results of agency). Thus work has to be done here in analyzing the links between the social location and the historical and current experiences of domination of Third-World women workers on the other. Reviewing the collective struggle of poor, Third-World women workers in relation to the above theorization of common interests provides a map of where our project is at.

The desire for international change through global linkages is the entity that defines what Mohanty refers to as 'our project'. This desire of course is also not beyond the realm of production, in the sense that it too contributes towards the production/ representation of third world women. It is however much more alert to noting the heterogeneity of objective locations and the contradictory nature of subjectivities. Whether it manages to escape a romantic association with the 'struggles' of third world women as workers is something that I am not however altogether certain of. Because texts in the mould of Marxist political economy tend to be seen to be much more 'political' and 'radical' than those informed by more culturalist persuasions, the type of subjecthoods and collective subjects they construct can all too often escape scrutiny.

Despite Mohanty's adeptness at locating latent trends in feminist analyses, even she manages to overlook the limited representation of subaltern women in the work of scholars who have only been too keen to stress the patriarchal/capitalism race mantra. Thus we have the cogs and wheels angle being surreptitiously fore grounded at the cost of profundity. Traditionally debates on production and consumption have at their worst been at loggerheads, or at best, being located in distinct fields, have spoken past each other; with accusations of 'economic determinism', 'identity navel-gazing', 'diehard realism' and 'free-floating subjectivities' flying between them in the exchange of political fire.

More recently, interdisciplinary efforts have attempted to re-think questions located in separate fields together through recognition of the connection between (1) commodities in the spheres of production and consumption and (2) the coexistence of bodies which produce and consume. While this can be grasped as an opportunity to re-think what it means to be a producer, to view '... the native - nowadays often a synonym for the oppressed, the marginalized, the wronged... [as] also the space of error, illusion, deception and filth', there is still a strong tendency within this new direction of thought, much of which is still in the making, to imagine the subaltern female producer as an absolute victim.

At a one-day conference on the global fashion industry, at the Institute of Contemporary Arts, in London, amidst a panel of journalists and academics, a South Asian woman was, rather like in the old anthropological sense of an exhibited spectacle, asked to talk about her life as a textile machinist home-worker. Crocodile tears of pity were once again rolled out for this occasion by a prominent white feminist in the field of fashion on the panel, while this woman sat in an alien space, totally out of keeping with her own habitus, to give testimony; a replay of the readers' reactions to Asian women 'giving voice' as observed by Parmar? Interestingly, debates on the production and consumption of fashion somehow seem to congeal problematic postures towards South Asian women.

So much of the analysis of the globalized condition, in a social and cultural, as well as an economic sense, is seen to reside with what is taken to be the condition(s) of the subaltern female, the contemporary 'heart of darkness'. It is amidst growing debates on globalization and its relationship to place-based identities and diasporic existences, that we have the fourth melodramatic moment. Here we find that the so-called hybrid, pastiched, negotiated and ambiguous identities of young South Asian second-generation women are the foci of attention and fascination.

The mixing and matching characterized in the simultaneous donning of saris and trainers are a somewhat exasperating site for academics, as these figures are seen to project the archetypal global cultural subject, one that is beyond borders, in flux and highly syncretic. And even those scholars who engage in the arduous and sophisticated hoops of dialogic research seem to rest the final word on the current state of the urban environment on the analysis of the young, second-generation South Asian woman. These figures raise unknown levels of excitement in academic ranks, because their bodies seem to bring the rhizomatic flows of culture and capital to the brink in one carnivalesque affair. Oh what a celebration!

In the last ten years or so we have witnessed a welcome move away from static binary notions towards more complexes and nuanced understandings. It is a move that has been particularly fruitful for freeing up the boundedness of groups and cultures for an appreciation of the interconnected, changing and fused nature of identities. Influenced by poststructuralist thinking, the academic conceptual toolbox for understanding life at the margins has become quite expansive. Discourses of hybridity, flows, borderlands, 'becoming minor', the nomadic, ambivalence are all to be found among the motley crew of concepts that are all too often called upon to narrate alterity as well as the path to alterity.

At the same time, there has been, at least in theory, a turning away from the old crude anthropological stance that sought to watch, observe and dissect the other under the cloak of scientific knowledge. Notions of mimetic realism have been displaced by an acknowledgement of the place of the researcher in the production of the knowledge. Thus the image of the scholar as a Mr Spock figure who is separated from the objects of the world by dint of his cold, rational, transcendental scientific demeanour has been dented, if not altogether replaced, by the recognition that academics are inside their research enterprises. That is, who they are affects their whole academic venture.

No one can escape, no matter how marginal, progressive, radical, organic and thus morally superior they position themselves as being in relation to their colleagues, their presence within their academically endorsed productions of statistics, philosophical quandaries, 'partial' stories and pictures or improvisational performances. At the same time, the looking-glass of reflexivity has been adopted to gauge the nature of the academic presence, leading some to produce lists along the traditional lines of the race, class, gender sing-song, while others offer in-depth confessional accounts from the field before offering the messy texts of the Other, with a full recognition of the meddling part played by the scholar. Thus we have the troubled and struggling all-knowing epistemic eye.

Although ethnographers will now (a) go to great lengths to make sure their narrations are outside the fixtures of previous taxonomies and as fluid and agile as possible, and (b) attempt to generate and present their research in the most dialogic and ethical terms possible, these mechanisms do not guarantee that the hitherto muted subaltern subjects can speak, in the sense of being heard. Furthermore, what is of particular note is that the desire to look, to see what life is like for those across the tracks or 'down under', has not gone away. Whether this desire is simply curiosity, or a search wrapped up in the politics of salvation, is neither here nor there. It is this desire, curiosity, whatever you want to call it, as well as the effects of it that I want to ponder on.

Here it is worth pausing on Patricia Williams's comments in her Reith Lecture, where she reminds us of the 'racial voyeurism' that propels 'bus loads of tourists [to] flock to black churches on a Sunday morning' in New York and Harlem. Williams sardonically remarks 'It's great theatre, according to the guidebook hit list of hits, all those black people dressed in their quaint finery, singing and swooning and singing some more'. Now, while researchers, unlike the average tourist, will declare sensitivity to the lives they look at (in the streets and clubs of metropolis, distant villages or cultural texts) nevertheless their gaze seeks also to travel, 'look', 'listen' and get a taste. In this sense they are all stomping the same territory, although the ethnographer is now, from time to time, fraught with twitches of reflexivity.

A refuge away from the troubled territory of ethnography is increasingly being sought in public texts (novels, films, art and theatre) by the other. The quandary of hearing/not hearing, re-presentation and symbolic violence is largely sidelined by feasting academic eyes on the other through already available texts. Academics are using art or novels, for instance, by those who have managed to utilize the means of representation for them. This safe position does however I think deserve further interrogation, as it is not without its power lines and institutional conditions of existence - especially as it is a form of academic feeding that has rather problematically become all too familiar in relation to conversations, syllabuses and textbooks on the subaltern female.

Philosophical turns (in short the onset of post-structuralism) and political struggles, in which the efforts of women in colour in the academy to push against the grain of the canon have been absolutely paramount, have all helped to engender an academic environment where the margin, as a text, has come to occupy centre-stage. We have moved from a time when the texts of women of colour were altogether absent or at best, in a spirit of guilt-ridden benevolent multiculturalism, tagged on to a course in the form of a little reading list and one or two lectures, to the following kinds of scenarios: bell hooks notes that 'the courses I teach on black women writers and Third World Literature are overcrowded, with large waiting lists'.

Today 'minority discourse' has become 'a hot topic' in the West. Working from within the black feminist movement in the States, which has fought long and hard battles to acknowledge outside-situated knowledges, specifically those of black women, Ann DuCille, vents her exasperation over the ways in which black women, as texts, sit within the sites of knowledge production as prized commodities. She comments on an 'occult' of 'black womanhood' whereby black women are now treated as a kind of 'sacred text': 'Why are they so interested in me and people who are like me (metaphorically speaking)? Why have we - black women - become the subjected subjects of so much scholarly investigation, the peasants under the glass of intellectual inquiry in the 1990s?'

OuCille sums up an academic genre - that haunts all subaltern women, in their heterogeneous locations, as objects of study. A recent conference titled 'Writing Europe 2001: Migrant Cartographies' exemplifies the ways in which the literary texts of women of colour have become common academic currency. Conferences can be great sites for highlighting gestures and genres; they are places where not only the content of analyses but the spirit in which the academic enterprise is conducted can come alive. Aside from being a lesson in how the academy is riddled by pecking orders, conferences can show how those scholars whose writings place them at the utmost radical edges of their disciplines, can together, within their own social milieu, generate a mood containing some not-so-radical after-effects.

Given the locations of the conference - Amsterdam - known to be one of the most 'cosmopolitan' cities in Europe - and Leiden as well as the subject-matter of the conference, I was most surprised to find that the participants at this conference were predominantly 'white'. I soon tempered my surprise with a quick reminder that this was just a replica of the whiteness of academia back in Britain, except that in Europe it was much worse and that, somewhat ironically, I needed to bear in mind that Britannia had some of the 'best' race relations throughout Europe.

As I went in and out of numerous sessions over the course of three days my ears became tuned in to a repetition of academic notes that produced a harmonic melody, a mantra that was caught in the rhapsody of the marginal, or at least talk of the marginal, in the most radical idioms. Thankfully, such was the sophistication of this conference that the demons of binary and essentialist speech were abandoned to the monsters of bad social thought in favour of a language that spoke of hybridity, ambivalence, the minor, the nomad, exile, border, etc. While the concepts themselves and the history of ideas surrounding them have allowed for new possibilities for thinking about the textuality of racialized immigrant and postcolonial existence, Coran Kaplan cautions that '... despite critiques of humanist categories, poststructuralist methodologies are no less prone to desiring the "other" or exoticizing difference'.

Since the racist murder of the black teenager Steven Lawrence and the publication of the Macpherson Report the expression 'unwitting' has perhaps been over-used for gesturing in the politest way possible: 'I know you have not deliberately caused damage, but that, I am sorry to inform you, has been the unintended consequence.' It is in this spirit that I would like to use the term 'unwitting' to refer to the effect of the academic rapping that prevailed through the repeated use of radical terms in relation to the literature and cultural works of people like Meera Syal, Meena Alexander and Zadie Smith.

These works come to function as second order mediations on the, still, mysterious world of Otherness. Even in the hands of complex analysis, women of colour become objects of knowledge, a fertile ground for theoretical feasting: spectacles for understanding the globalized and fractured conditions of the world. The pages of their novels, autobiographies and art works represent highly detailed and complex puzzles for academics to while away whole Sunday afternoons and sabbaticals. The effect of the continuous use of poets, filmmakers, writers, and artists from the 'margins' as raw material for theoretical acrobatics can so often be further marginalization. Even those academics who want to write culture otherwise can, as is noted by Cornel West, bring in debates on difference and borders 'in a way that it further marginalizes actual people of difference and otherness'.

Once again the 'Other' can be 'made object, appropriated, interpreted, and taken over by those in powers...' Michelle Wallace presents us with a vivid picture of this process when she captures the 'traffic jam' of intellectuals engaged in the analysis of the work of Zora Neale Hurston, who 'like groupies descending on Elvis Presley's estate' are engulfed in 'a mostly ill-mannered stampede to have some memento of the black woman'. With in the unwitting objectification of women of colour as prized objects of analysis a version of mythification can also prevail, as 'romanticizing nomad or guerrilla cultures is a frequent practice in contemporary poststructuralist theories'.

A romantic attachment to being minor and the hope of becoming minor can undermine the difficulty of existing on the borders. The cultural texts produced by the daughters of second-generation 'immigrants' seem to hold particular fascination. This of course is at a time when fashion has itself, in the world of music, media and clothing, shifted the image of the dirty, smelly, tradition-bound 'Paki' or Arab to the second-generation hip, hybrid, happening, mix-matching, bindhidenim- and trainer-wearing object of desire, with the 'Asian Babe' being a case in point. At the conference in Amsterdam it was pointed out to me that if academics want to make an original contribution to their disciplinary fields it is much harder for them to do this by specializing in the traditional canon, such as Shakespeare or Virginia Woolf, for instance. With these literary authors exhausted, the texts of newly discovered authors represent one route to academic recognition. Thus new voyages of discovery and 'virgin' territory can be found in the body of texts produced by women of colour. Once again, the East is a career.

No matter how loving and ethical the search for the 'heart of darkness' is, we need to be alert to the institutional conditions that enable the search, to what are often referred to as the 'conditions of articulation'. In a most obvious sense we take the journeys we do, reading novels, describing levels of capitalist exploitation, looking for exile, baggage and travel in the work of articles, taking the work of black female poets to new flights, and writings articles, like this one, that critique the search in the first place, because we can, because we have cultural capital and institutional mechanisms at our disposal, however minimal they may be.

This chapter is a call for pushing the politics of location and the research reflexivity that has ensued even further. The ways in which academics obtain a subject hood for themselves through melodramatic constructions of the female subaltern, in the case of the figure of the South Asian woman, by hemming this figure, no doubt unconsciously, even if she is not left altogether muted, like Spivak's subaltern, between victimhood, heroic struggle and romantic celebration, need to be interrogated. Now that we have got over replacing bad images with honourable good images, we need not only to think about the limited ways, in which subjectivities of others are constructed, but also to pause and think about the subject hood academics create for themselves, perhaps unconsciously through their very own creations.

In short, we need to ask: What do we think we are doing when we peer into, problematize and recognize the labour and cultural texts of women of colour? And while we can seek ethical responsibility with the subaltern through a one-to-one loving relationship where we systematically unlearn our privileges so that we 'speak to', not 'of, we must not escape the probing and uncomfortable question: Why are academics searching for an ethical relationship with the subaltern in the first place? If they hope to transform, save or protect, as many of them do in one guise or another, they must first debunk '... the illusion that, through privileged speech, one is helping to save the wretched of the earth'.

For my own part, I embarked on this journey because, when I, as a student, teacher and researcher, held up the academic images of South Asian women in Britain, to view myself, my sister, sisters-in-law, nieces, mother and neighbours I found that 'we' all almost slipped from view. Glimpses of recognition could be found in the murky waters of representation, but so much skewed and one-dimensional. What we find is that the figure of the South Asian woman is sandwiched between the voyeurism of the phantastically exotic and a 'rescue paradigm' underlaid by 'salvational motives', which are re-played and reformulated in a myriad of contexts, including the 'revolutionary tourism' and 'celebration of testimony' found in feminism.

While my mother and sister-in-laws or sister, for instance, are rather like the Chinese women who troubled Kristeva by their indifference to what she thought and saw, probably because I partake in the making of academic space, have found that it is absolutely imperative to my own sense of being to engage with the constructions and postures that hover around me. As the 'native' ethnics enter the academy, the academy is somewhat uncomfortably finding that they are no longer staying in the melodramatic 'frames' that they have come to know them over years of scholarly research. From the position of a 'native' who resides in the academy, with all the cultural, economic and symbolic capital that I embody, I am hopefully adding to that disruption - without slipping into the delusions of 'self-subalternization' or speaking about powerlessness from a position of power without an 'espistemological questioning of how it is that I am speaking'.

The problematic nature of the academic task of looking for the other, not only in terms of the frames that have been used, but also with the objectification entailed in the search for. This is the case for even those current re-framings that have gone beyond the limits of the tradition modern dichotomy and are now couched in the idioms of contradiction and hybridity. Though the task of resurrection in the face of erasure is compelling, gaps and silences are also constituitive of the defiled images that seek to replace the dichotomous good/bad, heroine/victim, and ethnic hybrid images. And anyway, while we embark on that process, there is also a need to make the academy the object of study without reverting to the insatiable academic desire for testimonies, in their current messy and muffled genres.

'A woman should never be independent. Her father has authority over her in childhood, her husband has authority over her in youth, and in old age her son has authority over her.' This statement is to be found in the famous Laws of Manu, the basic source of law in Hindu society. The book was composed in the early centuries A.D., and its application has continued up to recent times. It was written originally in order to preserve some of the finer values of Hindu society, but through the course of centuries the spirit of the book was lost.

The rigid application of ill-digested ideas, taken from this book, led to the emergence of a society which, ostensibly chasing an ideal, ended up by becoming a minor hell for some of its members. This was possible because political and social authoritarianism clasped hands with religious authoritarianism, as so often happens in the history of any civilization. The laws having been imbued with religious sanctions, there was no escape for those condemned to suffer in these societies. In the case of India, this social code affected not only the lowest of the four castes, who have traditionally been regarded as the unfortunates of society, but it also led to attacks on the position of women in society, and to their being regarded as inferior in every possible way.

This was the picture in India, in certain areas and at certain periods. It is certainly not possible to generalize from this and state that this was the picture for all time, or in all the countries under consideration in this book. The geographical area covered by these countries is far larger than that of the whole of Europe. Consequently there were many changes and modifications in each society, as new ideas arose. It is impossible to regard the region of South and South-East Asia as one unit. In tracing the emancipation movement of women in this region, I shall consider the area in three groups. The sub-continent of India, Pakistan and Ceylon comprises the first. This is the largest in the region and has been subject to two main waves of social thinking, one dominated by Hinduism, and the second and later wave dominated by Islam. The broader aspects of the Indian pattern are applicable to some of the other areas as well. Ceylon, with its Buddhist faith, provides a kind of bridge to the second group, which consists of Burma, Thailand, Laos, Cambodia and Vietnam. This region has been subject to only one religious code on the whole, that of Buddhism. The third group consists of the South-East Asian peninsula and islands: Malaya, Indonesia, Borneo and the Philippines.

The societies of all these countries have at some stage been moulded by one or two of the three main religious ideologies, Hinduism, Buddhism or Islam, though Confucianism in Vietnam and Roman Catholicism in the Philippines form exceptions. The development of social ideas has therefore been fairly similar in many countries, for example, there is a fairly close parallel between the position of women at various stages in Indian and Indonesian society. The urges for and against the emancipation of women, and the events connected with the spread of these ideas, have been remarkably similar. A representative example from each group may suffice. Indian society has been moulded by the impact of Hinduism and Islam. Indonesia presents in the main an Islamic society with elements of earlier Hindu and Buddhist culture.

The opening up of opportunities for women has been accelerated in the last decade in nearly all Asian countries. In ex-colonies which have now become independent, this is part of the process of national reconstruction, in which the role of women is being increasingly recognized. Nevertheless, traditional attitudes take a long time to pass away, and there are always traditionalists who insist on going back in time in order to provide the model, whether this model be relevant or not. Therefore, many Asian countries today show a strange mixture of enlightened ideas on the position of women co-existing with opinions that demand their rigid seclusion and subordination.

Contemporary India may be cited as an example. Theoretically the equality of women has been recognized, yet social opinion takes a long time to change and, in practice, the older attitudes are not dead. These attitudes still prevail in the middle classes of the urban centres, where modernization is either still a fringe development or else is an imitation of the West indulged in only by the men: in rural areas too, the better off families cling to these traditions in their entirety.

More often than not, the birth of a boy is welcomed with greater delight than that of a girl-at least one son being necessary for the various rites performed after the death of the father, and for the continuation of the family. A further rationalization of this lack of enthusiasm for too many daughters is that parents have to provide dowries for the daughters, which is a heavy financial liability, whereas sons bring in both money and goods. Starting life with this somewhat negative reception the girl has, however, a carefree childhood. This is the only time of her life when she is permitted liberty of movement and expression. At puberty she is considered ready for marriage and has to be trained accordingly. Now she can be free only with other young girls of her age. The company of boys is strictly forbidden. If she has been sent to school (and this is by no means the general pattern), then in most cases she will discontinue her schooling at this age.

Childhood in a joint family system or where many sections of a wide family live together, is not unpleasant. There are always many cousins and young relatives to provide companionship. But later it begins to be irksome when individual whims and fancies have to be suppressed. In Hindu families marriages have to be arranged in order to preserve caste requirements. Marriage has not only to be within the caste, but very often preferably within certain sub-castes, since a person's caste is determined by his or her being born into it. If young men and women were permitted a free choice in marriage it would be impossible to maintain caste endogamy. Once a girl is married, either she is absorbed into the large family of her in-laws or she lives with her husband. Her relationship with her husband is one of extreme deference towards him, since she has been brought up to believe that her sole purpose is to minister to his needs.

It is only when she becomes a mother-in-law in her own turn, or a grandmother, that she can assert her position and assumes some authority. Middle-class families in some cities are becoming a little less particular about following this pattern. A small percentage does send their daughters not only to schools, but even to universities, where the girls remain until they graduate. However, their activities at university remain circumscribed. Many admit quite frankly that they are there simply 'to mark time' until a 'good match' is found for them. Being at a university does not provide much opportunity for social activity unless it be at a college for girls alone. Mixing with male students is generally embarrassing to both sexes. In the few co-educational centers there are, on the whole, just a handful of students of both sexes participating in university activities.

This brief sketch of the average city-dwelling young woman applies only to present-day India. In the past a variety of social patterns existed. The process by which the present pattern was arrived at was a long and complicated one. In India the code of Manu did not prevail from the very beginnings of Indian culture; it was a later development. The earliest information available on Indian society is to be found in the famous Vedic hymns of the Indo-Aryan tribes; these go back to about 1000 B.C. From then until the early centuries A.D., it would appear that Indian society had a flexible social structure, which changed and took shape as the needs of the moment demanded. None of the rigid features known to later Indian society held sway at this time. There appears to have been no bar on young men and women mixing with each other before marriage. Marriages were determined by individual choice, and early marriages were not the norm. The remarriage of widows was permitted. Women were respected, and although it was a male-dominated society, women were given the privilege of being recognized as co-workers in the moulding of society.

The radical change which Indian society was to undergo was completed in the mediaeval period, that is, sometime after the seventh century A.D and after the invasion of India by the Arabs, Turks and other Islamic peoples to the West (post-A.D. 1000), the marriageable age for girls was made even earlier by Hindu theorists. Marriage was now to take place before puberty, and no woman was allowed to remain unmarried. By the seventeenth century A.D., early marriages had become the vogue. This was followed by the other practices which were to be condemned by later reformers. Women were reduced to a subordinate position both socially and legally, and the code of Manu was cited as the theoretical basis for this subordination.

Perhaps it was because of current attitudes to sexual life that Hindu social legislators were insistent in precipitating this situation. The Hindu attitude to sex had been an enlightened one in the past. There was no guilt complex with regard to sex, such as there is in the Judeo-Christian tradition, since there was no belief in original sin. The purpose of early marriage was theoretically explained to be the preservation of caste. Another reason may be suggested, that of avoiding sexual frustration among young people, a problem which European society has up to now failed to solve. But the comprehension of this idea appears to have been lost at a certain stage in India, when perversions such as marriages before puberty (even if they were not consummated) were introduced. The sexual guilt complex first came to India via Islam, which had borrowed it from the Judeo-Christian background in which it originated.

The impact of Christian Europe on India intensified this new development. Today the idea has permeated fairly deeply into Hindu society, particularly amongst the urban middle classes, who are now incapable of even appreciating the earlier Hindu attitude, let alone practicing it. The position of women further deteriorated in this period when the consolidation of family holdings became a regular feature of Hindu life. According to the various laws regarding property rights which governed the joint family system, daughters could not inherit the family property, since it was the maintenance of the family property as joint property that was the material basis of the family structure, and daughters always left their natal families at marriage.

Women were compensated by being given a dowry at marriage. A portion of this was regarded as their personal property which no-one could take from them without their consent. In point of fact, a woman was hardly ever able to maintain her rights over this property once she had gone to the home of her in-laws. Being in a subordinate position, she could not fight to keep intact her own possessions. The treatment of widows was another stigma on latter-day Hindu society. In certain circles the widow was held responsible for the death of her husband and was treated as an outcast. She was not permitted to marry again, and was denied normal social activities. Her head was shaved and she was expected to wear white all the time, so that her widowhood was immediately apparent. She was believed to be an inauspicious person and was therefore excluded from family ceremonies and festive rites. It is not surprising that some preferred to die by becoming *satis* (that is, attaining merit by 'voluntarily' being burnt alive on the funeral pyre of their husbands), rather than live in this fashion.

The coming of Islam to India did not in any way alleviate the position of women. It brought with it the *purdah* system, which merely continued the downward trend at a faster rate. *Purdah,* which means literally a curtain, required the complete curtaining off or seclusion of women. Even close male relatives in a large family are often not permitted to look upon all the women in the family. The women usually live in a separate part of the house, known as the *zenana* (women's quarter). When in public, the women have to veil their faces or else wear a large tent-like garment called a *burkah,* which covers them fully from head to toe. In the case of well-to-do families there is at least a garden attached to the house where the women can move freely, but in the poorer sections of the cities this fencing in of women was harmful to their health as well.

Yet the surprising thing is that legally Muslim women had a better status than Hindu women. They were permitted religious education (not that this stressed anything but their subservience), divorce and remarriage should the marriage not work, and rights of inheritance. The divorce or *talak* is thought to be unfair on the women, since it was the husband alone who had the right to divorce his wife. The divorce itself is a fairly straightforward matter; the husband merely repeats the word *talak* thrice in the presence of his wife and a few witnesses. It meant that a wife had no real security in the marriage. The inheritance laws were about the only real privilege that the Muslim woman had, though the application of these is also a debatable point.

The laws were not always applied in her favour, nor could she always gain her rights. Polygamy was allowed in both the Hindu and the Islamic systems, the difference being that the Islamic code limited the number of wives to four, whereas the Hindu code did not specify any limit. Polygamy has generally been a luxury indulged in only by those who could afford to keep more than one wife. This naturally tended to reduce the status of the wife officially, if more than one wife was possible in an otherwise largely monogamous society. Indonesia has followed a pattern similar in some ways to that of India. Indonesia is a predominantly Muslim country and Islamic ideas had a constraining influence on the women. Many of the modern emancipation movements among Indonesian women have been for the abolition of the *talak* or divorce as envisaged by Muslim law. In some places it has been modified.

A wife can now make a petition before a judge, and the husband may be called upon to explain why he wishes to divorce his wife. The *purdah* system was also common to both India and Indonesia, but in the latter country the veiling of women was not insisted upon so strictly, and they were not kept in seclusion as soon as they were of a marriageable age. Thailand presents a different picture from those of India or Indonesia. Theoretically women are subordinate to men, but owing to the absence of the joint family system, women have a considerable say in family affairs. The family units are small and the position of the wife and mother is one of privilege and independence.

There are no caste restrictions either, so that young people are more in a position to choose their marriage partners, although the parents influence the choice. The ideal Thai woman may be described as hard-working in the rice-field, a capable woman in the house, respectful to her husband, efficient with children, devoted to religion and a shrewd businesswoman in the market. This stress on being a good worker is not without fortunate effects on the status of women. Much of the trade in the small country markets is handled entirely by women. This results in their providing a sizeable portion of the family's income. The knowledge of this financial independence creates in the women the necessary self-confidence, and in the men the necessary respect, for there to be a fairly equal relationship between the two sexes.

Inheritance laws provide equal shares for sons and daughters, so that there is no need to give a large dowry to the daughter. A similar situation exists also in many sections of Burmese society, and in Laos and Cambodia. Part of the reason why Thailand has managed to avoid a rigid social code is because it has not been subject to orthodox Hindu or Islamic codes. The main religion in Thailand today is Buddhism. The type of Hinduism which earlier received favour amongst the Thais was a much modified religion that found its way into folk sentiment. Ceremonies were adopted largely because they were believed to be auspicious. The more authoritarian aspects of Hinduism, particularly its social code, were dropped.

Although Buddhism accepted the idea of women being an inferior species, it had a far more humane and liberal attitude towards the female sex than either Hinduism or Islam. Women were not thought of simply as child-bearers. It is the only one of these three religions that permitted women to become nuns. Although nuns have the lowest rank in the religious hierarchy, nevertheless the fact that a woman was permitted the alternative of becoming a nun is significant. In Laos, Cambodia, Thailand and Burma, the attitude to marriage is based on a considerable amount of commonsense. Young people meet at local gatherings and on festive occasions. Courtship is permitted provided the parents of the girl are in the vicinity.

Choice of a marriage partner is not restricted by any caste rules. The marriage itself is regarded as a secular and social affair, and there is no necessity for any religious sanction. In most cases an elder of the community presides and blesses the union. Divorce is regarded as a solution to a marriage that has failed. The termination of the marriage may be announced to the village headman or the heads of the two families concerned. A complete separation lasting for a period of about three years can also be regarded as sufficient ground for divorce. Inheritance laws are generally simple. In Burma, property is held jointly. The surviving partner inherits the property and, at the death of both parents, the property is equally divided between all the children.

Countries such as these have not seen any marked agitation in favour of female emancipation. Within the existing socio -economic framework, women have long had a position of prestige and respect. When the occupations begin to change in large numbers, for example, when women stop being merely petty traders and take to professions of various kinds, there may well be social upheaval, but it is likely to be of a less fundamental nature than in other countries, since the condemnation of working women as such is not found.

EARLY REFORMERS IN INDIA

The unequal position of women in India had its critics even in the early stages. Mediaeval India saw a number of movements, which, though often religious heresies in origin, advocated social reform. Religious reformers of the time attacked the rights which the priests had assumed as the guardians and interpreters of religion. In some ways similar to the leaders of the Reformation in Europe, they wished to bring true religion to the uneducated. They used the everyday speech of the people and not the court language, and were thus able to reach a large audience. It is significant that women were encouraged to participate in this new religious expression and to attend gatherings for prayers, and so on.

Unfortunately, none of these movements conducted systematic campaigns against the various social injustices. Thus, their protest weakened through the years, and orthodoxy once more established itself. Organized movements for social reform did not start until the early nineteenth century. The impetus then came from a group of thinkers of remarkable perception, and also from the fact that the socio-economic structure of Indian society had begun to change, as indeed had that of practically all Asian societies. The intrusion of Europe into the history of Asia in the seventeenth century had hastened the downfall of the traditional social structures in Asia, and had introduced a new set of ideas, those that were current at the time in Europe.

It was to take a couple of centuries for these ideas to grow in Asian soil, but by the nineteenth century Indian society had begun to respond to them. In India, the history of the emancipation of women began with a number of people who questioned their existing status in Indian society. The questioning originated in two sources of thinking. One, known as Revivalism, objected that the existing status of women was not in keeping with the very ancient tradition, which was far more liberal. This group spoke of a Utopian past and desired a return to it. They stressed the gentle and submissive qualities of a woman, assuming that emancipation, or rather liberalization, was to come as a gift from the male section of the community. But the second group, known as the Reformers, objected to the subordinate position of women because they believed in the equality of the sexes and individual liberty. They took it for granted that a society was not healthy as long as women were kept in a state of subjugation.

The Reformers were impressed by the humanism and application of rational thought in the European philosophy of the eighteenth and nineteenth centuries. The works of Mill and Bentham were favoured by this group. They were interested in the speculations of European intellectuals on society and social patterns. They were convinced of the necessity for social and political reform in India, and of this being the only means by which India could once more emerge with a civilization that she could be proud of. By far the most outstanding person amongst the Reformers was Ram Mohan Roy. Roy was, in a way, the man who launched the ideological movement for the modernization of India.

He published his own journal in which he discussed his ideas and explained the controversies that were current at the time. In 1828 he founded the Brahmo Samaj, an organization of people who had ideas similar to his own, and who were in favour of reform. Roy and his supporters strongly attacked inhumane practices such as the burning of widows. They supported the social reforms planned by Lord Bentinck, the then Governor-General of India. It had been suggested that the government should forbid such customs as female infanticide, the burning of widows, and so on. Roy also demanded that the inheritance laws be changed so that women should have the right to inherit property.

Another vexed question on which the early Reformers spent much time and discussion was that of the age of consent.

Some were of the opinion that the marriage of a woman could be arranged any time between the ages of 16 and 24, and that the marriage should conform to the old ideal of *svayamvara* (free choice), under which eligible bachelors were selected by the parents and the young woman was permitted to choose from among them. The possibility of divorce was not allowed at this stage even by the Reformers. According to Hindu custom marriages are sacred and only death can part a husband and wife. In 1860, after much agitation, the age of consent for girls was raised to 10 years. Previous to this it was permissible to marry a girl below the age of 10. In 1891 the age of consent was raised to 12 years.

During the latter half of the nineteenth century, the debate continued with men such as Ranade attempting to change public opinion. Ranade attacked not only child marriages but also the ban on the remarriage of widows. The orthodox were willing to grant that a child widow (i.e., a girl who had been widowed before reaching puberty) could be permitted to marry again. But any other widow would be regarded as an adulteress if she remarried. Between the years 1860 and 1901, a total of 138 cases of widows remarrying were recorded, and this in itself was an achievement.

Another supporter of widow remarriage was the novelist Premchand regarded as among the most outstanding writers in Hindi and Urdu during this period, this writer's novels and short stories, generally carrying a theme in support of social reform, were another factor in influencing public opinion. Ranade was also keen that there should be an organization devoted to the cause of the emancipation of women, so that the movement should cease to be a local battle in certain areas, and should become a national cause. This was achieved to some extent when the National Social Conference was inaugurated in 1887. The founding of this organization was assisted by the emergence of another aspect of the main problem-the demand for education for women.

The lack of facilities for the education of women had already caused much controversy. It was recognized by some thinkers, such as Vivekanand, that women should be fully educated so that they could participate in social reforms and assist those who were propagating these reforms. His argument was that women alone know best what improvements are most urgent. In 1875 the Arya Samaj was founded by Davananda Sarasvati. Although this group had a traditionalist (Revivalist) character, it mobilized opinion in favour of reform. Education for women was one of the slogans of the Arya Samaj. Dayananda himself insisted that girls should be educated until the age of 16. The educational course was to emphasize languages, sciences, practical handicrafts and physical fitness. It is interesting to notice that he did not advocate domestic science alone for women, but demanded an all-round educational background, similar to that given to men.

Traditionally if women were given schooling at all, it ceased at the primary school stage. The nineteenth century saw the opening up of a few private institutions for girls. These were organized by various societies, such as the Brahmo Samaj, the Arya Samaj and also by some of the Christian missionary societies. The latter were made somewhat ineffectual by the fact that no girl from a 'respectable' family was permitted to attend them. It was also feared that the mission schools would try to convert the girls to Christianity. It was not until fifty years ago, when a 'European-type' education became a definite asset in upper-class society in India that convents and mission schools began to enroll a large number of girls from 'respectable' families.

The biggest obstacle in the way of large-scale schooling for girls was that of early marriages. Thus, the two problems went hand-in-hand. The raising of the age of consent also meant the possibility for more opportunities of higher education. The British-India Government was on the whole slow in encouraging women's education. In the main, government-sponsored schools were for boys only. It was not until the last quarter of the nineteenth century that emphasis was placed on the possibilities of encouraging schools for girls.

The real advance in this direction had to wait until the twentieth century. It has been suggested that the Indian uprising of 1857 was partially responsible for the timidity of the British-India Government in matters relating to social reform after 1857, for the government thought that earlier attempts at reform had been interpreted as unnecessary interference in Indian society, and that this had been one of the causes of the uprising. A more probable reason for the slowness of development is that the emancipation of women even in Europe was still a comparatively unheard-of idea. In 1865, when John Stuart Mill placed women's suffrage in his election address, it was thought to be quite revolutionary.

The situation was similar in both the Hindu and Muslim communities. The nineteenth century saw a number of Muslims, prominent among them Sir Sayyed Ahmed Khan, advocating more educational facilities for women. But this consciousness took a somewhat longer time to mature in Muslim society, and the concessions were, therefore, granted at a later period. Another argument in favour of educating women was that if women were encouraged in this activity, it would provide a means of employment for them; and once women were given economic independence, then their social equality would follow as a natural course. Facilities for women's education were, until fairly recently, restricted to school education. In 1916, a Women's University was founded in Bombay by Karve, the idea coming originally from a similar experiment which had been tried out in Japan. In the first year only six candidates appeared for the examination. Gradually the numbers grew and it became a centre for women who wanted university education.

2

Women in India and Spread of Mass Culture

Women in India today have legal equality with men in political and civil rights. Of all the revolutionary changes in modern India, it is safe to say that nothing will have more far-reaching significance than this change in the legal status of women. Political equality for women was written into the new Constitution of India, as the natural result of the tremendous service of women in the struggle for independence. Equality in civil rights was gained in 1955, when the Hindu Reform Code bill was passed, eradicating the traditional inequities affecting women in respect to marriage, guardianship, adoption and maintenance. This basic social legislation, for which women had worked over a long period and which was vigorously supported by the Prime Minister himself, will stand as a major achievement of the first Parliament of the Republic of India.

The new status of Indian women is the consummation of over a hundred years of individual and collective effort on the part of Indian social reformers and educational pioneers, liberal religious movements of India, and Christian Missions-all deeply concerned in the advance of Indian women. The final impetus to this effort was given by the passive resistance movement for Indian Independence, under the great leader of India, Mahatma Gandhi, who called women out of their sheltered lives, imbued them with the spirit of sacrificial service and showed them the way of non-violence. Inspired by Gandhi's example and his message of passive resistance, women responded to his call. At first a core of deeply committed leaders, then thousands of women of all classes, young and older, shared hardship and imprisonment in the common sacrifice for freedom. "Theirs was a key role," wrote one of the great leaders, Sarojini Naidu.

"Without their help, the movement could never have been a success." Gandhi's call to national service inspired women not only to active political participation in the national struggle but also to social welfare service. In order to promote the social and educational advance of women, a number of women leaders from the different religious communities organized the first All-India Women's Conference, a widely representative gathering of women, which has been a remarkably effective instrument of national service.

Through the widespread efforts of the All-India Women's Conference, and under the leadership of Dr. Muthulakshimi Reddi, the notable Child Marriage Restraint Act, commonly called the Sarda Act, was passed in April 1930. In the preliminary referendum of public opinion, made by a Government Commission that included two women members, men and women of all classes, even women just out of *purdah*, fearlessly registered their protest against child marriage and urged legislation. These years of active participation in the Independence Movement and in the political campaigns and campaigns for social welfare and reform prepared the women throughout India in a remarkable way to share in the building of the new State.

Immediately after partition, women leaders in Delhi were called upon to assume major responsibility for the refugees from Pakistan, spreading like a tidal wave over North India. A body of devoted, efficient volunteers and trained social workers, in close association with the Minister of Health, Rajkumari Amrit Kaur, for two and a half years carried on a well-organized camp service for thousands of refugees and later helped to develop rehabilitation plans for the refugee population. During this first decade of the Republic multiple social services for women and children were carried on by individual leaders and organizations in order to sustain and promote national welfare. Noteworthy in this impressive development of national welfare are several main trends: promotion of rural welfare; training women for social work of various kinds, especially for rural welfare, and cooperation in social welfare between the Government and voluntary social agencies.

As already mentioned the full participation of women in political life is of signal importance in the total development of India today. With equal status, women are enabled to assume responsibility and materially affect legislative decisions, in the whole gamut of political issues, national and international. The Deputy Foreign Minister today is a woman, and the rights and responsibilities of women so freely accorded by the Constitution are fully recognized and further promoted. Their complete political equality with men and their recognized capacity have given women a position of unusually strategic influence. Also of great importance for India today, is the fact that not only the educated minority of Indian women have political equality but the great illiterate masses as well.

The two elections held on the basis of universal suffrage were a dramatic evidence of the political awakening of the Indian people. This awakening of India's former voiceless millions has incalculable meaning for the future of India, as the basis of a potential free democracy. The atmosphere of India today is vibrant with opportunity and the sense of freedom. As one travels one sees women and girls actively taking part in the new life and work of the nation-girls at school in classes and at sports, Girl Guides, clerks in government bureaus and in railway stations and travel offices, airplane hostesses, women in professions, women in the fields, in factories and in cottage industries. And everywhere are women volunteers in social welfare. These Indian women, older and younger, are the leaders of today and tomorrow, and evidence of the new freedom and new status of women in India.

Immediately after Independence, India assumed the tremendous task of establishing a new system of education based on the long past but reoriented to the needs of a new democratic society. At the beginning of the new State, barely thirty per cent of the children in India were in school. With a sense of urgency, and in the midst of the vast upheaval of partition, a program of vigorous expansion of education was immediately begun. The record of results is impressive, as shown in the Government summary of accomplishments. From 1948-1954, the number of primary schools in all the major provinces (the Part A States after Independence) increased by 37,000 and the enrollment to 4.6 millions. For all India the total number of primary schools was 221,082 and the number of pupils 19,296,840. With the continued expansion of primary education, it was estimated that by 1955-56 fifty per cent of school age children had school privileges. Based on this, the Second Five Year Plan has allowed for sixty-three per cent of school-going children by 1961 and hopes to reach eight million in the major provinces by that time.

Progress has been made in literacy since Independence, from 14.6 in 1941 (omitting the 0-5 years group) to 18.3 per cent in 1951, the latest census. Since then there has been steady advance. Remarkable advance has also been made toward compulsory primary education. The number of areas in which primary education is compulsory has risen from 224 towns and 10,010 villages in 1948, to 598 towns and 21,260 villages in 1953. These figures reveal the willingness of the villagers to accept the economic sacrifice necessary to have their children benefit from compulsory schooling. Parents give up the small potential earnings of their children so that they may attend school. The villagers in many areas have given labor, land and money freely for building their own village schools.

The expansion in secondary education has also been extraordinary. The increase in the number of secondary schools (middle schools and higher) in the first six years of the new Republic, 1947 to 1954, was nearly fifty per cent, and for high schools, seventy-seven per cent. The increase in the enrollment was also arresting-in the middle schools an increase of thirty per cent and in high (higher secondary) schools an increase of more than sixty per cent. The number of students who took the School Leaving Certificate more than doubled between

1948 and 1953.In this vigorous expansion of education, the importance of promoting the education of girls and women is widely recognized cause of their essential contribution to the life of India.

The difficulties of achieving comparable numerical results in girls' education, on all levels, are inherent in the situation, because of the lack of a unified system of boys' and girls' schools. But the obligation of the State to realize in practice the constitutional legal equality is accepted. Moreover, the urgent necessity for a country like India, at has universal suffrage, to educate the female population (female literacy, 9.3 per cent, 1951 census) is not debated. In 1950 the total number of girls enrolled in secondary schools was 700,000; by 1953 the enrollment in middle schools alone was 774,148, and in high schools, 256,456: The increase in enrollment of girls in secondary education indicates the collective effort of the State Governments to promote girls' education beyond the primary level, and also the awakened desire of girls for further educational opportunity.

The opening of certain professional careers-nursing, medicine and teacher training-to secondary school graduates has met an economic need. Attendance at middle schools and high schools has been encouraged by free transportation, hostel accommodations and financial assistance scholarships. In certain less progressive areas, some scholarships are allocated for girls starting from the primary), grade and continuing into the university, in order to build up) educated women leaders for the backward community life. The total advance in women's education in less than a decade from 1947-48 to 1953-54 is an illustration of the successful effort to equalize educational opportunities of women and men, an essential part of the basic goal of democratizing education.

The over-all summary of women's education, at all stages, points up the remarkable progress that characterizes India as a whole, but particularly in some seven States. Statistics show an increase of 4,000 separate institutions for girls; 3,000,000 enrolled, double the number three years earlier; and a budget increase of 67,000,000 rupees over the period. Progress in the education of girls and women is also evident in the increasing proportion in the total enrollment of students at all stages, from the primary school through the university. During the period from 1950 to 1955 the total number of girls in all educational institutions increased from 6.1 million to 8.1 million.

This marked progress in girls' education during less than a decade, however, when compared with the advance in boys' education, presents clearly the major problem of disparity between girls' education and that of boys. Two-thirds of all boys (six to eleven years) are in primary schools and only one-third of all girls. Only three per cent of girls go to secondary schools. The problem of disparity is obviously the result of the segregated system of girls' education. It is not a new problem in India. But today the problem is being attacked in India in a new spirit of determination, with the conviction that the disparity is not inevitable but can and must be solved. The new nation cannot be built on the present adverse ratio of educated women to educated men, roughly one to five.

That the disparity is being reduced is indicated in an educational survey of 1954-55. A comparison of the total enrollment for two years of men and women students, including all categories of teaching institutions, shows that women students increased approximately ten per cent and men students slightly more than five per cent. This is a hopeful trend for the future. The adoption of coeducation would undoubtedly have a material effect on the solution of the problem of disparity. According to an official report, coeducation has been discussed and the position generally adopted that "there should be common schools for boys and girls at the elementary stage, but that schools should be separated at the secondary stage."

A growing trend toward coeducation is apparent in the number of State Governments that have already adopted the system, especially in the primary schools. In 1953, there were eight states that had coeducation. Since then, doubtless, others have also endorsed it for the primary schools, and some for secondary schools on a voluntary basis. Coeducation is a subject of discussion among educators, who have clear convictions on coeducation, both for and against, based on their educational experience. The advance in primary and secondary education during this period has been evident not merely quantitatively, but qualitatively in the changing pattern and new content of education itself. Two aims have been steadily related and are being carried out: to give educational opportunity to all, in accordance with constitutional equality, and to reconstruct the educational system to meet the needs of the new nation.

For primary schools, the principles of Basic Education have been adopted as offering the right type of education for young children. New primary schools on the Basic Education pattern are being built as rapidly as possible. Meanwhile the present schools are being improved and the content enriched by introducing crafts and creative activities, and better text books. The change to the Basic Education pattern for primary schools was accepted by the States of the Union in 1948 and in spite of difficulties, financial and otherwise, the number of such schools has steadily increased.

The chief difficulties are the dearth of trained teachers and the special training needed for "Basic" schools. To meet this need, a large scale, brief in-service training was carried out in 1957. This required primarily an intensive training in crafts, as the schools are craft-centered and aim to harmonize the regular school work with crafts chosen in relation to the children's background. The general objective of Basic Education is to promote a better standard of life and to lead to some earning. The joyous atmosphere of freedom and creative activity of these schools is evidence of the value of this method, which, it is hoped, will eventually be the general pattern of primary education in India.

The plans for reconstruction in the secondary field were made by a Commission appointed by the Central Government. The major recommendations stressed the need "for varying educational courses to suit different aptitudes and to enable the large majority of persons to fit into some vocation after completing their school career. A large number of multi-purpose high schools are therefore needed, where encouragement may be given in particular to agriculture and allied activities and to cottage and small-scale industries." Improvements are being made in the current curriculum through new courses in civics, music, and home science. Training courses in recreation activities and voluntary social service are offered, as well as vocational guidance.

Women educators consider that the diversified courses in the multiple high schools will have great practical value for many girls and young women, in directing them into useful employment and in offering opportunities for vocational training and guidance. Such courses, it is felt, will result in stimulating the desire of secondary school graduates to enter certain courses not requiring university professional preparation in fields in which there is special need and opportunity for well-trained workers. This body of young women from the secondary schools constitutes a very large potential for a number of national services, such as health visitors, of whom there are only 800 in all India. The plan would also serve the needs of young women for a general education and prepare them to take their places as citizens in their own home towns and in society.

Three hundred and thirty-four multi-purpose schools were established by 1956. The Second Five Year Plan will add about four times that number. A group of experimental Teacher Training Colleges has set up extension services to help secondary teachers improve methods and curricula. The need for vocational guidance and training seems to be widely felt. A young Muslim student in Osmania University expressed a keen desire for guidance and her feeling of futility in not having a sense of direction in planning for a career. The Principal of the Women's College of Aligarh University, speaking especially of Muslim young women, stressed the need for more vocational direction of students still in secondary school.

"There are always," she said, "a number of young women for whom useful careers along non-academic lines should and could be found." She emphasized also the lack of available resources for vocational guidance for the use of student advisers. Since Independence the pressure for higher education has steadily increased. Before partition there were twenty-one universities in India; after partition two were transferred (Lahore and Dacca) to Pakistan. The number in India in 1957 was thirty-two. During the First Five Year Plan the enrollment in the universities increased from 396,745 to 720,000; the number of State colleges from 695 to 965.

At the beginning of this new period of rapid expansion, the Government of India appointed an Indian University Commission to make an exhaustive survey of university situations under changed conditions. Some of the suggestions were: the establishment of a University Grants Commission to allocate funds and promote better standards; more emphasis on agricultural education and on higher education in rural areas; a better examination system; changing the system of recruitment for public service to one of competitive examination without requirement of a degree and raising the status of teachers.

The Second Five Year Plan includes provision for seven new universities, and new buildings-libraries, laboratories and hostels -for the present institutions; also the development of a new Rural University specializing in citizenship training, research on rural problems, and village extension service. Broadening the life of the universities has been the growth in extra-curricular activities. Universities and colleges have promoted training in the National Cadet Corps for both men and women, in close relationship to the regular university program and under university control. Extra-curricular activities are planned also by the students themselves, and have included all the activities common to universities elsewhere.

Inter-university debates and oratorical contests of men and women students are popular. Student information and travel bureaus have carried on useful service in counselling on courses of study in India and available scholarships, as well as in promoting overseas contacts and study. Students have international contacts with the World University Service, the Delhi Student Committee being the liaison center for India with the World Organization in Geneva. In the First Five Year Plan, women's higher education received special consideration, not only assurance of equal opportunity with men but provision for their particular interests, opportunities for private study and for taking necessary examinations as private candidates. Short-term courses in general education were also set up for women.

All universities are open to women as a constitutional right. Present statistics on the enrollment of women university students are not available, but in 1957 they were 13.6 per cent of the total number registered. Of the thirty-two universities in India, all but one has general education courses with women students enrolled. The Thompson College of Civil Engineering, the Roorkie, the only engineering institution in India (established over a hundred years ago and since 1948 a residential institution) is primarily a men's college but women are free to attend. The response of women to higher education opportunities is shown by the fact that 4900 were completing courses in 1955-56 in certain professional fields-education, medicine, law, commerce, music and fine arts, and library, science.

Independent women's colleges have made and are making a noteworthy contribution to women's higher education. Especially significant are the pioneering professional colleges-Christian Medical College, Ludhiana, Principal, Dr. Eileen R. B. Snow; The Lady Hardinge Government Medical College for Women, Principal, Dr. H. Patil, and the Christian Medical College, Vellore, Founder Principal, Dr. Ida Scudder, present Director, Dr. John Carman. They have exerted a marked influence on the medical profession for women for many years and without which a number of young women of conservative families, especially Muslims in *purdah*, could not have studied medicine.

Noteworthy also is the Lady Irwin College for Home Science in New Delhi, founded by The All-India Women's Conference with University affiliation, which has given training in home science the status of a profession, under the leadership of the first Principal, the late Mrs. Hannah Sen, for more than twenty years, and of the present Principal, Mrs. Bijur Tara Bai. The Higher Schools of nursing in Delhi and Vellore, founded later, are successfully raising the professional status of nursing. The development of the general field of higher education for women is also intimately associated with a number of pioneering women's colleges for general education, each worthy of special mention. These colleges exemplify modern scientific education for women, liberal culture and general education and especially character training for leadership.

The founders and leaders of these institutions represent different cultural and religious backgrounds, mostly Indian, some foreign, all united in promoting the advance of women through higher education. Throughout the years trained women of all communities have gone out from these colleges as teachers, doctors, homemakers, social workers, civic leaders, and women prominent in political life to serve India at home and abroad. Since Independence the number of women's colleges has increased in all areas. These new women's colleges, together with the colleges of long standing and distinction, form today a solid basis for the continued impressive educational development of Indian women.

The thousands of women students today in the colleges and universities of India, enjoying without effort the atmosphere of freedom and educational opportunity, are scarcely aware of the vision and long-sustained struggle of the pioneer leaders who made this possible. The record of progress in the education of girls and women in India from the primary school through the University naturally does not indicate the specific educational advance of the different religious communities. As a secular state India offers equal opportunities for education to all alike and is concerned primarily with the total unified result.

The advance of Muslim girls in education is an integral part of the total advance and cannot be measured separately by statistics. Prior to 1947 there was a special chapter on Muslim Education in the Report of the Director of Public Instruction; it has since been discontinued. If there were still statistical material available, it would show that Muslim girls are in a retarded situation as compared with others, but that the gap is undoubtedly narrowing. Hopeful development in the field of education for Muslim girls and women is, therefore, worth special attention. Of primary significance is the fact that the conservative attitude of many Muslim parents toward girls' education is changing.

A growing number of conservative parents are now willing to send their daughters to school and some to college, as girls have started earning their livelihood and helping the family. Education for girls is now increasingly recognized as an economic asset to their parents or husbands, as the case may be. This change is now apparent in the usually conservative middle class. Although indifference and apathy and conservatism characterize the Muslim community in respect to girls' education, the more liberal trend in public opinion is without doubt gaining ground, girls' education is being recognized and the provision of more girls' schools is being urged. An obvious evidence of change is the decline of the *purdah* system and decrease of the *burqa* in many areas, especially for the younger generation.

This progressive trend will increase the number of Muslim girls who can enter mixed primary schools and take full advantage of the government's opportunities for education and will mean a basic change in the extent and freedom of the educational development of Muslim girls. The most hopeful sign of advance is the eagerness of Muslim girls to have their full opportunity of primary and secondary schools and college. Their urge for education reflects a sense of need to be prepared to play their part in the new India. Muslim youth, girls as well as boys, share with all Indian youth the common desire to be identified with the new development of national life. Educational urge and the newly awakened spirit of patriotism are closely related in the minds of youth. For Muslim girls this fact has special meaning for their future.

In the education of Indian girls as a whole, including Muslim girls, private schools of Indian and foreign agencies, for many years have made an important contribution. In almost every large city the Muslim community, long before the partition, had organized Muslim educational institutions, both for girls and boys, to give Muslim children Urdu and religious culture. In various areas Muslim girls' schools, some of long standing is being carried on by individual Muslim effort and by organizations, to meet particularly the needs of girls in *purdah* communities. Strict *purdah* observance, as has been said, is diminishing but the covered conveyances-curtained carts, tongas, and motor cars at the entrance of a Muslim private girls' school in a crowded street in Lucknow illustrate the continuing need for private schools for the *purdanashin* (girls in *purdah*).

This school, started by Begum Habibullah in 1930 as a pioneer elementary girls' school, and now with a partial junior college program, has served a special continuing need. Many Muslim girls of conservative families would be deprived of education if *purdah* arrangements were not safeguarded and an atmosphere of seclusion assured. These Muslim private girls' schools, because of the current serious economic situation, face great financial difficulties. They can receive government subsidies if they meet the standards of a secular state and are on a non-communal basis. As many Muslim private schools desire to maintain their communal basis, they must depend on non-governmental financial support.

A noteworthy, contribution to Muslim education is being made by two Muslim foundations in Bombay. The Diamond Jubilee Trust Foundation established by the late Aga Khan III provides for an extensive program of boys' and girls' primary and secondary schools, including domestic science schools and industrial classes for women; and also scholarships for secondary and college education and vocational training for girls as well as boys (800 scholarships of all kinds in 1957-58). The major responsibility of the Diamond Jubilee Trust Foundation is carried by the Honorary General Secretary, Mrs. Zarina Currimbhoy.

The Anjuman-I-Islam Trust, which is supported by individual subscriptions and contributions from Muslims and non-Muslims, also has a comprehensive education system of boys' and girls' schools on all levels. One of the well-known institutions of this Foundation in Bombay is the Anjuman-I-Islam Girls' High School, which has a full academic modern program, and also emphasis on home-training, physical education and extracurricular activities. As the principal, Mrs. Simpson noted, its growth in twenty years (founded in 1936 with three students; 1956 enrollment, fourteen hundred) is a significant illustration of the response of Muslim girls to modern educational opportunities.

The majority of Muslim parents prefer Muslim primary and secondary schools for girls, as already indicated, to preserve *purdah* conditions. The more liberal Muslim public also prefers separate Muslim girls' primary schools. The question does not arise in secondary school as there is little public secondary coeducation. The preference for Muslim education in general, boys as well as girls, is based on the desire to maintain Urdu as the medium of instruction and preserve Islamic tradition and culture. The question of language is a major problem especially for some areas. In the government schools Hindi is the prevailing language of instruction. The choice of government schools with the use of Hindi, it is feared by some Muslim parents, may mean a loss of Urdu and a decline of Muslim culture.

Others, however, feel that Muslim students without knowledge of Hindi may be handicapped economically and remain without relationship to national development. Currently, however, the Muslim schools as well as other private primary and secondary schools, are needed and desired and apparently will be, in the foreseeable future, in view of the lack of public educational facilities and the increasing pressure of demand which the government is financially unable to meet. The provision of universal, free and compulsory education up to fourteen years of age (Constitution of India, Art. 45) is obviously not yet possible but is an ultimate goal.

The higher education of Muslim girls has been slowly but steadily developing for over thirty years in women's colleges in India. In 1925 two Muslim students of Isabella Thoburn College at Lucknow in *burqas* were awarded their degrees at the Convocation of Lucknow University and in 1928 three Muslim women on the same platform, unveiled, received degrees with the other women and men students. Since Independence the number of Muslim women students in colleges has greatly increased. Today Muslim women are entering coeducation universities all over India, primarily for graduate study.

A private, *purdah* college, such as the Muslim Women's College, Lucknow, which has a well-known Principal - Kumari Roshin Jahon-faces a difficult problem because of the decreasing need for strict *purdah* on the college level and serious decline of Muslim landlord wealth since partition. The price of conservatism is too high. The Women's College, Muslim University, Aligarh, is a pioneer effort in Muslim women's education, which began as a high school in 1907 and became a B.A. college in 1939. Under the leadership of Begum Mumtaz Haidar, the Principal, it has, for more than twenty years, had a major influence in promoting higher education for women of conservative as well as of liberal Muslim families.

The student body, which has grown steadily since partition, has a Muslim majority, but always has a number of non-Muslim students. Urdu and English are used as well as Hindi. The College combines studies in Islamic culture with modern education along various lines, including special emphasis on science, to give women pre-medical training in preparation for the Medical Faculty of the University. The students attend classes for the B.A. degree in the College; and for higher degrees, in the University. At the University Convocation in 1957 eighty Muslim women appeared for degrees, of whom twelve were in *burqas*, and remained veiled throughout the awarding of degrees. One mounted the platform twice to receive high science awards. Some wore the characteristic Islamic white head veil and a number were entirely unveiled.

Aligarh College graduates often pursue further studies in science or higher mathematics and sometimes continue post-graduate study after marriage. Important teaching positions are held by graduates of the Women's College throughout India and also, especially, in women's colleges in Pakistan. Two women's colleges in Hyderabad contribute especially to Muslim women's education. The Hyderabad Women's College, affiliated with Osmania University, has a mixed student body of Muslims, Hindus, Christians and Parsis. In 1957 one-half of the enrollments of 1250 were Muslims. The medium of instruction, originally Urdu, is now English, which is in great demand, and Hindi is also used. A relatively small number of Muslim students take M.A. courses at Osmania University.

The Nizam College, closely connected with Osmania University, has always been coeducational and uses English as the medium of instruction. The staff includes both men and women. The college, which is open to all religious communities, caters to a liberal public. A considerable number of Muslim women students enter the University for M.A. courses. The most recent advance in higher education for Muslim women is the new Women's College at Madras, founded in June 1955 by the Southern India Education Trust, and started in July of that year with eighty students. Provisional affiliation with Madras University was secured. The College is steadily expanding; an institution for possibly a thousand students is envisaged in the plans. The Southern India Education Trust's (SIET) Women's College will benefit, primarily, Muslim women, because of their special need but is open to women of all religious communities in accordance with the non-communal objectives of SIET.

It will serve not only Madras but a wide area, including Muslim communities in Southeast Asia which have liberally contributed to its establishment and support. Closely associated in promoting the SIET college project is the South India Muslim Education Association in Madras, which has vigorously campaigned for Muslim and non-Muslim donors and shares in the College administration. Muslim women leaders are actively participating in this Association, especially in raising funds for the College. The new Women's College at Madras will materially advance the future development of Muslim women's education not only, in Madras but in all of Southern India. The presence of Prime Minister Nehru and the late Education Minister of India, Maulana Azad, at the Foundation Ceremony of the College was an evidence of the concern of the leaders of India for the advancement of the education of Muslim women.

The Prime Minister's strong endorsement of the SIET Women's College confirmed the confidence of the public in his support. "If a country is going to make progress," he said, "as we are determined to do, it is quite essential that education should be widespread among men and women." From the status, position and education of women in a country, one could draw a sure deduction about the rest of the country. The Education Minister in his address stressed the basic objective of the College "to serve all sections of the population without distinction of religion, community or caste" and expressed the hope that the promotion of education in this liberal spirit would "bring about among women irrespective of religion a true awakening to their role in society and in the building of the nation."

In the total educational program of the Government of India, social education has claimed major attention, since a literate population is an urgent necessity for national development. Social education, the new term used instead of adult education, includes in addition to literacy, the central objective, general education in health, home life and recreation, economic activity and citizenship training, with special emphasis on women. "The importance of social education of women," as expressed by Mrs. Durgabai Deshmuk, Chairman of the Central Social Welfare Board, "is tantamount to education of two generations of a community, because educating the women amounts to educating the whole family and this work can most effectively be carried out by women workers."

The success of the Social Education Program depends upon the cooperation of the people. Its expansion, as pointed out in the Second Five Year Plan, will be conditioned by the joint efforts of all local groups in rural life-the cooperatives and labor groups, the village *panchayats* (councils), the village cooperatives, and village education centers. The program of social education, which has been promoted directly by the Ministry of Education during the first plan, included setting up community centers and libraries, wide distribution to the State Governments of adult education pamphlets (10,000 produced by the Adult Education Department of Jamia Millia University near Delhi), a planning conference of experts on audio-visual education, and the establishment of Social Education Department in the State Governments.

The Ministry of Labor promoted a literacy program among industrial workers and the Defense Forces, a successful two-year program which reduced the number of illiterates in these groups from 19,344 in 1949 to 5,780 in 1951. Two very interesting social education projects were carried out in a rural area in Delhi State-an intensive literacy campaign and a social education caravan project. The first was a concentrated effort to liquidate the illiteracy of 124,000 persons in a chosen area through primary and secondary schools and teacher training institutes for men and women. The Caravan Project comprised several jeeps, a mobile stage, a library, an exhibition van and a projector.

The caravan settled temporarily in a central village, presented an exhibition of health, agriculture, etc., and staged a dramatic performance with local talent, using educational propaganda and puppets for the themes, organized athletic contests and general village recreation. Soon the whole village was a part of the project. Then literacy classes were organized, local leaders recruited and eventually the caravan moved on. The concentrated social education program, which has been carried on since 1947, is bearing results. General literacy, which was 12.2 per cent in 1941, was 16.6 per cent in 1951; the female literacy, 9.6 per cent in 1951, marks an increase over earlier estimate of fewer than eight per cent.

The 1951 census gives the latest measure of progress. Noteworthy in this advance is the growth in the number of educational centers for adult women, and the eager response of women to the opportunities offered them. For the further development of social education the Second Five Year Plan suggests expansion of facilities on all levels: (1) for the State programs, the opening of more Social Education Centers, training of social education organizers, publication of literature, audio-visual education and founding of Rural Institutes; (2) the establishing of an education center for training social education organizers and for research in social education problems.

An interesting voluntary project is Literacy Village, a literacy plus program, at Saksharta Niketan near Lucknow. It is widely known as a unique social education center for training in literacy, techniques and research, and for the production of reading materials for new literates- the trainees-teachers, village workers, men and women but mostly men-come from all over India. Hundreds have had the four-week course. Puppets and

Khaddargraph (like the Western flannel graph) are successfully used. The book distribution covers all parts of India. Voluntary effort has made an inestimable contribution to the promotion of literacy and adult education. It is impossible to enumerate the countless services of individuals and groups working independently, especially women with literacy classes for women.

In every area of India there are illustrations of voluntary personal service. To mention only one-the remarkable adult education program for illiterate women in the crowded Bombay tenements, carried on for thirty years by Mrs. Kulsum Sayani, a Muslim leader. The crucial problem of education in India is the shortage of teachers. 2.8 million teachers were needed in 1947 for compulsory education; only 560,000 primary teachers were available and of these only 58.2 per cent were trained. Women teachers in 1953-54 were only seventeen per cent of the total number of teachers in primary and secondary schools. Substantial progress was made under the First Five Year Plan but the number of trained teachers is still far from adequate. This lack of women teachers is a major deterrent to the attendance of girls at school and keeps village women away from the Social Education Centers, as rural women can be reached only by women.

Without women teachers it will be impossible to expand girls' primary education. To this end, the maximum age limit for recruitment has been raised from forty to forty-five and the minimum educational qualification has been reduced. The utilization of women teachers for village work presents two main problems: lack of living quarters the need to arrange for part-time service of married women. The training of more women teachers is an immediate necessity because the Third Five Year Plan will give priority to women's education. A wide-scale, quick, in-service plan was carried out in 1957 by various colleges with Teacher Training Departments. In some cases mobile training squads gave courses in different centers for groups of local leaders.

The in-service training plan has been welcomed by the colleges that have participated. The Director of Teacher Training at Isabella Thoburn College, Miss Doris Wilson, in a personal letter wrote with enthusiasm about the invigorating effect of this plan of national service. A number of Training Institutes have been set up in the States for training in Basic Education; some with experimentation in village relations to serve the villages nearby and train village leaders; others as experimental centers, combining Basic Education and the conventional program and studying the distinctive principles of both types.

Preparation is being made for the specific emphasis on women's education under the Third Five Year Plan. At the suggestion of the Education Panel of the Planning Commission, the Government set up a National Committee on Women's Education in 1958, made up of highly representative leaders-educators in schools and colleges and specialists in social education, editors, social workers and others - under the Chairmanship of Mrs. Durgabai Deshmuk. The Committee has wide terms of reference to investigate the major problems of education of girls, the need for increase in vocational and social education, the contribution of voluntary organizations, etc., and to recommend the necessary measures to expand and improve education for girls and women.

An over-all view of education in India since Independence leaves an impression of great progress. There has been remarkable expansion on all levels, and at the same time a steady adaptation of methods to meet the changing needs of modern India. New ideas have become dynamic in action, as is evident from the spread of social education, nation-wide; the extension of education to all classes; the training of thousands of teachers and village workers, many of them women, for health and rural welfare; and marked advance in the education of girls and women, with plans for its wide and carefully considered promotion in the next Five Year Plan. All these developments have been made possible through the cooperation and eager response of the Indian people themselves, and especially through the efforts of women.

Education in this period has steadily advanced toward the achievement of the major objective-to equalize the educational opportunity for all classes in order to build a democratic society in free India. Women's organizations and voluntary groups-local, state and national-have made a marked contribution to educational advance in India, especially the education of women and girls, both in rural and urban areas. Women's organized effort has been evident on all levels: primary, secondary, and higher education; social education-literacy, general training of women for home and family life; vocational education, training for clerical service and industrial employment; and citizenship education through lectures, seminars, conferences.

The scope and volume of the voluntary educational activities of women in India make a detailed enumeration of the specialized services of individual organizations impossible. The national organizations play a considerable part in the general educational program, stimulating the voluntary effort of their local branches, interpreting the national education plans of the government and promoting effective cooperation. A number of official and private agencies have cooperated with the Indian Government in the development of its extensive national programs in education through material aid and technical assistance in India and scholarships and fellowships for study abroad

These participating agencies include the United Nations-UNESCO and ILO; the Colombo Powers (the members of the Commonwealth); the Technical Cooperation Mission of the U. S.; the U. S. Education Foundation in India (the joint Indian and American administration of the Fulbright fellowship program); and private philanthropic groups such as the Ford, Rockefeller and Asia Foundations, American Friends Committee, and the British Council. The sum total of the contribution in material and technical assistance of these various agencies represents a considerable volume of fruitful international cooperation.

An hour with the Minister of Health in India, Rajkumari Amrit Kaur, in 1957, left an impression of the overwhelming health needs of India, a dark picture but one with highlights of hopeful change. To establish the new health program of India was and still is a tremendous task, two-fold in character and aim-to intensify the fight against communicable disease, and continue the long-range effort to build a sound foundation for national health. Remarkable progress has been made in eliminating several of the major enemies of India. Two hundred million Indians live in malarial areas. One-half have been protected by a mass-scale campaign against malaria, probably the largest in the world, which will continue until all have been reached. In the fight against tuberculosis, eighty-two million persons have been tested and over twenty-eight million vaccinated.

There are 2.5 million active cases of tuberculosis; one-half million die each year. The Second Five Year Plan proposes to open new training centers and clinics and to reach the entire susceptible population under twenty-five years of age. Leprosy is a menace to other million and a half in India. Already, through research and teaching, advance has been made. The Second Five Year Plan will provide eighty-eight more subsidiary centers, as well as isolation care and rehabilitation. The struggle against disease is accompanied by an active campaign to eradicate the causes - contaminated water, improper waste disposal, poor housing, and low standards of sanitation and of public health. Only six per cent of the population has protected water and three per cent protected sewage.

Progress was made during the First Five Year Plan in sanitation in certain selected areas; 100,000 drinking water wells were built or renovated, and thousands of feet of drains constructed. To improve the environment, sanitation must be taught, which means that training facilities for public health engineers, sanitary inspectors and other workers must be provided. Along with this continuing campaign against disease and a low sanitary standard, a Positive Health Program for rural India was steadily, promoted during the First Five Year Plan, and continues to be a central objective. A network of Health Centers or units, 725 in all, a part of the Community Development Block Plan, was established. One health unit is located in each "block" of 100 villages, called a "National Extension Service Block," of which it is planned to have, eventually, 5,000.

These health units are the center for the curative and preventive health services in the various areas, and will meet the need until the full medical care of hospitals can be extended to reach the 500,000 villages. The Second Five-Year Plan proposes to add more than 3,000 health units in national extension and community projects and in other areas, serving some 60,000 persons in each area. A number of mobile teams will carry out the over-all program-maternal and child health work, sanitation, preventive inoculation and health education. A central necessity in the intensive rural health development is promotion of the Maternal and Child Health Program (MCH). During the period of the First Five Year Plan a hopeful index of change in the health situation was the decrease in infant mortality from 127 per 1,000 births in 1950 to 113 in 1954. Maternal mortality likewise decreased.

This is encouraging, yet at the same time it points up the appallingly high infant mortality, and emphasizes the need for continuing effort to provide maternal and child care. The number of MCH Centers was increased from 1,651 to 1,790. In this number are 136 centers in the backward areas of sixteen States. In solving the difficult problem of recruiting and training health workers such as nurses, midwives, health visitors, auxiliary nurse midwives, the Government midwifery service has had the full cooperation and assistance of WHO and UNICEF-material help to the schools and stipends for women medical officers and midwives taking refresher courses, and considerable financial aid from UNICEF in addition, in establishing the widely known Maternal and Child Health Training Center at the All-India Institute of Hygiene and Public Health in Calcutta. This Institute provides training for MCH personnel, not only from India but the whole of South East Asia.

The courses include both academic and field training in maternal and child health work, public health nursing, public health education and related fields. A number of fellowships have been established. In discussing their MCH service, the nurses and midwives always stress both the decline in traditional attitudes toward modern health care and the slow but steady growth in the active interest of the village people. Many Centers have been built with the financial help and labor of the village people themselves, women bearing their share.

The eager response of village women to MCH care and also their urgent needs are evident from the waiting rooms in any of the MCH Centers or Clinics, which are always filled with mothers and their children, patiently waiting their turn for the service of the over pressed staff.

The multiplication of MCH Centers and an increase in health workers are interdependent and urgently needed. The Second Five Year Plan provided for 2,100 more MCH Centers, to be directly attached to the rural units. The work for mothers and children provided for pre-natal care, domiciliary midwifery, post-natal follow-up and care of the child during its first year. Thirty-six thousand local hereditary midwives, *dais*, were to be trained; five centers for pediatric training were to be set up for instruction of health workers in regular and refresher courses. These workers would give both ante-natal and obstetrical service in MCH Centers, and teach health education in the elementary schools.

Nutrition teaching in the use of protective foods, especially for children and expectant mothers, has been an important part of the MCH program in rural areas, where the low standard of living is the result not only of poverty but of ignorance. Family planning in India is being vigorously promoted as a central government policy related to the basic problems of food, health and general welfare. The limitation of population is regarded as both a primary health service in safeguarding the life of both mother and child, and a national necessity, in order to stabilize population on a level in balance with national economy. The Government promotion of family planning represents the fruition of the efforts of individuals and agencies for many years to awaken concern on birth control. The All-India Women's Conference, held in Trivandrum in 1936, called the attention of women especially to this problem.

The First Five Year Plan began the family planning program with an allocation of sixty-five lakhs (100,000 rupees=1 lakh; 65 lakhs=6,500,000) for research on basic problems, field experiments in different methods and financial assistance to voluntary agencies for family planning. Through the Family Planning Section of the Ministry of Health the Government has carried on an enormous education program through broadcasts and visual aids, pamphlets, exhibits, demonstration centers with distribution of free materials. By 1957 every city in India had at least one clinic; some ten to thirty. By 1961 the Second Five Year Plan expects to set up 2,000 rural and 300 urban centers. Family Planning is the core around which other health programs are being built or developed for the social and economic well being of India. The fact that the present increase in the birth rate is 4.5 million each year makes Family Planning imperative.

The Family Planning Association, with men and women members, established in 1949 under the Chairmanship of Lady Dhanvanti Rama Rau, is cooperating closely in its thirteen branches throughout India with the government program. With financial assistance, the Association is able to develop effectively an extensive program of welfare services and carries on valuable research in relation to the basic problems of population control. The program includes family planning clinics, parents' classes and guidance centers, widespread education and research in specific Indian problems. The Association publishes the bimonthly Journal of Family Welfare and sponsors the Family Welfare Bureau, financed by the Government. It exerts wide regional influence through contacts and national conferences.

The Family Planning Association in India is affiliated with the International Planned Parenthood Federation, which held its first meeting in Bombay in 1952. The Federation met in New Delhi in 1959. The most serious problem in the development of the health program in India, particularly in rural areas, is, as has been said, the shortage of trained medical and health personnel. At the beginning of the First Five Year Plan there were 59,000 doctors, or about one to every 6,200 population; in rural areas one to about every 15,000 persons, because of the concentration of doctors in cities. By 1956 there were 70,000 qualified doctors in India; 12,500 more will qualify by 1960. The number of medical colleges increased during the First Five Year Plan from thirty to forty-two and the annual admissions from 2,500 to 3,500.

The Second Five Year Plan will provide for more colleges, the upgrading of certain of them for graduate training and research, establishment of preventive medicine and psychiatric departments in several colleges, and an All-India Institute of Medical Science. The number of women doctors in 1950 was 4,552 (medical graduates 2,214, medical licentiates 2,338). The number of women doctors in 1958 was 7,299 out of a total of 69,605. Women students consider medicine a priority profession because of its prestige and professional opportunity, and because of its strong service appeal. They have equality of access to all medical colleges and universities, but the number of women applicants for entrance exceeds the possibilities of admission.

There are three well-known, long-established women's colleges, Lady Hardinge and the two Christian medical colleges-Ludhiana Medical School and Christian Medical College, Vellore, both of which now admit men. Currently there is a marked trend toward coeducation, as is shown by the growing number of women in coeducational medical schools. The Central Government, after long consideration, adopted the policy of coeducation for medical training. However, the specific government proposal to convert the Lady Hardinge Medical College into a coeducational institution met with such vigorous opposition by the Association of Medical Women and other women's organizations that the College has been allowed to continue exclusively for women.

The opposition of the women's organizations was made on the basis that the discontinuance of Lady Hardinge College "was a premature step, as social conditions had not changed overnight with the acquisition of Independence." The Association of Medical Women in India is affiliated with the International Association of Medical Women. India has some 600-700 qualified dental surgeons and six dental colleges. The Second Five Year Plan will add four colleges, double the admissions and raise the standards. This is another profession in which the number of women might be increased. Women are very much needed.

During the First Five Year Plan marked advance was made in the training of health personnel of all categories-nurses, midwives, health visitors and nurse-*dais*. The number of nurses increased from 17,000 to 22,000; midwives from 18,000 to 26,000; health visitors from 600 to 800 and nurse-*dais* or midwives from 4,000 to 6,800. The goals for 1960 for the several categories increased, respectively, for nurses to 31,000, midwives to 32,000, and health visitors to 2,500. The training centers for nurses increased from 141 to 324 and for midwives from 156 to 259 and for health visitors eight other institutions in addition to the Lady Reading Health School at Delhi were expanded. In 1955 there were in training 2,030 nurses, 2,170 midwives, 2,070 *dais* and 600 auxiliary nurse midwives.

The minimum education requirement for nurses' training is matriculation (high school education), which is not yet enforced in some States. The three-year course, plus six months midwifery, combines nursing care and domiciliary service with public health instruction and village work-a special emphasis in the States' training program. The Director of the New Delhi College of Nursing in 1957, Miss Margaretta Craig, stressed the hopeful trend in nursing away from merely bedside care of the sick: "Today," she said, "nursing is a service to maintain positive health of body, mind and spirit-a great challenge to nurses' training." For many years the training of nurses was largely given in Christian hospitals. Nurses' training today is a major Government responsibility.

There are two higher schools of nursing in India, in New Delhi and Vellore. The New Delhi College of Nursing is affiliated with the University of Delhi; the School of Nursing in the Vellore Christian Medical College is accredited for the B.S. degree in nursing by the Medical College of the University of Madras. The Dean of the School of Nursing is Miss Florence Taylor. Both New Delhi and Vellore require a minimum of two years of intermediate college (some students have had four years of college) for entrance to the four-year integrated college course of regular nursing and full public health instruction. A new post-graduate course for nursing administration and teaching, open to experienced registered nurses, leads to the certificate issued by the Ministry of Health.

The demand for entrance to the two colleges far exceeds their capacity, which is limited because of lack of hostel space. As Government colleges, all of their admissions are by examination. The financial status of nurses in hospitals is low but the basic pay-100-185 rupees per month, plus allowances for board and room, uniform and laundry-may equal the earning of the average level of teaching. There are very few private nurses with independent earnings, mostly in large cities. The attitude toward nursing has been steadily changing, especially since Independence. The general loosening of fixed social lines has helped to lessen the prejudice against it, and the two Colleges of Nursing are raising the status of nursing to the University level with other professions. Thus nursing can attract the type of woman needed for the increased responsibility envisaged by the Second Five Year Plan. The changing attitude toward nursing is reflected in the enrollment of these two nonsectarian colleges, which include a large Hindi majority, many Christians and a few Muslims.

The marked increase in Hindus and the attendance of even a few Muslims mark hopeful advance. The Trained Nurses' Association of India is affiliated with the International Council of Nursing. The entrance requirement for midwifery training is seven years of schooling. The two-year course includes, in addition to the usual training, some elementary nursing and more hygiene, to prepare the midwives in rural areas for simple nursing duties as required. Also, experience will be provided in organizing and conducting ante-natal clinics in order to improve preventive service.

"Midwifery does not have the status of an independent profession," as explained by Miss T. K. Adranvala, Chief Nursing Superintendent, Ministry of Health, probably because it has been traditionally practiced by untrained women of low social standing. Most women nurses are qualified midwives but very few practice midwifery except in their hospital service. Upper class women prefer to use the hospital, a maternity home, or call a doctor. Training in midwifery alone is often selected by candidates not eligible for nurses' training.

The Second Five Year Plan of increasing the number of trained midwives should lift the level of midwifery as an independent career service.

Trained midwives are used largely in maternal and child welfare clinics and in domiciliary service in limited areas. Only the untrained local *dais*-the traditional hereditary midwives, the Sairy Gamps-is available for the midwifery needs of the great mass of village women. The Second Five Year Plan provides for the training of 36,000 *dais* in a six-month course prescribed by the Indian Council of Nursing, to be given by the public health nurses or health visitors qualified in nursing, with supervision in their service by health visitors and trained midwives. Untrained *dais* attends eighty-five per cent of total yearly births (eight million).

The health visitor service has contributed effectively to the development of the maternity and child welfare program in India. It was started by the Lady Reading Health School, originally under the Red Cross, and later a Government institution. There are now ten other Health Visitor Schools in India, either Red Cross or Government State schools. Matriculation is required for the health visitor training. The three-year course-eighteen months in midwifery and eighteen months in public health-prepares for work with children up to five years, in ante-natal and post-natal clinics, home nursing and midwifery; and since 1955 with an integrated course in mid- wifery and public health. Health visitors receive the same salary as trained nurses, without the nurses' allowances for living, uniforms, etc.

The career of the health visitor, according to Miss M. Korah, Director of the Lady Reading Health Service, is preferred by most parents and young women to that of nursing for various reasons: higher social status, freedom from the régime of hospital living, and more freedom to work after marriage, as the health visitor has a daytime schedule. Moreover, the profession of health visitor is a new profession and free from any inherited prejudice. In the further development of the Maternal and Child Health Program,

Dr. S. Bhatia, Advisor on Maternity and Child Welfare, Ministry of Health, stressed the need to utilize more fully the MCH officers for technical advice in institutions, consultation and training services, help in administrative problems in the MCH, and for participation in the school health service.

Securing women personnel for health service in rural communities presents the familiar problem of the shortage of women candidates willing to enter service in rural areas, in view of prevailing social conservatism. All candidates, in varying degrees, face the same difficulties in living conditions and a generally adverse social climate, especially for unmarried women. In order to achieve the goal of greatly increased numbers of women in rural health service, the official promotion of a change in social conditions is a necessity. The crucial need of health personnel is evident in the 1951 census: one nurse for 43,000 populations, one health visitor for 400,000, and one midwife for 60,000. In 1956, health personnel (other than doctors), in spite of progress, was only twenty-five per cent of the number needed. In 1961 it will be forty per cent, in view of the increased provision for health personnel in the Second Five Year Plan, which envisions steady progress toward a still distant goal.

Builders of the health program face with realism these tremendous difficulties but are nonetheless encouraged by the signs of hope. To quote from an address to the YWCA International Seminar by the Minister of Health, Rajkumari Amrit Kaur, "Until ignorance and poverty are overcome, health standards will remain below the optimum. However, the efforts we have put in during the last few years have been rewarded with results which give us hope and confidence that we will in due course find a place among the healthy nations of the world." The Government health program has been capably promoted by women's organizations and mixed voluntary agencies. Various national organizations-the Red Cross, All-India Women's Conference, National Council of Women, Family Planning Association, National Association of Medical Women and the YWCA-have carried on varied nationwide health services through their branches in cities and towns and particularly in rural areas.

The composite of health welfare comprises child welfare

clinics, maternity welfare centers, dispensaries, mobile medical vans, voluntary hospital care, and distribution of vitamin tablets and milk powder from UNICEF, and training of women rural welfare workers. The various welfare programs are carried out cooperatively and in close relationship to the over-all government plan. The following international and foreign agencies have cooperated with the Government of India in developing the health program: WHO, UNICEF, FAO, the Colombo Plan, Technical Cooperation Mission, and the Rockefeller and Ford Foundations.

In the rural development program, the welfare of women and children has claimed the major attention of the Government and also of voluntary agencies. After the community development program was inaugurated, it became evident that village women would have a determinative influence on its success, and, moreover, that it would be impossible to raise the level of family living, a major objective, without the cooperation of women. A development program for village women was obviously necessary, as were also women workers, since the men workers in the community development program had no contact with village women.

The National Home Science Extension Program, accordingly, was set up in 1954 in the Food and Agriculture Ministry, to train rural women workers and the training program was started in 1955 under the direction of Dr. Rajammal P. Devadas, Chief Home Economist of the Ministry of Agriculture. Twenty-five training centers-home economics wings-were established and at the same time an extension bureau to supervise these centers-the first National Home Science Bureau in India. By 1956, two home science extension training centers had been established, and within a year these centers had all been staffed, each with three trained home economists, to a total of eighty-one.

In each center twenty women annually have had a one year training course and then been assigned to village service in the development Block, two workers in each Bloc of 100 villages. The *gramsevikas* (village workers) select a few villages at a time for their service. By December 1961, it is hoped to have 3,300 trained *gramsevikas* to supply two per Block in about 1,650 Blocks. The one-year training course includes food and nutrition, clothing for the family, mother and child care, health and sanitation, handicraft and cottage industries, agriculture, cooperatives, civics, community recreation and psychology. Agriculture and handicrafts have special emphasis. Practical field work includes kitchen gardening, bee keeping, dairying, poultry raising, farming and horticulture. This course is the basis for the work with the village women in helping them in their home and family life and in the community.

The major requirements for admission to the course are: age, between eighteen and thirty-five; education, ten years of school; a village background, and special desire to work in rural India. The Home Science Wings throughout India are located usually in the general training centers of the National Extension Services, where various types of training are given, or in an Agricultural Extension Center, as at Sarojini Nagar at Lucknow. Wherever located, these Home Science Wings are developed along the same lines. A visit to Sarojini Nagar with the social welfare adviser from Lucknow gave a clear idea of the general training plan-a group of young trainees and teachers living and working together as a family in a fairly large Center, recently built, which combines living quarters and rooms for teaching.

This group of eighteen young women, all from villages, was made up of Hindus, the majority, Christians, and six Muslims. (The number of Muslims was noted as unusual since relatively few enter rural service.) Several in the group were married. The trainees were responsible for the housekeeping, which was considered an essential part of their training. The staff was the usual number-a director, an experienced older woman who was a university graduate with a number of years in Government work, and three associates, well-trained younger women. Temporarily the Center was having the assistance of a mobile team for one week, to train in fruit preservation. The regular program had been changed to concentrate on this special subject. Other teams teaching embroidery, tailoring, horticulture, and medical care, frequently "services" the Center. Specialists from the Agricultural Center are also available for technical assistance.

The day's schedule at the Training Center, from 5.00 a.m. to 10:00 p.m., is very full. There are household duties (classes beginning at 8:00 a.m.), field work, recreation, study and rest periods, crafts, prayer time, and the evening free for reading and discussion. The Training Center gave the impression of a well-organized program and a well-adjusted group living and working together. The *gramsevikas* seemed to enjoy their full, disciplined life and the free atmosphere of the center. One could easily envisage this group in village service later. After the training course the *gramsevikas* begin their village work. In their training it has been emphasized that they must move slowly, get acquainted with the women in their homes, learn their needs and interests, and let the program gradually take shape.

Through their contacts and the various classes the *gramsevikas* are able slowly to improve home practices, food habits, sanitation, and the basic standards of living. Special effort is made to develop in the village woman a sense of economic responsibility for the family and for the community as a co-partner with her husband in agriculture and food production, helping to raise the economic standards of rural life. The objective is to break down the segregation of women in the village, and encourage them to take part as responsible citizens in community life. One of the leaders summed up the response of the village women to the help of the gramsevika. "Village women are eager to know modern techniques and apply them in their homes, provided they are profitable to them and do not violate their cultural background and religious belief. The *gramsevikas* are inspired by the response of the village women."

Women social education organizers contribute to the village welfare program for women in connection with literacy and increased participation of women in village life. Their work with village women is part of the general social education program carried on jointly by men and women workers. The women social education organizers are college or university graduates, usually with teaching or social work experience. Training for social education in the villages is coeducational, and includes theoretical subjects-psychology, sociology, etc.-and practical preparation for general community activities-recreation, group work, and civic education.

Estimates of the Second Five Year Plan are that 200,000 workers of all types of village service are needed. Provision is being made to cover the large-scale training requirements by the increase of extension training centers from forty-three to sixty-one. In order to mobilize and develop the nation-wide social welfare resources of voluntary agencies, the Government set up the Central Social Welfare Board as part of the First Five Year Plan, to assist them to carry on their welfare program for women, children and handicapped persons. The work the Central Board of Social Welfare, under the Chairmanship of Mrs. Durgabai Deshmukh, covers all of India-but the beginning period was concerned primarily with rural India. In cooperation with the State Governments, the Central Board has set up State Social Welfare Boards throughout India. These Boards are composed largely of non-officials, all women, with much experience in voluntary welfare work.

The Central Board is empowered with large funds and a great deal of administrative authority to implement its expanding program and the welfare network of the State Boards. In the first Five Year Plan the Central Social Welfare Board assisted 2,128 private welfare organizations-grants for general welfare about one-third, women's welfare a little less than a third, and the remainder for children and institutions for the handicapped. The grants of the Central Social Welfare Board, which covered the whole country, were made to existing voluntary organizations to consolidate their activities and to new organizations to help them begin their program on sound lines. The general purpose is to facilitate the establishment of voluntary organizations throughout India.

The Central Social Welfare Board, in addition to the grants to voluntary agencies, has also launched a program of Welfare Extension Projects or extension areas, one in each District with twenty-five villages to each extension area. In 1956 there were 291 of these Welfare Extension Projects. By 1961, under the

Second Five Year Plan, there will be 1,320, four in each district, the total reaching 50,000 villages with welfare services for women and children. The program, which is carried on largely by local women welfare workers, volunteers and officials in the welfare field, includes nurseries and nursery schools, maternity and child health services, social education for arts and crafts, recreation and cultural activities. For the Welfare Extension Projects it is estimated that 6,600 *gramsevika* village welfare workers will be needed by the end of 1961.

To meet these multiple needs for trained women workers the Central Social Welfare Board has organized and carried out large scale training schemes with the cooperation and assistance of the Kasturba Gandhi Memorial Trust, the pioneer agency in rural welfare training. By the end of 1961, through Government and private agencies, 400,000 villages will have the services of trained village-level workers, home science and social education organizers-an impressive body of trained women united in the community development of rural life.

The Central Social Welfare Board, in its over-all organization with the network of State Branches and tireless individual members promoting the welfare services of hundreds of local leaders in remote centers all over India, represents graphically the remarkable expansion of social welfare through voluntary effort. But beyond its concrete success, in terms of national social welfare expansion, the Central Social Welfare Board has unusual meaning for India. It marks the recognition by the Government of the essential necessity of women's voluntary agencies in promoting national welfare and is an evidence of official confidence in women's ability to plan and administer large financial enterprises.

The Board is evidence also of the basic value of cooperation and partnership between Government and voluntary agencies. Furthermore, it clearly illustrates the integral relationship in community development between social and economic progress and specifically demonstrates that social advance in the life of village women is the key to change in the life of the homes and village, and rural life as a whole. Associated with the Chairman of the Central Social

Welfare Board, Mrs. Deshmukh, are a number of outstanding national leaders including Mrs. Achamma Matthai, Begum Ali Zahir, Mrs. Mary Clubwalla Jadhav, Mrs. P. N. Haksar, Mrs. Currimbhoy, Mrs. Sengupta and Lady Rama Rau.

Of distinct value in the welfare program for village women are the student vacation camps of girls and young women from schools and colleges, which the Bharat Sevak Samaj (Indian Service Union) is conducting as a part of the Youth Camp Program. From April 1954 to March 1957, the camp organization included 185 girls' camps (attended by 9,560 campers) compared to 904 boys' camps (attended by 75,000 campers. The disparity in numbers reflects the effect of social conditions. However, as the number of girls' camps indicates, the difficulties are being overcome.

The over-all objective of the youth camps of both sexes is to promote national reconstruction and the spirit of service through definite lines of work. The boys' camps help in building roads and schools, in slum clearance and sanitation, and in other lines of reconstruction. The main objectives of the girls' camps are to help change village conditions and to improve the personal well-being of village women-their home and family life, and life in the community. Better homes and brighter villages are the goal. The program of the girls' camps, a brief period of only two or three weeks, is planned closely with the other village workers, home economics workers, social education organizers and health workers, so that the campers can successfully supplement the regular services.

At the beginning the villagers are somewhat aloof, but after the campers have made contacts with the village elders and with women in their homes, the entire community responds, and regrets the campers' leaving, as youth brings new life to the village. The Government allotted considerable funds during the First Five Year Plan for camps organized by the National Cadet Corps and Auxiliary Cadet Corps, State Governments, the Bharat Sevak Samaj and other voluntary agencies. Cooperating with the organizers of these girls' camps for rural reconstruction in the recruiting and training of leaders are two national organizations that have had long experience in this field -The Girl Guides, headed by Mrs. Lakshmi Mazumdar, Chief Guide Commissioner of India, and the YWCA, of which Miss Ivy Khan is National General Secretary.

Of the present number of social welfare agencies and institutions in India, estimated at 10,000, women's agencies form a large part, as women have always been concerned, especially from religious motives, with charity and relief. During the past forty years since the social awakening of women began, the volume of social welfare activities has steadily grown, and since Independence, under the pressure of growing needs and opportunities, the voluntary activities of women have increased even more, and new types of work and new emphases have been developed.

There has been a special increase in child welfare services and a fresh approach to the needs of children, as illustrated by a number of pioneer projects, such as-to mention only a few- a children's recreation center and a children's cooperative (*Bal Sahyog*) for street boys and destitute in Delhi; children's vacation libraries and recreation outings in Bombay; and the model Seva Samajam Boys' and Girls' Home in Madras. In these varied child welfare agencies the problem of juvenile delinquency is a common concern, either in preventive or rehabilitation services. The organization of Child Welfare Services was promoted by Rajkumari Amrit Kaur as Health Minister in 1947 through the Indian National Committee of the United Nations Committeee for Children (UNAC).

This was later developed under the vital leadership of the late Hannah Sen and Indira Gandhi into the Indian Council for Child Welfare, which was registered in 1952 and, in 1953, affiliated with the International Union of Child Welfare. The Council stimulates and coordinates the various voluntary child welfare efforts throughout India. Emphasis is being given by Government and voluntary agencies to special welfare services for *Harijans* (outcasts), the so-called depressed classes, and physically and mentally handicapped children. The majority of institutions for the handicapped are run by private agencies with Government aid. The Second Five Year Plan provides for increased facilities, some model schools, and scholarships.

Noteworthy service is being carried on by individual women leaders for handicapped children in several fields-the mentally retarded, the blind, and the crippled children.

A widely known example is the result of the long pioneering effort of Begum Fatima Ismail for the rehabilitation of her own child, a victim of polio, which inspired the promotion of clinical and hospital care of all children stricken with polio and finally brought the achievement of the Children's Orthopaedic Hospital in Bombay, the only one of its kind in India. Among the problems frequently discussed by women leaders in India is the social evil of prostitution, which has long been a subject of major concern for women's organizations, specifically the Association of Moral and Social Hygiene. This long sustained effort gained fresh impetus three years ago through the Report of a Study of Prostitution, its cause and the present situation, made by a women's committee which was appointed by the Central Social Welfare Board.

Through this report public attention was sharply focused on the dangers of this social vice and the necessity for legislation. The Association of Moral and Social Hygiene led a vigorous campaign for drastic control of prostitution. A comprehensive new law supported by women Parliament members was presented to the Parliament but is not yet passed. The active promotion by women in Parliament of legislative social reform gives assurance of future success in eradicating social evils. Attention is being given to the aftercare services for men and women released from correctional institutions and needing homes and rehabilitation assistance. A Women's Advisory Committee appointed by the Central Board of Social Welfare has helped to plan the aftercare provision for women, for which Government funds have been provided.

Homes and care for three types of women will be provided: for women needing a long period of social and environmental adjustment before vocational training is possible; for women discharged from correctional institutions, and for women from non-correctional and care institutions for short rehabilitation periods. The aftercare program opens a new field of social work for which special training is needed.

Economic help to home women in urban areas is being provided by the Family Welfare Service, a voluntary society started in 1955 by the Central Social Welfare Board and the Ministry of Industry. It arranges for home employment, on a part-time basis, through contact with neighboring factories that can use home labor. A committee of volunteers is the liaison between the factory and the workers.

The Family Welfare Service, which provides not only home work but home welfare, child care, medical aid, and family counseling, has become a popular movement with prospects for further growth. Unique in the various voluntary activities for national welfare has been the work of the Women's Savings Campaign, a scheme to increase Government funds for the Five Year Plans by promoting thrift among women and the investment of their savings in the national cause. Under the remarkable leadership of the late Hannah Sen, 188 women's organizations have helped to carry out the plan, and 681 volunteer workers have been appointed as "agents" of the Government. The sales figures for eight months-October 1956 to May 1957-were 203 lakhs of rupees.

Social welfare leaders call attention to the marked development in coordination and cooperation among welfare agencies, which is recognized as a necessity in order to meet the increasing pressure of social needs. The Madras Guild of Service is a unique example of the efficient coordination of more than one hundred social welfare agencies under the dynamic chairmanship of Mrs. Mary Clubwalla Jadhav. The Guild was established over thirty years ago and has greatly increased its activities since 1948. It represents a wide cross section-men and women's organizations and Indian and foreign representatives of voluntary and governmental agencies for the welfare of women and children. Its over-all functions include administration of emergency relief programs, social planning and supervision of projects, information and public education.

Madras is the only city with a central coordinating body like the Guild of Service. In other cities there are many different types of cooperation and coordination of activities-inter organizational relations, group councils on special interests such as child welfare and youth problems, joint studies and surveys, training projects, etc. Similar types of cooperation are developed on national lines through All-India organizations. Among voluntary organizations there is an important new field of cooperation in respect to their relationship with Government planning. An excellent illustration is the Seminar on the Role of Voluntary Organizations in the Second Five Year Plan, which was held May 16-20, 1957, at Anandigiri Ootacamund, the YWCA Summer Conference Grounds.

It was attended by representatives of seventeen voluntary organizations, a number of Government officials and two coordinators-the Field Director of the Delhi School of Social Work, Mr. Meher Nanavatty, and the Social Welfare Adviser, Technical Cooperation Administration, Miss Evelyn Hersey. The Seminar was organized jointly by the YWCA and YMCA with the assistance of the National Social Welfare Organization in Delhi and the active support of Mr. L. R. Nair, Adviser, Five Year Plan Publicity, Ministry of Information and Broadcasting. The program comprised the presentation by Government officials of the Second Five Year Plan in main outline and specific phases-Education, Health, Social Welfare, Community Development; and the discussion by seminar groups of the Second Five Year Plan in reference to the role of voluntary agencies.

A major development in social welfare since Independence has been the establishment of six new schools of social work, making now a total of seven. The Tata Institute of Social Science, founded in 1936, was the first in India. The Delhi School of Social Work was the second, founded in 1946 and affiliated in 1948 to the University of Delhi. The Tata Institute gives a diploma in Social Service Administration and the Schools of Social Work, related to the Universities, give an M.A. degree. The other Schools are on the college level.

An increasing number of trained social workers, men and women, from these schools are carrying on outstanding social work throughout India. In a brief period the profession of social work has become firmly established and widely recognized. Commenting on the outlook for social work Mr. M. S. Gore, Principal of the Delhi School of Social Work, expressed the view that "the development of new programs for general welfare and the growing recognition of the need for professionally trained social workers give hope for increased job opportunities for those who are properly equipped." Education and training in one of the accredited schools is now required by the Government for employment as labor welfare officers and medical social workers, and also by the Central Social Welfare Board for work in the field of aftercare services and moral and social hygiene. Social workers hold positions of high responsibility and have influence in social planning.

With the School of Social Work has come an awakening to the sense of need among voluntary social welfare leaders for professional training and for knowledge of the scientific principles of social welfare. The tremendous plans of India as a Welfare State require reorientation in the concept of social welfare from the idea of charity to that of service based on self help. This means a redirection of social policy from curative to preventive social services.

To quote from Mrs. Hansaben Mehta, the President of the Indian Conference of Social Work: "Social security consists of providing preventive measures for social health. The focus of preventive social policy should be to provide against the social insecurity of people-we must realize that social service is not a form of patronage. Social security is the birthright of a welfare state. Social justice and social security have to be transformed into concrete realities. This requires a large body of qualified welfare workers who can utilize limited resources to the best advantage," Commenting in personal conversation on future trends, Mrs. P. Parjatham Naidu, Deputy Director, Social Services, in the Planning Commission of the Government of India, expressed the opinion that "one of the most hopeful elements in the social situation is the growing measure of understanding and cooperation between professional and voluntary social workers.

This is the natural result of their common need for training, their mutual appreciation and unity of purpose in the service of India." And Mrs. Naidu added, "We [in the

Government] are making more attempts to bring official and non-official agencies closer still, because we have realized in the light of our experience in these two Five Year Plans that this intimate collaboration is most essential in the field of social services." In the development of social welfare in India, the Indian Conference of Social Work has been a potent force. Bringing together each year five hundred or more professional and volunteer social workers, men and women of different communities, it provides a free forum for an exchange of information and experience, and for social planning. Through the Conference, social problems and needs are studied.

All-India Expositions are held, seminars and symposiums on various aspects of social welfare are planned-nation-wide and regionally and also internationally, as for example, the International Conference of Social Work held in Madras in 1953. Women are playing an important part in the development of the Indian Conference of Social Work. Mrs. Mehta has been its President for several years. The Indian Conference of Social Work is affiliated with the International Conference of Social Work, which has set up a permanent South East Asia Regional Office in Bombay.

Of tremendous importance in the development of Indian democracy is the new economic position of women. Women of all classes are today participating in the economic life of India. For women in professional life, independence has not meant a radical change, as they have been well established and long recognized as a national asset. It has brought them, however, an increased sense of responsibility and the inspiration of new demands and opportunities. Nor for women in industry and rural life has there been marked change in their economic position. Women in rural life have always carried a heavy burden in the rural economy, helping in the family support with no idea of economic independence.

But to the women of the urban middle class the decade of Independence has brought a radical change. The urge toward economic independence has been awakened, and also economic necessity has led them into public employment of various kinds. Their presence is an accepted fact. They move about with a sense of assurance, working easily with men, enjoying their equal rights and responsibilities.

The economic position of women of all classes rests on the sound foundation of equality, as defined in the Constitution, which provides for equality of opportunity for all citizens in matters of employment, stating that "no citizen shall on grounds of religion, race, caste, sex, descent, place of birth, residence, or any of them, be ineligible for or discriminated against in respect of any employment or office under the State." In addition to this full charter of equality accorded in the Constitution, women have also the strength and confidence that comes from the Prime Minister's recognition of their value to the State. His liberal plans for women's training and education and employment are a constant incentive toward action.

The professional life of women in India before Independence included four professions-teaching, medicine, law and nursing. Since Independence there has been marked development in these professions and rapid progress in opening new ones for women. The opening of teaching to women over one hundred years ago was the first step toward their economic independence. In 1957, about twenty per cent of the total number of teachers was women. Women occupy major positions in the field of education, as inspectresses, principals of girls' schools and colleges, and specialists in various fields. There are two women Vice-Chancellors of Universities, Mrs. Hansaben Mehta, of Baroda University and Mrs. Sarada Mehta, of the Indian Women's University in Poona, also a woman Principal of a men's college in Madras, Mrs. S. Parthasarathy. In 1957 there were 2,083 women members of university faculties, out of a total of 23,920.

Women entered the medical profession more than fifty years ago. In 1928 one-fourteenth of the total number of medical students in India was women (683 women-8,937 men). There were in 1957 over 7,000 women doctors in India, as heads of hospitals, university professors, in private practice and carrying on research. There are many well-known women specialists, particularly in the diseases of women and children.

The women's medical profession has had a marked influence on social reforms affecting the life of women. The law profession for Indian women had a difficult beginning. The first woman was graduated in law in 1894, Miss Cornelia Sorabji; the second in 1916.

Women were not allowed to practice in the Courts until 1923. In 1956 there were only seventy-eight women in a total of 5,755 advocates from Bombay University. (There are no statistics covering all India.) Women lawyers today have full rights to plead and preside as barristers, magistrates, judges, members of special tribunals. Women lawyers are needed as specialists in labor legislation affecting women and family law. The nursing service has now a key position in the wide program of rural welfare through the Maternal and Child Health Centers and the extensive training of health workers. In 1956 there were 22,386 registered nurses.

Allied with the medical and health fields are several professions which have only recently been entered by women: dentistry, in which women are needed for women in conservative areas and for children in preventive and corrective work; physiotherapy, women physiotherapists (probably not more than thirty in India) are needed for children's hospitals, visiting service, and care of the handicapped; pharmacy, for regular service and for employment as assistant chemists or analysts in pharmaceutical factories, hospitals, and in the manufacture of cosmetics, confectionery and plastics.

Social work is a promising new field. Women have equal opportunity with men in the various lines of social work: labor welfare, medical and psychiatric social work, as social education organizers in community projects, case workers in family and child welfare, and in administrative service. As yet the employment of social workers depends almost entirely on the Government. Few private organizations have paid staff. The financial status of the social worker is comparable to that of a well-trained teacher. Vocational guidance, one of the newest professions in India, offers a special field for women. The one-year course in scientific techniques for teachers is given in universities or Government departments. The Bureau of Vocational Guidance includes on its staff testers of aptitudes, disseminators of occupational information, and counsellors. The Director of one bureau is a woman.

Journalism is a developing field for women. There are many women reporters and feature writers; editors of the women's sections on most papers and journals are women. Women's newspaper work is usually limited to women's affairs. They are rarely used as sub-editors "because of the night hours, till two or three a.m." Training in journalism is available at most universities and in the School of Journalism sponsored by the United States Information Service. Women's magazines and journals employ a large number of women in responsible posts as well as young girls. There are some women business managers. A number of women are free lance writers for the radio and newspapers, both English and Indian.

Architecture has attracted a few women, who are working in private firms or teaching, though one is assistant director in the National Buildings Organization. In interior decoration there are also a few women of artistic ability. Advertising offers promising careers for women with special skills in imaginative and attractive layout and copy. Many women are in the radio field as broadcasters, script and feature writers and news commentators, and also in the technical services. A young woman graduate in telecommunications is in the control room in the maintenance section of one company, and the wireless engineer of the Calcutta transmitter is a woman. Women also are in charge of large stations. A woman holds the highest administrative post in the All-India Radio, Miss Mehra Masani, Director of External Services, covering a worldwide network in twenty-three languages. Before assuming her present high administrative post she had already organized and developed the foreign program.

A few women have entered engineering. A mechanical engineer, formerly assistant foreman at the Ordnance Factory at Dehra Dun, is now a lecturer at the Delhi Polytechnic. A civil engineer studied concrete bridge building in Germany; a hydraulic engineer studied flood relief in the United States. Writes one: "The patience and perseverance that a woman generally has can after training, be applied to prepare the minute details of structures; creative talent is very essential to the advancement of engineering. Women will find this profession very interesting and revealing." An Indian woman aviator has achieved national and international distinction. She now has her license as pilot and navigator and her radio license, but she was refused the pilot's license for civil aviation because of lack of public confidence.

The question of the films as a career for women is still debatable. "It is considered to be below the dignity of a decent woman to work in the films and few are prepared to consider films in the light of a career," is one comment. A second comment is also interesting: "A great deal is said about moral standards in the industry. Those who wish to work with dignity can do so. It is the harder way but worth while. Because of the limelight in which the actors live, everything good or bad is grossly exaggerated." A number of women of the upper class have entered the films and are breaking down tradition.

In the development of the professional life of women in India since Independence, a marked evidence of fundamental social and economic change is the steady increase in the number of Muslim women who are entering professions. Even more noteworthy is the increasing number of professions which Muslim women have entered for full-time careers. This important development is the result of the fact that Muslim women as well as those of the other minorities are an integral part of the advance of women in India. The rapid growth of higher education, the expanding social freedom, the increasing economic independence of women and recognition of the value of the economic contribution of Indian women and its urgent necessity-this composite of progressive influences in the life of Indian women has especially benefited Muslim women.

The statistics of women in professions and in all lines of economic employment are not differentiated by the religious communities. Muslim women are included in the total body of professional women and represented in practically all professions-in education and medicine (the two long-established professions always considered suitable for Muslim women), in various lines of urban and social welfare work, journalism, broadcasting, and law-to a limited degree. Muslim women in the professions are a small but growing numerical minority. The number in teaching has rapidly grown in the past decade, both in general and in various specialized fields.

The medical career has a high priority among Muslim women students, as also among other students. The demand for medical training, however, exceeds the present government facilities. Entrance into the medical profession is severely limited by examination and competition is very keen. Muslim women are handicapped by their lack of educational background and experience. Increase of medical training opportunities for Muslim women is of special concern to the Women's College of Aligarh University. A new medical faculty, coeducational and non-communal, is now being promoted. The new faculty will benefit especially Muslim women students.

Women of the middle class entered employment rapidly after Independence, as the natural result of several factors: the influence of the Women's Army Corps of India (WACI), the National War Service Body of over 10,000 young women, mostly of the middle class; the awakened urge of women to be actively identified with national life; and increased economic pressure, which made economic independence of women a necessity. The question was no longer whether to work but what to do. Today thousands of women are employed in business as receptionists, stenographers and clerks in firms and private offices, large and small, all over India. Statistics are not available, but a view of the crowded streets in any of the large cities in the morning, at noon, or in the evening, when young women stream out of their offices, is convincing evidence of the number of women engaged in business life.

The whole field of clerical service is the major source of income for women earning their own living or adding to family support. Many are employed in the main public services, namely telephone 2,623, postal 2,047, telegraph 416, wireless 67. Large numbers are also in Government service - the Central Government, the State Governments and in the municipalities in large numbers, the non-professional category as well as a considerable number of women of professional rank. In the Central Government, 20,668 women were employed in 1957. In six of the Ministries (Railways, Defense, Production, External Affairs, Information and Broadcasting, Food and Agriculture) the total number of women employed was 13,998, include both professional and non-professional categories.

Thirty women held high ranking secretarial jobs. In the Ministry, of Transport, which is not included in the list above, more women than men were employed. A number of women held responsible posts. There were four managers of large regional offices, seven of smaller offices. All careers in the Administrative Services are open to women on a competitive examination basis. In 1959 there were seven in the IAS (Indian Administrative Service), six in the Foreign Service, a Deputy Commissioner in Simla, five district or assistant district magistrates and five deputy secretaries in the Central Secretariat. A woman was Director of the Indian tourist office in London. The tourist and travel business offer special employment opportunities for women, in the regular customer service as well as clerical. Young women serve as registered guides after a training course given by the tourist bureau.

A young woman working with a travel agency has developed a Tour Guide Service, conducting foreign groups through India. The Air India Hostess Service has opened up an attractive career for young women, carefully planned by Air India-a temporary flight period with an age limit followed by ground service. Knowledge of English is required. The rapidity of increase of women of the middle class seeking employment is shown by the Employment Exchanges' registry. The number applying for assistance rose from 1,500 in 1948 to 4,500 in 1951 and to 40,000 in 1957. This graphically indicates the growing necessity and desire of women to earn their livelihood and gain economic independence. It also highlights the serious problem of the "educated" unemployed, the term used for those with high school education or more.

The present number of educated unemployed is estimated to be a half-million men and women; in five years another one and a half million will be educated and needing jobs. The solution of this problem through training and recruitment for new fields of employment is a major emphasis in the Second Five-Year Plan. The urban training and employment plan, similar to the current plan which is being carried out in rural India, will provide employment and useful careers for a large number of these. Of the twelve million jobs which will be provided in the plan, Shrimati Lakshmi Menon, the Deputy Foreign Minister has urged that four million be allocated to women.

The number of women running their own business is increasing. In the cities women have their own tailoring shops, food shops, beauty parlors and various miscellaneous concerns. There are also women in responsible business positions as directors of shops or housekeepers in hotels. On the higher business level, in the executive category and independent enterprises, a growing number of women have achieved success, as directors of publicity and business promotion, of public relations and personnel management in factories and large business concerns. An illustration of the business capacity of women is the establishment of a chain of inexpensive restaurants-called Anapoorna from the name of the Hindu Goddess of Plenty.

These restaurants were organized by the Woman's Food Council whose chairman is Mrs. Lilavati Munshi, a Member of Parliament. They operate in the large cities and also have a catering service on trains. These are non-profit public services and a very successful business enterprise as well. In the revival of cottage industries and handicrafts, women hold important positions, which require business ability and technical skill; for example, in departments of design, in the promotion of production, in export marketing, and in the management of exhibitions, especially abroad. The All-India Handloom Society and the National Small Industries Organizations have women directors.

The Cottage Industries Emporium in New Delhi has a woman manager and the staff and board are for the most part women. Many women of the less educated group are in miscellaneous lines of employment: as saleswomen in all kinds of shops, in hotels, restaurants, beauty parlors, as caretakers in schools and household employees. The number of women seeking these various types of employment, either for part-time or full-time is steadily growing with the increased economic necessity. The shortage of jobs is shown by the fact that there were over a thousand applications in reply to an advertisement for the position of caretaker of a municipal school.

In the countryside women are an economic asset. Over seventy per cent of the population of India lives in villages. Indian economy is primarily agricultural and women have always shared equally with men in agricultural production. Accordingly, agriculture is quantitatively the most important occupation of Indian women. Twelve and a half million women are reported as supporting themselves by agricultural work, with wages as hired labor on part-time and full-time work, and twenty million as "earning dependents" on their own land, and over million non-earning dependents. But the participation of women in agriculture is not uniform throughout India. For example, the percentage of female agricultural workers varies from thirty per cent of the total in Madras, to less than ten per cent in Punjab and Uttar Pradesh, and was 2.33 per cent around Delhi-predominantly Muslim areas under the control of *purdah*. Economic necessity and social conservatism are here in conflict.

Rural women carry the double burden of the home and family and the daily toil in the fields, sharing with men the usual farm tasks-planting and weeding, irrigating, manuring, harvesting and threshing. Men do the heavy work of ploughing. A special problem of many village women is the separation from husbands who have migrated to the city to enter industry, leaving the women behind to maintain the farm. Village women are thus the stable factor in the rural economy which helps to make possible industrialization in India. The idea of economic independence of women has had no meaning for the village woman. Typically, she is a part of a family unit-more than seventy per cent are married and ninety-three per cent are, if one counts the widowed or divorced. She works by the day for the support of the family on a margin of low subsistence, perhaps with meager savings and no security against famine or other disasters.

Yet throughout the years these underdeveloped and untrained village women have been a sustaining force in the economy of India. Today the village woman is being trained for a better level of living through the community development program with all of its resources to which reference has already been made. Her latent power is being developed for her home and family, her community, and especially for her fuller contribution to the economic life of her country.

The number of women employed in factories was 280,947, or 11.33 per cent of the total labor force in factory work. Most of them were textile workers (cotton and jute), workers in tobacco, in ginning and presses, food and chemical products. The largest number of women employed in any one occupation was on tea, coffee and rubber plantations, 479,983 or 43.53 per cent of a total labor force of 1,102,686. Women are also working in mines-coal, manganese and iron ore. Most of the women employed in the factories do manual or semi-skilled work. In the textile factories they do mostly winding and reeling; in the jute industries, batching, preparing and sack sewing; the mines, loading the surface wagons; on the plantations, plucking the leaves and carrying loads of tea from one place to another. They are in road work and in building construction, where they carry heavy loads.

The basic wages of women are fixed at a rate lower than men's wages, but on piece work the rate is the same. Equal basic rates for certain industries have been fixed in some large centers, i.e., Bombay, Madras and Calcutta. Under the standardization scheme, certain tribunals now have set basic wages. Extra facilities, such as maternity benefits and crèches, are provided for women workers. As in agricultural work, there is little idea of personal economic independence. The workers, husband and wife, or the members of a family, coming from the same village, try to get work together, the women supplementing the men's work. Sometimes the group receives a joint wage. These groups retain their relationship to their original village, often contributing to its support. Their employment is regarded as temporary or migratory.

The difference in the employment of women in different areas of India, concentration in some and lack of women in others indicates the cultural and religious variations in India, which is not a homogeneous country. For example, in Muslim areas women, because of *purdah,* do not work in factories. In recent years there has been a progressive diminution in the percentage of women employed in textile and other mills. In 1939, women in textile factories were thirteen per cent of the total labor force; in 1950 only nine per cent. According to labor inspectors, officers and social workers, the reasons were: (1) the statutory obligations imposed upon employees, namely, the protective legislation and welfare provisions for women, and standardization schemes for wages, thus reducing possible exploitation of women's cheap wages; (2) nationalization of industries, and (3) new machines which have eliminated manual tasks hitherto performed by women.

Since Independence the Government has taken legislative and other measures for the protection of women workers, as follows:

1. The ratification of the International Labor Organization Conventions, prohibiting the employment of women underground and in night work.
2. The Factories Act (1948), limiting women to nine hours' work per day, between 7 a.m. and 6 p.m. in factories, mines and on plantations, and the Mines Act (1951), prohibiting the employment of women underground.
3. A law forbidding the lifting of heavy weights in excess of 65 pounds for adult women, 45 pounds for adolescents, and excluding women from dangerous operations.
4. Welfare facilities, i.e., improved sanitation, maintenance of crèches for children under six years in factories employing more than 80 women or even where any women are employed (as in the Mines Act), and providing rest periods for mothers to feed their babies.
5. Maternity benefits are now being absorbed in the nationwide Employers' State Insurance Schemes.

The main difficulties in enforcing the legislation outlined above are the paucity of trained personnel, especially in remote places like plantations and mines, and the lack of payment adequate to secure an efficient inspectoral staff. There is an encouraging increase in the effort to introduce welfare activities for all workers, especially for women. Village and small industries, as yet an undeveloped asset, are being promoted and strengthened because of their potential value to Indian economy. Eleven and a half million people, twenty-nine per cent of all those working outside agriculture, are engaged in small enterprises. They produce about one-twelfth (eight per cent) of all of India's goods and services, which about equals the total production of the large and medium-sized industries.

Village industries are being encouraged to produce more goods and more jobs in the next five years in order to help rural people earn a better livelihood. Village craftsmen are being mobilized to improve their skills and to learn modern techniques and the use of modern machinery. The Second Five Year Plan will allot four times the amount allowed for the First Five Year Plan. No special attention apparently is given to the training and employment of women in these small industries. Hand and cottage industries have a long history in India, some dating back, it is said, five thousand years. In these industries women have always had an essential part since the working unit is the family.

Some of the handicrafts by tradition have been carried on exclusively by women. Today, thousands of women are engaged in these-traditional hand and cottage industries which include: hand-loom cloth from mill-made yarn and khaki cloth hand woven from home-spun yarn; silk and sericulture, handicraft (art metal work, toys, ivory, carving, bidri ware, decorative ceramics). Other "village" industries are hand pounding rice, pressing vegetable oils, manufacturing raw sugar and matches, canning and shoe making.

Handicrafts will be further developed through training centers, craft museums, art schools with scholarships, internal sale and export trade. Cottage industries and handicraft are being promoted by the All-India Khadi Board, the All-India Handloom Board, the All-India Handicraft Board and the Indian Co-operative Union. Women serve on all these Boards. The Chairman of the All-India Handicraft Board and also of the Indian Co-operative Union is Mrs. Kamaledevi

Chattopadhyay. The Honorary Director of the All-India Handloom Board is Mrs. Pupul Jayakar.

A glance at the past gives meaning to the present full participation of Indian women in political life. The agitation for equal political rights for women began more than forty years ago, in 1917, when a women's deputation of fourteen members, led by Sarojini Naidu, met Mr. Montagu, the Secretary for India, and Lord Chelmsford, the Viceroy, and formally requested that women be given equal representation with men when the franchise was granted. They also asked for more educational opportunities for girls and more medical colleges and referred to their political equality in the Indian National Congress since 1885.

The "Constitutional" reforms, when announced, did not mention women. However, the request was referred to the provincial legislatures with statutory authority to grant suffrage to women. The women's organizations gained the support of public opinion in favor of women's suffrage in one province after another. Madras in 1921 endorsed women's equal rights of election to municipal councils and the legislatures. Other provinces followed this example. By 1926, women in all the provinces had the right to vote on the same basis as men-property and educational qualification-but because of the limited property rights of women under the Hindu law, few women could qualify for voting. Between 1921 and 1933, only 315,651 women were enfranchised, in contrast to 6.8 million men.

After political rights were granted in the provinces, the number of women entering political life as members of the legislative assemblies and as magistrates steadily grew. In 1930 the leaders of the women's organizations were actively concerned with the work of the Franchise Committee headed by Lord Lothian, which was appointed to extend the current franchise, especially to include more women, and also to formulate a basis for the franchise under a new Constitution of India. The women's organizations presented their views to the Lothian Committee, urging adult suffrage equal for men and women, and opposing communal electorates and the preferential basis with reserved places for women.

Three outstanding women leaders-Rajkumari Amrit Kaur, Dr. Muthulakshmi Reddi and Begum Hamid Ali, of different faiths-gave evidence to the Joint Select Parliamentary Committee of the Round Table Conference in London, opposing the idea of communal electorates. Their views, however, were not incorporated into the Parliamentary Report, and therefore did not influence the franchise basis of the new Constitution. A memorandum of protest was sent jointly from the All-India Women's Conference, the Women's Indian Association and the National Council of Women to the Joint Parliamentary Committee. The substance of the protest was that the preferential suffrage basis favored certain classes and vested interests, and that sex equality had not been granted. The memorandum closes with the statement:

We wish to make it quite clear that even if we had secured for ourselves all that we have wished to secure and if, at the same time, we felt that the recommendations as a whole were not in the true interest of India, we would as women, feel it our bounden duty to deny all privileges for ourselves, for the sake of the common good. While protesting the basis of suffrage, the Conference urged women to use their vote. The Government of India Act, which instituted the new Constitution, increased the number of enfranchised from 8,744,000 under the Montagu Reforms, to 35,000,000. The act also increased the proportional suffrage rights of women by a ratio of one woman to six men instead of one woman to twenty men, and admitted women to the Federal Assembly, with six places reserved for women in the Upper House, and nine in the Lower House. Two of these seats were reserved for Muslim women and one for a Christian.

Women took an active part in the new elections for the Provincial legislatures and the Central Legislative Assembly. Eight women were elected to the Lower Houses from the general constituencies; forty-two elected from the reserved constituencies, and five nominated to Upper Houses. The first woman Minister of a provincial government was elected, Vijayalakshmi Pandit, as Minister of Local Self-Government and Public Health in the United Provinces, which marked the beginning of a brilliant national and international career. Five other women took office as Deputy Speakers and Parliamentary Secretaries. A number of well-known women were elected to the Central Legislative Assembly.

After Independence, twelve women were chosen to the Constituent Assembly set up by the Interim Government after Partition to frame the Constitution for independent India, and there were eleven women members out of a total of 313 in the Provisional Parliament, which was dissolved before the first election. With the final adoption of the Constitution on November 26, 1949, the goal of full equality of rights of all citizens, irrespective of caste, creed or sex (Article 15) was achieved. The world's two largest elections, which were held in 1952 and 1957, were a massive demonstration of democracy in action. A free election of 193 million persons (the estimated number of the second election) with perhaps eighty-five per cent of them illiterate, covering a sub-continent and extending over a period from February 4 to March 26, 1957, may well be considered a world phenomenon. Observers commented on the orderliness of the elections, the interest and intelligence of the people.

In the second election there was a marked increase in the number of women voters. In Uttar Pradesh women outnumbered the men in some constituencies. Many Muslim women in *burqas* went to the polls. There were many polling stations for women only, and women were the polling clerks. Also, in the 1957 election more women candidates actively campaigned than in 1952. They traveled constantly, covering wide rural areas, making countless speeches-a hard job but a necessity. Women candidates competed with men as well as with other women. They were very well informed, keenly interested in all welfare problems-refugees, mothers and children, education and health. "Women politicians inspire confidence," was the comment made by Mrs. Renuka Ray, the Minister of Rehabilitation in Bengal and a successful candidate in 1957 for the Federal Parliament.

"They attract huge crowds, especially in rural areas, as the community development programs have greatly increased the political consciousness of village people. There is doubtless conservatism in some areas about women in politics, but women are always well received." A large number were successful in their strenuous campaign efforts. The fact that some were, of course, defeated was not interpreted by them as any derogation of the position of women in politics. Their presence is an accepted fact as is also their public campaigning. The results of the second election, compared with the first show the following increase: in the Lok Sabha (House of the People, or Lower House), from twenty-three women in 1952 to twenty-seven in 1957; in the Rajya Sabha (Upper House), from nineteen in 1952 to twenty-three in 1957. In the State Assemblies, which total 2,906 members, 195 women were elected of the 342 women who stood for election.

Women members of Parliament participate ably in all fields, not merely in social legislation affecting general welfare, relief, and women and children, but in a wide range of interests including finance, defense and labor. Women naturally have specialized knowledge and experience in social questions, contribute impressively in this field, and are an active force for reform, as was evident in their vigorous and successful support of the Hindu Code Bill and in the continuing struggle to control prostitution. There are some excellent women speakers. An observer commented, however, that women in Parliament contribute more by action than by speaking. They are held in high esteem by the general public as a body of thoughtful, serious citizens genuinely concerned in the national welfare.

Indian women political leaders are active in their political parties. There are women members of the Congress Working Party and a strong Women's Section; women members of the Communist Party (none on the Politburo); women members of the National Executive of the Socialist Party. To meet the needs of women members of Parliament, training seminars for legislators, conducted by prominent women political leaders in high parliamentary positions, were initiated by Mrs. Indira

Gandhi, the Prime Minister's daughter, then Head of the Women's Section of the Congress Party. She was elected President of the Party in February 1959 and has demonstrated her ability as a dynamic national leader.

Women are represented today on elected and appointed bodies on all levels-the village councils (*panchayats*), local and district boards, state and federal legislative bodies. One village in south India elected a *panchayat* made up entirely of women members in order to bring harmony to the village, as the city fathers had always failed to agree. Women have also received unusual recognition in political life in municipal, state and central government. Begum Khadija Tyabji was for many years an elected member of the Municipal Corporation of Bombay. Delhi had a women mayor in 1957-58, Mrs. Asaf Ali; Bombay has a woman sheriff (but not for the first time), Mrs. Gulistan Billmoria, appointed in 1957; Madras also has a woman sheriff appointed in the same year, Mrs. Clubwalla Jadhav.

In State service two distinguished examples are Dr. Sushila Nayar, formerly Health Minister of Delhi State and Speaker of the Delhi State Legislature, and Mrs. Renuka Ray, formerly Minister of Rehabilitation, West Bengal, and since 1957 a Member of Parliament. Two women governors have been appointed: Sarojini Naidu to the United Provinces immediately after Independence and Padmanja Naidu, the daughter of Sarojini Naidu, appointed the Governor of Bengal in 1956. Distinguished examples of women in high positions in the Central Government are Rajkumari Amrit Kaur, the former Health Minister, and Mrs. Lakshmi Menon, the present Deputy Minister of External Affairs, both already mentioned, and Mrs. Violet Alva, the Deputy Minister of Home Affairs.

A woman now has the highest ranking Indian diplomatic post, as present High Commissioner to the United Kingdom in London, Vijayalakshmi Pandit. She is also Ambassador to Ireland and Spain and was formerly Ambassador in Washington and Moscow. Indian women have served on many international missions and one or more are usually appointed to the Indian delegation at the United Nations. The steady campaign for political equality carried on by Indian women in the years before Independence was unusually free from any sense of conflict or sharp feminist struggle, in the usual sense of the word. Women knew that they were not alone in their campaign but supported by liberal leaders among the men, who worked with them and for them. Their political emancipation was regarded as an integral part of the total movement for freedom. Suffrage was not a goal in itself.

"The vote was never looked upon as a yardstick of progress or emancipation," said Lakshmi Menon. "It was important, of course, in the eyes of the law that women should get the vote. It enabled both sexes to work in cordial cooperation in the framing of the Constitution in 1950, and in implementing the political and social legislation that has followed since." Because of this atmosphere of cooperation and freedom from sex conflict, Indian women were able to enter political life with an immediate sense of confidence, free from any feeling of inferiority or necessity for self-assertion.

Women leaders in India appreciate their advantage. To quote again from Lakshmi Menon, "The relative ease with which women came to their present position is due to the successful termination of the struggle in progressive countries of the West, where women acquired these opportunities the hard way." This comment illustrates the growing sense of relationship of women leaders in India with leaders in other countries and the realization of mutual benefits in their common aspiration toward the full participation of women in national life.

The Hindu Code legislation, the landmark of legal social equality of women, represents the achievement of fifteen years of concentrate effort by a legal committee appointed by the Government in 1941, to improve the status of Hindu women in respect to property rights (Hindu Women's Rights to Property Act 1937). This involved eventually drafting a comprehensive Hindu Code of Law, which was presented to the Provincial Parliament in 1948, but was not passed. The different Acts were then taken up separately and passed after prolonged struggle by the first Parliament of the Republic of India, 1956.The Hindu Code Bill comprises four separate bills: The Special Marriage Bill, 1954, the Hindu Marriage Bill, 1955, the Hindu Succession Bill, 1956, and the Adoption and Maintenance Bill, 1956. The legal social status of Hindu women under the Hindu Code Bill is as follows:

a. Monogamy-enforced, polygamy outlawed and punishable by fine and imprisonment;
b. Marriage age-minimum is fifteen for girls, eighteen for boys;
c. Divorce-equal basis for both sexes through the Courts;
d. Inheritance rights for women-absolute control of her property and rights of the daughter and her children to succeed equally with the son and his children to the property of either parent;
e. Adoption-right of both parents to adopt, son or daughter;
f. Alimony-regulated by law and paid to both sexes.

The serious inequities in social law and custom suffered by Hindu women before the Hindu Code Bill indicate the revolutionary significance of the reform. Child marriage and the dowry system prevailed. Polygamy existed. No divorce was allowed. Women could not inherit property, except that a widow might use personally money left to her by her husband or son, but without the right of disposal. Women had no right of adoption and girls could not be adopted. The most vital reform in the Hindu Code Bill was the recognition of and provision for divorce through the Courts. This represented a radical change in the Hindu concept of marriage, affecting both men and women. Other Code Bills provide specifically for the equal rights of women. The Hindu Code, as a whole, is based on a new attitude toward women. Legally no longer dependents, their equal rights bring also equal duties.

Women leaders in India realize that the achievement of legal social equality is not the end of their effort to lift the status of women. They stress the fact that the new legislation now makes possible tremendous social change but laws are not automatically translated into practice. Social custom is stronger than law where conservatism and ignorance prevail. The Hindu Code presents to educated women the urgent need and the opportunity to inform and enlighten Indian women as a whole on their legal social equality and new responsibility. The Hindu Code does not apply to the religious minorities, which have their own family and marriage laws.

However, if desired they may adopt the Code, as it was formulated on a nonreligious basis so that it might serve as a uniform Code for all citizens which is a primary objective of the new India as a secular state. But the principle of religious liberty protects the minorities in maintaining their own codes. The Hindu Code reforms are not relevant in respect to legal social equality of women in the Christian and Parsi communities. The Christian law is based on monogamy and equality of divorce, as is also the Parsi law. Islamic law, the Sharia, gives permission for four wives at the same time, under the Prophet's injunction of equal treatment for each. If the Hindu Code, which outlaws polygamy, were applicable to the Muslim community, the major barrier for the legal social equality of Muslim women would be removed.

Polygamy is definitely decreasing in urban life particularly in the middle class because of economic pressure and in the educated upper class because of the adverse opinion of the enlightened public regarding polygamy. The spread of education has steadily undermined the institution. A new leverage against polygamy is the Government policy, adopted since the Hindu Code Reforms, that Muslims who choose to take a second wife are debarred (or disqualify themselves) from government employment. The Muslim legal right of polygamy is not questioned. The responsibility rests with the individual. The decline of polygamy in the younger and middle generation is evident. In the urban lower classes polygamy persists, in spite of adverse economic conditions. In rural life polygamy is prevalent, as it has always been. An additional wife is an economic asset, not a liability, and also has a certain prestige value.

There is currently no agitation against polygamy and no movement among Muslims for legislative modification of Islamic law and practice regarding polygamy. The legal inequity of the social status of Muslim women is a cause of deep concern among Muslim women leaders but any Muslim legislative reform seems improbable. Some liberals believe the only desirable solution would be the unification of law in a secular state, which is now made possible by the Hindu Code. But while desirable and logical as a reform for social injustice, this solution is far from simple. "You cannot," to quote from a Bombay woman leader, "force this upon the ignorant and unwilling masses. Education for change is a time-consuming process. We must work towards this goal."

Social equality, for Muslim women, is being steadily advanced by the decline of *purdah* and the discarding of the *burqa*. Tremendous social changes have taken place in the past ten or fifteen years. Through the pressure of external events the restrictions of *purdah* have been loosened. A large number of young Muslim women of orthodox middle class families during the war years were drawn into the public services of the Women's Army Corps of India. This marked a total break with their traditional way of life and opened a new future. In the upheaval of the partition many sheltered prrdah women were uprooted from their homes, and forced out of their seclusion.

Often they lost their *burqa*s in the confusion, and found themselves with hundreds of other women in the pitiless publicity of relief camps. Some of the older women, after the shock of partition, were able to return to their secluded lives. But many Muslim women, formerly under the restraint of *purdah*, after Independence were forced by economic necessity to earn a livelihood and became a part of the general working force of women. An increasing number of younger women without awareness of restraint have advanced with full equality of government higher education into the widening field of professional life. Many Muslim women today have moved outside the framework of *purdah*. The steady movement toward social equality in the life of Muslim women is an evident fact in cities all over India.

Purdah and the *burqa* are the symbols of a passing way of life and no longer primary questions for debate and agitation. To gauge the totality of change is impossible. Centers of conservatism and *purdah* pockets persist in certain cities and the influence of conservatism dominates particularly in rural areas, which are always the stronghold of orthodoxy and tradition. But "*purdah* is bound to lose ground; eventually, it will disappear. There will probably be no direct attack against polygamy, no legal regulation," was the opinion expressed by Begum Qudsia Zaidi, a leader in contact with the student generation and with modern cultural movements in India. "Gradually the changing social climate of a secular state and the strong influence of the Government, as well as economic forces, will cause the practice of polygamy to cease." Liberal Muslim leaders share this opinion and realize that the future of Muslims will depend on their adaptation to the new way of life in modern India.

WOMEN'S ORGANIZATIONS IN INDIA

The development of women's organizations in India began about 1900. Already before this, however, as indicated in an earlier section, women were actively engaged in various welfare activities as a result of the influence of certain liberal Indian social movements and Christian Missions. The inspiring example of Pandita Ramabai, who founded the first Hindu widow's home, Sharada Sadan, in 1899, gave impetus to women's voluntary welfare service for the sociail uplift of women and the care of children, which steadily developed after that time. Between 1895 and 1920 a number of national women's organizations with international affiliations were founded by women leaders from Great Britain, the USA, and India, including the YWCA, the National Council of Women, the Association of University Women, the Medical Women's Association, the Trained Nurses Association and the Girl Guides, each with its specific purpose to promote the advance of Indian women and girls; and the Women's Indian Association in Madras, a special advocate of social and political equality with an all-India outreach through its magazine, Stri Dharma.

In 1926 the All-India Women's Conference was established by some of the leaders in the women's organizations (Hindu, Christian, Muslim and Parsee) as an instrument to promote their common aim of social and educational advance. The immediate impulse for the establishment of the All-India Women's Conference was an appeal made by the Director of

Public Instruction in Bengal to the women of India "to say with one voice what they wanted and to keep on saying it until they got what they wanted." Following this appeal, a conference of representative women leaders from all over India was called in Poona, 1927, by Mrs. Margaret Cousins and a small group of leaders. At that gathering the All-India Conference was established.

Since its inception the All-India Women's Conference (AICW) has become recognized as the voice of the forward movement of Indian women and has helped to develop friendship and understanding among women of widely different groups. "The AICW," as interpreted by one of the leaders, "is neither a political nor a feminist organization but a small attempt to organize the women of our vast society and to educate them to a realization of their duties and responsibilities." This organization has had a tremendous educational influence on public opinion in regard to women. The leaders of the Conference, during the period before Independence, each year presented to the Government of India, on behalf of the All-India Women's Conference, the pressing needs of Indian women and the necessity for Government action.

Since Independence the annual Conferences have interpreted to the Government of India the current specific problems of Indian women, as a guide for Government planning and action. It has also interpreted to the women the specific needs of the Government for their support in its far-reaching plans for national welfare. The resolutions passed at the annual Conferences (twenty-six were held between 1927 and 1956) cover a wide range of women's concerns and reforms needed; such as in facilities for girls' education, maternal and child health, abolition of child marriage (The Marriage Restraint Act), abolition of *purdah* and polygamy and of traffic in women and children, political equality and improvement of rural life.

The promotion of these various concerns has been carried on by special committees in education, social welfare, medical relief, industrial training and legal affairs. A number of practical projects have been promoted through the cooperation of the various branches. Notable among them is the Village Medical Relief scheme, with eight centers equipped with mobile vans. Each of the local branches has had its own social and educational projects, carried on in cooperation with the States' welfare program. The All-India Women's Conference with 54,000 members, thirty-nine main branches and 250 constituent branches, is well organized for collective effort throughout India.

For the women's organizations as a whole, the All-India Women's Conference has been and is a most effective instrument for promoting collectively the advance of women in India. It is an impressive mass education movement. For hundreds of women it has been the main channel of their social education and has prepared many for intelligent citizenship in the new India. To an unusual degree the All-India Women's Conference represents not only the work of individuals but the collective cooperation of the national organizations of the different religious communities. The development of women's organizations has been greatly increased since Independence, the natural results of the widening of women's interests and the realization of the need for combined effort. The scope of this women's organizational activity is evident from a study of the varied purposes of the national organizations.

There is no registry of women's organizations, and this list may not be complete. The national organizations are widely representative of all India, through their local branches. The varied purposes of the organization in the list, reflect as a composite the following concerns: promotion of the professions-medicine, nursing, home-science, social work; training of voluntary workers; education and social development of rural women; training of rural welfare workers; family planning; moral and social hygiene; family and child welfare; housing for young women; refugee relief service; youth interests-student camps for boys and girls; care of juvenile delinquents; industrial welfare of women; promotion of cottage industry; food conservation; financial support for government welfare schemes; citizenship education and the promotion of peace. A number of the organizations are multi-purpose but the increase in specialization is evident.

In the development of women's organizations in India a change has occurred since partition in the voluntary dissolution of the All-India Muslim Women's organization formerly a strong movement with a number of outstanding leaders. This association from its inception was actively connected with the All-India Women's Conference and also worked independently for the advance of Muslim women. The cessation of the National Muslim Association seems to be the result of the new trend away from centralized Muslim activities. The continuing concern of Muslim women leaders for the welfare of Muslim women is being carried on in various centers by special local Muslim welfare societies; for example, homes for abandoned or abducted women, the victims of partition; as in Calcutta (the All-Bengal Women's Association), in Lucknow (The Women's Home) in Bombay (a Home and Muslim Orphanage), also in Delhi (*Purdah* Home) and elsewhere in orphanages and other Muslim welfare institutions.

The Muslim Women's Association in Madras, a regional organization (founded in 1927 as the Madras Presidency Ladies Association), which recently celebrated its Silver Jubilee, has a long, distinguished record for emergency relief, promotion of girls' schools and higher education, and general social advance. This Association in Madras has continued to carry on what seems the normal program of an effective Muslim minority. From various parts of India at the time of partition a certain number of leaders migrated into Pakistan-to East Pakistan from Calcutta and Lucknow, to West Pakistan from Lucknow and Delhi particularly and also from Hyderabad, Bombay and elsewhere. Since Independence Muslim women leaders remaining in India have participated actively as before in several previously established All-India organizations, in new women's organizations, joint women's committees, notably the Central Social Welfare Board program for Community Development and on State Boards.

An outstanding example is Begum Anis Kidwai, an unassuming member of Parliament, with multiple responsibilities in social welfare, especially for women and children; in the executive of the Congress' Women's Committee; the Jamia Millia Islam Rural Welfare Project; and in Lucknow as Trustee of the Muslim Girls' College and the founder and sponsor of the Recovery Home for Muslim Women. Two examples of leadership in Hyderabad may be mentioned-the well-known Begum Hussain Ali Khan, a member of the State Legislative Assembly, recently, elected against keen Communist competition and a leader in civic welfare; and a young Muslim women, Mrs. Munir Zuhire, with varied national interests-a State Girl Guide Commissioner, active in the Indian Conference of Social Work and representative of the All-India Women's Conference.

In Madras are a number of women leaders in civic and educational affairs and Muslim welfare, who are associated with the Muslim Women's Association-the pioneer leader, Begum Nazir Hussein, President of the Association, formerly President of the AIWC; Begum Shah Khaleeli, Honorary Secretary, of the Association, and Begum Bashir Ahmed Sayed, the first Muslim woman member of the Madras University Senate. Women in India generally participate actively in mixed organizations, for example, The Indian Child Welfare Council, Indian Conference of Social Work, the Cottage Industry Organizations, the Red Cross, etc. In these various organizations women work along with men on the basis of an equal partnership of common interests, mutual recognition and equal responsibility.

Women as well as men are elected or appointed to high policy-planning positions. This does not mean necessarily equal number of leaders but equal sharing by women in the responsibilities of the organizations. Of special interest is the development of women's organized effort in direct support of the Government, for example, the Women's Small Savings Campaign. The Family Planning Association and All-India Food Council also in different ways illustrate the close relationship between Government policy and voluntary activity. The Central Social Welfare Board, with the fourteen State Boards, assisting Social tary agencies throughout India to assume increased welfare responsibility, is a unique demonstration of the value of the partnership of government and voluntary effort. This represents a new social welfare pattern characteristic of a democratic welfare state.

3

Malaysia in the Front-Line State

If you stand at the top of Pitt Street in downtown Georgetown, Penang, you stand athwart the intersection of three of the world's great civilisations. Penang is a small, bustling island off the northwest coast of the Malay Peninsula. To the west is India, and the teeming multitudes of the subcontinent. To the north is China, the oldest civilisation extant, and the largest. And to the south is the vast Malay world. Modern Malaysia is a result of this intersection. Its population is a composition of the three civilisations-more than 60 per cent of its people are ethnic Malays or belong to the indigenous races of East Malaysia; something less than 30 per cent are Chinese and a little under 10 per cent are Indian.

Pitt Street itself embodies this diversity. Amidst the rumbling traffic and elegant traces of colonial architecture are two big mosques, two Chinese clan houses (where ancestors are worshipped), a Buddhist temple, a Hindu temple, and just a few blocks away a magnificent Sikh *gurdwara*. If ever a nation was itself going to suffer the 'clash of civilisations', to be torn apart by ethnic and communal hostilities, it is Malaysia. And indeed in the late 1960s it did experience murderous race riots in which hundreds of Chinese were killed.

As a majority Muslim state it satisfies every criterion of Western paranoia-ethnic division, Islamic predominance and a developing economy. Yet for 30 years, through good times and bad, through the oil shock of the 1970s, the recession of the mid-80s, the political upheaval of the late 80s, the rapid social change associated with the boom years of fast economic growth during most of the 90s and then the most recent savage regional economic downturn of the late 90s, Malaysians have kept the racial calm. Peace among the races, an accommodation at least if not a profound harmony, has been secured. This is no mean achievement anywhere. For a developing nation making the transition out of poverty and buffeted by the cruelties of market mood swings and radical capital flows, it is worth more recognition internationally than it usually gets.

For an outsider like me, Malaysia's racial mixture and cultural diversity are its most delightful aspect. It is not diverse in the same sense as the United States-you don't have the experience of finding people in substantial numbers from all over the globe in Malaysia. You don't have the experience, as you do in the US, of running into Armenians in North Hollywood, Vietnamese in San Jose, Poles in Milwaukee, and Ethiopians in New York. Malaysia doesn't set out to be a universal nation in the way the US does. But even so, its diversity has a quality which is lacking in the US. In most situations in the US, the affluent visitor will find himself in a basically white environment most of the time. In Malaysia, in virtually every social setting, you find yourself dealing with Malays, Chinese and Indians simultaneously.

This is an unusual diversity in South East Asia, too. Thus while the vast archipelago of Indonesia is in an absolute sense more ethnically and linguistically diverse than Malaysia, Malaysia often feels more diverse because of the ubiquity of the three races. In so far as the West has a view of Malaysia it tends to be defined by the nation's high-profile prime minister of such long standing, Mahathir Mohamad. Mahathir's caustic lectures to the West and his determination never to be trod on or told what to do by outsiders deserve attention. But Malaysia is much more than Mahathir. The man who had been his deputy for so long and who was jailed by Mahathir, Anwar Ibrahim, was a balancing voice to Mahathir's. Anwar's profile in the South East Asian region was especially strong.

It is beyond the scope of this book to explore fully the criminal charges brought against Anwar, some of which were still proceeding through the courts at the time of writing the struggle for power between Mahathir and Anwar. Instead the contribution of both men to the Asian values debate is examined. On racial issues the two men have mostly been as one. Not the least of the ways in which Mahathir has been misunderstood and misrepresented in the West is that his role in racial reconciliation is never adverted to. Admittedly, the situation is a little too complex for the ready stereotypes with which we like to categorise people. Is Mahathir a racial conservative or a racial liberal?

He started out as Malay 'ultra'. His 1969 book, *The Malay Dilemma,* was a cri de coeur of Malay dispossession and a determination to reassert Malay pride and control. Yet Mahathir developed as almost an avuncular and unifying figure within Malaysia, ever willing to deliver stern lectures to his countrymen, but looked to as a protector not only by Malays but by ethnic minority groups, in much the same way that these groups once looked to Malaysia's first Prime Minister, the aristocratic and paternal Tunku Abdul Rahman. Anwar Ibrahim started out as an 'ultra' too, but he was concerned more with the assertion for Malaysia of an overtly Islamic identity rather than Malayness as such.

In truth the two are profoundly intertwined, for in Malaysia it is assumed that all Malays should be Muslims, and ethnic issues are often subsumed in religious issues. But on religion, as on race, Mahathir and Anwar have in recent years both been apostles of moderation. When they fell out, it was not over issues of race. Not long before the outbreak of the regional economic crisis in 1997 I asked Anwar what he thought of race relations in contemporary Malaysia. He argued then that Malaysia's economic success in the 1970s, 80s and 90s, especially the creation of a Malay business class, had resulted in a profound change in race relations.

In particular he thought the growing Malay self confidence generally had resulted in the evolution of a more relaxed racial atmosphere: 'It has improved tremendously. Growth and prosperity have contributed to easing tensions. There is less feeling of insecurity among the races, particularly the Malays, because their economic achievement is considerable. Race relations have entered a new phase. Cultural and religious differences are now seen in a new light. It is considered strength rather than a source of conflict. This reflects the maturing process in race relations.' For a self-consciously Islamic leader like Anwar to hail Malaysia's racial and religious diversity as a positive strength is itself a sign of how far Malaysia has travelled.

It was at the time of the holiest Muslim feast, Idul Fitri, in January. That year the feast fell at the same time as Chinese New Year, the most important celebration in the calendar for the Chinese. The atmosphere in Malaysia at the time was not one of racial tension but of a determined official, and apparently popular, effort to promote interracial good feeling. The Chinese New Year greeting-*Gong Xie Fa Chui*-was everywhere amalgamated with the Muslim celebratory *Selamat Hari Raya* to form *Gong Xie Raya*. Restaurants and hotels across the country featured Malay and Chinese figures, dressed in elaborate traditional costume, in joint celebration.

Anwar was making the most of this happy conjunction: 'This is a great experience for us. All analysts, including those in the media, seem to assume economic difficulties will incite racial disharmony. We have not seen any signs of that in Malaysia.' The official campaign was at times a bit corny. Typical was a widely screened community service television advertisement of the time. The scene opens on a Chinese teenager. He looks a typical overachieving Chinese 'nerd', head bowed over his books, deep into complex mathematical problems. He is disturbed by a series of noises, the last a lively Hindi song from an unknown radio. He stumbles out of his studious lair, blinking his eyes in the unfamiliar sunlight.

Has he been studying all night? He stumbles around in search of the source of the noise, enacting a few slapstick falls and misadventures on the way. Finally he knocks at a door nearby and it is opened by a Malay girl of ravishing beauty, whose eyes sparkle and who smiles beatifically upon him. The Chinese student is invited into an Edenic garden full of exotic tropical fruits. The Malay girl entices him to try one, which he finds a little bitter but perseveres with anyway (though how a Chinese living in Malaysia could be unfamiliar with its fruit is unknowable). Meanwhile, in the background a famous ethnically Punjabi Malaysian singer, who has converted to Islam, is crooning, in Hindi, a love song about 'the first time I ever saw you'.

This advertisement is almost terminal schmaltz but the interesting, perhaps even important, thing about it is its official promotion of interracial friendship. In this case the advertisement even seems to be promoting interracial romance. Interracial marriage is quite common in Malaysia, but I have never before seen it officially promoted. This commercial was in its way a powerful symbol of government and corporate determination to keep race relations civil. In a globalising economy ethnic diversity is a comparative advantage and it is smart and true of Malaysia's leaders to stress this aspect. Penang is the perfect example. Penang State consists of the small island and a little strip on the mainland linked by one of the longest causeways in the world. It is Malaysia's only majority Chinese State, although the ethnic scales are balanced somewhat by the predominantly Malay population in the mainland part of Penang.

Penang's chief minister, Dr Koh Tsu Koon, the only ethnic Chinese long-term chief minister of any Malaysian State in an inevitably antiseptic conference room in the ultramodern Penang Development Corporation office tower on the southern end of Penang Island, near the airport. Dr Koh leads the predominantly Chinese Gerakan party but is in coalition with the United Malays National Organisation (UMNO), the dominant political party in Malaysia, which spearheads the Barisan coalition, which governs nationally. For much of the 1990s Penang had an annual economic growth rate of 12 per cent, making it, with southern China, one of the fastest growing regional economies in the world.

The Japanese management guru, Kenichi Ohmae, nominated it in his book *The End of the Nation State* as the very model of an effective internationalist city, inviting the global economy and taking full advantage of location, cost, infrastructure and human resources. 'Penang is a microcosm of South East Asia,' Dr Koh told me. 'People have come to see our multicultural and multiracial aspect as an economic asset. Malaysians can easily move into China, India, and Indonesia. They are used to dealing with complex, intercultural situations.' Koh is particularly proud of those multinationals that have located their sales and marketing or customer service regional headquarters in Penang, in order to take advantage of the diverse linguistic skills of its inhabitants. If a customer rings from India, China, and Indonesia or virtually anywhere in the region they can find an operator who speaks their language.

For Koh, his ethnicity does not compromise his civic loyalty. 'I'm first and foremost a Malaysian. We're very fortunate to inherit the major religions and cultures of the world without losing our own particular cultural heritage. You are no less culturally a Malay, or a Chinese, while still being Malaysian. We all have the chance to accept, appreciate and adopt the good aspects of other cultures. Our diversity is a big virtue, a big asset, which if we didn't manage it well could be a big liability, it could lead to friction. There is a greater sense of confidence in every ethnic group. There is less feeling of threat or insecurity. The late 60s and 70s were very divisive. Now it's more natural for people to interact, to appreciate each other's cultural forms and religious beliefs.'

Koh's fellow Penangite, Anwar Ibrahim, contributed to this by being the first national Malay leader to use a brush to write Chinese characters, an important gesture of cultural appreciation of the Chinese. Anwar would quote the Koran in Arabic and the Analects of Confucius in Chinese.

Like many Malaysians, Koh does not think Western societies are necessarily in a position to lecture Malaysia: 'On my first trip to Sydney in 1980, on my first day there, a group of white kids in a car stopped and shouted at me: Go home!'

Of course, Koh is a chief minister, so he is obliged to be polite. Some others are more sceptical. Of Tamil background himself; Maniam has often drawn on his own background to depict the traditional Tamil existence in Malaysia of life on a rubber plantation. His works are understated but densely poetic and allusive. They sometimes have a dreamlike quality. They are among the most beautiful works in English in the 20th century. His stories often deal with racial issues, or at least have a consciousness of race as a strong background. I sought him out in a quiet, old-fashioned bar on the edge of Chinatown in Kuala Lumpur.

A small, gentle man, his dark face deeply lined, his hair and moustache flecked with white, Maniam loves his country but that day at least was full of melancholy reflection: 'There's a race rather than a race riot these days can smash someone's face or more likely make them lose face. After World War II the races were separated geographically. When you come to the 1990s you still get the idea of different locations, but locations defined in a different way, sort of like computer locations. It's a sense of separate mental spaces-the separate physical spaces have substantially eroded. But mental spaces are harder to break down. It's easier to enter a Chinese area than a Chinese mental space. And the media is always telling each race what it should be.' Maniam also attributed much of the racial calm to economic growth, but his warning was dire: 'If economic growth stops, it will be horrendous.'

Maniam is somewhat depressed about the prospects for his own Indian community in Malaysia. As Koh pointed out, the Indian Malaysian community has a peculiar structure. It has a strong professional class, a narrow middle class and a huge working class inherited from the days when Indians were overwhelmingly rubber tappers working on the plantations. The Indian politicians have insisted on preserving Tamil language schools, often within or on the edge of plantations. But while Indians are justly proud of their cultural heritage, Tamil is a language which gets them nowhere economically Moreover, preserving the Tamil schools, while useful for Indian politicians in that it preserves their support base, tends to ghettoise the Indians, narrowing their horizons and limiting their opportunities.

Urban Indian friends of mine in Malaysia refuse to send their children to Tamil schools for this reason, preferring the national Malay or even the Chinese schools. Overall, Indians remain the most marginalised of the major ethnic groups in Malaysia. Much less marginalised, but still placed in a slightly equivocal position, are Malaysia's many Eurasians. Anne, a young writer with a British father and a Chinese mother in her small Kuala Lumpur townhouse. A typical middle-class Malaysian house-downstairs for eating, entertaining and work, upstairs for sleeping, with a car space out front-it is the kind of suburban accommodation that is common throughout Malaysia and a testament to the embourgeoisement of Malaysian life. Anne is an attractive young woman; she looks relaxed in slacks and a smock and, like most Malaysians at home, is sensibly barefooted. She is full of energy, full of smiles.

Anne is interesting for many reasons, not least because she has chosen to live in Malaysia, to be Malaysian, although she had the opportunity to live in England and indeed looks European. She was born in Sabah, in East Malaysia, and educated partly in Penang and partly in England. Her early years were spent in Malaysia, but then from age 11 to 20 she lived in England, returning to Malaysia for holidays. 'When I came back I thought I'd have to speak Bahasa [Malay] fluently to get a job. About three years later I had to decide whether I wanted to be in Asia or in Europe, in IQ or London.

'I guess I'm a sunshine kinda gal,' she says jokingly of her decision to choose Malaysia-but then adds: 'I'd rather deal with the problems of a developing country than a country that seems overdeveloped. There are opportunities here; it's up to you to make something of them. The Malaysian point of view fascinated me. I wanted to be part of the action. 'There is a drive to modernise here. But there's also this concern that we remain ourselves, that we don't lose our Asian values. There's a tension there in accepting the paradox-how do you modernise but maintain values, such as the family, which are important? For women the question is how do you reconcile the freedom you get [from economic development] with the place you have in the family Women friends of mine who are Muslim are very liberal, but they pray regularly each day and have an inner spirituality.'

Anne was conscious of her unusual racial status while she was growing up: 'I'm from Sabah where there's a lot more intermarriage, not the automatic Chinese, Malay and Indian division. With economic development there is a multiracial middle class. But there are also multiracist stereotypes-that the Malay government workers are slow, that the Chinese would sell their mothers that Indians are low achievers. 'My school in Penang was truly multiracial and multi religious but there were all kinds of intricate hierarchies among the Eurasians. For example, if your father was *mat salleh* [white] rather than your mother, that was one point more, and if your father was American that was half a point less than if he was English.

'From my non-Eurasian cousins there is one of two reactions. Either they imagine that you think you're so great, such a big deal, because you're *mat salleh,* or they have a kind of awe, a great interest in you.' Anne has had plenty of incongruous racial experiences. When she went shopping with her mother as a child, people often assumed she was with her *amah,* that her mother was the family servant. Similarly, in a small traffic accident she is assumed to be a foreigner, and the locals are astonished when she speaks Bahasa and the Chinese dialect Hakka. But for all that, she loves Malaysia and bounces her own energy off the swirling social energy, the social-hybrid vigour, around her.

Ivy sees another side of Malaysia's multiracial life. She runs a women's shelter in Kuala Lumpur for battered wives and it is there, after having promised faithfully never to disclose its precise location, that I meet her. There is a locked gate, high walls and strong physical security. There are lots of little kids running around, mainly Indian, like Ivy; they are all as cute as can be, very shy, not used to *mat sallehs* [white people]. My heart melts-how can anyone abuse these kids? The way Ivy sees it, spousal abuse is a terrible problem in Malaysia. It is most often associated with the Indian community, and with alcohol, but Ivy's work has shown her that it cuts across all races and all classes.

She discusses racial issues in a complex and nuanced fashion, recognising the advances that have been made but also the limitations, frankly discussing the special privileges Malays get which other races do not. But there is one comment Ivy makes that strikes me very strongly: 'When I walk down the street in Western countries, in New York or Sydney, I'm acutely aware that I'm brown. When I walk the streets here I don't feel that I'm Indian all the time. As a kid I was told not to go to the Malay *kampungs* [villages] or I might get beaten up. Now I never hear anything like that. This country provided enough plates of rice for my father, a Sri Lankan immigrant, for him to give his family opportunities. I'm a great optimist about Bangsa Malaysia.'

Bangsa Malaysia literally means 'Malaysian nationality' and is intended to connote a diminished emphasis on ethnicity and a heightened emphasis on the unity of Malaysian citizenship. Ivy would like to see greater progress in the status of women in Malaysia. She points out that it is not just Islam, but most other religions too, that afford women an inferior place in the social hierarchy. Economic progress has helped Malaysian women in achieving some economic independence but it has also led to great dislocation as women have migrated from rural to urban areas in search of work, often as a result becoming cut off from the support network of the extended family.

These of course are problems familiar in many developing countries. Part of Malaysia's uniqueness lies in the way these problems are blended with its predominantly Islamic identity. The West has a cockeyed view of Islam. More Muslims live in India than in any country in the Middle East. More Muslims live in Indonesia than in any other country in the world. The world's vision of the typical Muslim ought thus to be, say, of a Javanese woman, yet it is almost invariably of an Iranian mullah. Malaysia is one of the most economically developed of all Muslim societies. And it has to confront the challenge of building a decent compact with its large (nearly 40 per cent) non-Muslim minorities.

The Western media tends to demonise Islam, especially by an exaggeration of what it labels Islamic terrorism. There are just as many examples of insane and destructive behaviour carried out by nominal Christians, in Kosovo or Northern

Ireland or Latin America, or by nominal Confucians, in Tibet or Tiananmen Square, or by nominal atheists-the Khmer Rouge, the North Korean communists-as there are of such behaviour from nominal Muslims. One problem in Western analysis of Islam is that in Islamic society's actions tend to be carried out in an Islamic idiom even when these actions cannot in any meaningful way be attributed to Islamic teaching or even serious Islamic organisation.

When someone like Branch Davidians leader David Koresh of Waco fame embarks on lunatic paramilitary civil disobedience, which results in appalling death and destruction, we write him off as just an American nut that got out of control. But if Koresh had linked his nuttiness in any way to Islam, or worse, actually called himself a Muslim, the world would have been filled to saturation with learned articles denouncing the threat of the new international Islamic menace. It is even more absurd that Malaysia should be caught up in these Western stereotypes, because the Islam practiced in Malaysia is overwhelmingly tolerant, sensible and socially beneficial. Even when it does seem to constrain civil liberties it is more in the essentially trivial category of such things as banning participation by Malay women in beauty contests rather than the imposition of onerous constraints on the society as a whole. And Malaysia is such a diverse, sophisticated society that even limited moves such as these become hotly contested and is often reversed.

More importantly, the Western media, in its generally one dimensional rendition of Dr Mahathir, misses one of the most complex, subtle and important dynamics at work in any Islamic society: his attempt to harness the traditional moral virtues of Islam-thrift, honesty, family fidelity, obedience, abstemiousness, communal solidarity-with the traditional Chinese and Japanese ingredients of East Asian economic success. This was particularly embodied in Mahathir "Look East" policy in which he urged his countrymen to emulate Japan. This in itself was a strong assertion of Asian values, the very idea that a developing country could look to an Asian society for inspiration rather than always to a Western society. The Japanese development model has been shown to have its flaws and its limitations, but it served Japan well for 40 years and it served Malaysia well for at least two decades.

The larger reality was that Mahathir was trying to reconcile Islam with the modern world. There is a vigorous debate about how to adapt Islam to the needs of modern life and the modern economy. This is of course a clumsy outsider's way of expressing a complex intellectual process. One might just as well say the attempt is being made to adapt modern life to the needs of Islam. But the important, the essential, point is that the attempt is being made with basic goodwill towards both Islam and the modern world. The two are not seen as antithetical. Of course, not everything practiced under the guise of 'modernity' needs to be accepted, and Mahathir's robust rejection of the bits of Western modernity he doesn't like earn him the most publicity in the West, but there is no feeling that Islam and the modern world are at war. Rather there is an attempt to see what an authentic application of Islamic ethics to the realities, the good and the not so good, might produce.

Malaysia's endeavour here is of global importance. If Malaysia succeeds in becoming a fully developed nation it will not only demonstrate the viability of multiethnic, multireligious societies but may offer a new vision of how an Islamic society can reconcile Islam and economic modernisation. The exciting aspect of Mahathir's endeavours is that he tried to use Islam as a constructive force for modernisation, rather than succumbing to the Western stereotype of Islam as a force for feudalism or at least antique Arab chauvinism. This remains just as true despite Mahathir's harshly critical statements concerning Western hedge fund managers and the United States, in connection with the Asian economic crisis. Mahathir was most certainly not rejecting modernity in those statements, he was blaming hedge funds and criticising US policy.

None of this means that there are no difficult Islamic issues to manage in Malaysia. All my Malaysian friends acknowledge that there has been an Islamic resurgence over the last 20 years. Rehman Rashid, in his marvellous book, *Malaysian Journey*, describes how the success of the Ayatollah Khomeini in overthrowing the Shah of Iran initially produced a burst of support and applause among Malaysians, especially students. But now the Islamic societies in the Middle East are recognised in Malaysia as basically unsuccessful, certainly not models Malaysia should follow. Yet Malaysia is still more consciously Islamic than it was 20 years ago. Malay friends in the civil service tell me that 20 years ago, during the Muslim fasting month of Ramadan, most Malay civil servants still ate lunch.

Now virtually no one does, certainly not in public. I asked Anwar Ibrahim about the Islamic resurgence in Malaysia. 'We do not see religiosity, be it Islamic, Buddhist, Confucian or Christian, as a threat,' he said. 'What we are against is extremism and intolerance, particularly if it has a violent tendency. The resurgence of religiosity is a global tendency and not confined to Islam. It is something we should view positively because it gives a sense of fulfillment beyond materialistic pursuits and strengthens the moral fabric of society and the family.'

Indeed, Anwar has argued that the role, the respect, given to organised religion is one of the essential Asian values, and distinguishes East Asian societies from the West. This is a difficult argument to sustain for Japan, China or even Korea, but in different ways it does apply to South East Asia and even to South Asia. In taking religion seriously, Asian societies actually resemble the way the West was for most of its existence. It is only recently that mass atheism has come to be a hallmark of advanced Western liberalism, and Anwar has identified this as the source of some of the social malaise to be found in many Western societies.

As for his own society, he told me: 'The problem is with militancy. The solution is to promote tolerance and a universal perspective among religions. In Malaysia we certainly view Islam as a modernising force. Islam promotes rational thinking and orderliness. The role of Islam's critical values such as justice, respect of human dignity, the rule of law-these are crucial in the formation of a modern nation state and a democratic and multicultural community.'

Both Anwar and Mahathir have been trenchant opponents of Islamic fundamentalism, though both have problems with the term itself. One reason for opposing fundamentalism is its incompatibility with the modern economy. When the Islamic fundamentalist Parti Islam SeMalaysia (PAS) won control of the State government in Kelantan it decreed that women could not work at night. As a result, factories in Kelantan were effectively limited to one shift per day. Some of them closed and Kelantan lost outside investment to other States. Of course, Mahathir and Anwar have made in-principle arguments against fundamentalism as well as pragmatic arguments against it. But the vision of development is also important to the vision of the good life, meaning a moral and fully rounded human life, which both Mahathir and Anwar have promoted for Malaysia.

In an important speech to the UMNO General Assembly in September 1997, Mahathir directly linked economic development to religious dignity: 'To really redeem the dignity of race and religion, our progress must at least be on a par with those said to be advanced in this world, those respected, even feared, by all, including Muslims and Islamic countries.' In this same speech, which caused something of a sensation in Malaysia at the time, Mahathir also made the case, which he has made so many times, for a moderate and tolerant Islam:

I realise that what I am saying will not make many people comfortable, including UMNO members. But we are facing a problem of increasing intolerance to anyone who does not give priority to the form and shape of Islam...In several other Muslim countries, the fanatic groups are prepared to kill people of the same faith because they want to seize power to implement their opinion. In Malaysia, groups like these have already reached a level of slandering and denying the 'Muslimness' of others. If left like this we will also become like certain Muslim countries which are already weak and oppressed by foreign powers. We have to defend the true Islamic teachings before tragedy befalls us.

The reason they [other Muslims] are proud of Malaysia is not that we have exhibited the kind of Islam which is extreme but that we practice moderation in Islam. Malaysian Muslims have successfully dealt with the problem of ruling a multiethnic and religious population...Although from the beginning there were attempts to split the Malays through religion, this attempt failed. The majority of Malays had a moderate attitude as is required in Islam and not an extreme attitude that is condemned in Islam. This side of Mahathir, it is fair to say, gets far too little international recognition. The leaders of Islamic fundamentalist groups such as PAS are locked in an endless struggle with the moderates and the modernisers for the soul of the majority Malays. Having spoken at length with PAS leaders I find them, by international standards, a pretty moderate sort of Islamic fundamentalist.

Their critique of modern Western society is the same as would be made by any conservative religious person of virtually any faith. They even make a reasonable case for the role religious values should have in crafting state laws. Although for many Islamic thinkers the intertwining of state law and religious law is very intimate, while in the West we pride ourselves on the separation of church and state, the truth is that most societies have some profound historical connection between law and religion; they just strike a different balance. Most Western laws have their origin in some Christian ethical concern, or even, distantly, in natural law theory, an explicitly Christian idea. That is not to support the PAS agenda of implementing Islamic law much more rigorously and pervasively in Malaysia (most Malaysians clearly don't want it) but simply to recognise that even religious fundamentalists occupy more a different point along a continuum than a different solar system.

A spokesman for PAS, at the end of a long discussion, made one especially revealing comment: 'Among Muslims the understanding and commitment [to their religion] is increasing much better than before. But foreign influence and the influence of non-Muslims are also increasing. In the past non-Muslims never interfered in these matters but now they talk much more and we can't say openly what we think.' The point which perhaps PAS does not like to acknowledge is that non-

Muslims are right to participate in the national discussion about how to give expression to Islamic values, because although in Malaysia specifically Islamic laws governing such areas as marriage, divorce and custody of children, or observance of fasting laws and a ban on alcohol, apply only to Muslims, they indicate the nature of the relationship between the state and the individual citizen and non-Muslims have a huge and legitimate stake in the definition of that relationship.

Nonetheless, it is worth pointing out that PAS spokesmen generally do say that while they would like to implement Islamic law if they gained political power, they would not force its observance on non-Muslims. As my PAS interlocutor put it: 'Of course, non-Muslims might have a wrong idea of Islam and be frightened but this is not realistic. Chinese and Indians are Malaysian citizens-we cannot expect them to follow our religion.' I spent an afternoon in a suburban Kuala Lumpur coffee shop with a very different group of Islamic thinkers and *Sisters in Islam* was formed in 1988 and it sprang from the concern of a handful of women about the status of women in Islam. The group's spokes- woman, a feisty, unveiled, highly articulate, middle-aged academic, Norani, told the story: '*Sisters in Islam* came about because we were concerned that Islam had so often been used by men to promote bad practices.

We began with a concern about the implementation of Islamic family law. Very often men are saying things like "Islam gives men the right to beat their wives", or "Wives must be obedient to their husbands". 'Some of us women went back to the primary source of Islam, to read the Koran. Everything we believe in concerning the rights of women was validated in the Koran. It's all there in the Koran. It didn't come about just with Western feminism. Islam was regarded as a very liberating religion 1400 years ago. It gave women lots of rights. We had never heard these rights in our religion before but they are explicit in the verses of the Koran. This was so exhilarating and a wonderful experience for us.

'But the professional literature, the literature about the Koran, had been written by men. Men read the verse on polygamy and interpret it as a universal right to have up to four wives. Women read the same verse and see the injunction that if you can't treat them all justly you should marry only one. Polygamy is allowed in Malaysia. In some States you need the first wife's permission but if you are having trouble you can just go across the border to another State (where the religious courts always rule in the man's favour) and marry there. 'Many women have been very happy to hear themselves reaffirmed. You don't just cower into silence because some men say it's all just Western feminism and you're not allowed to say it.'

Sisters In Islam believe that lack of education in Islamic matters for Islamic women has been fundamental in denying women power: 'There is this exclusive group of men who, because of their training and their ability to speak Arabic, can say what it is to be a woman. We've had informal links with women's groups in the Middle East and many have taken the same route as Sisters In Islam-they've gone back to the Koran and worked within the religious framework. There's nothing radical or revolutionary about it although the traditional Ulama [religious teachers] view it as such.' Nonetheless, the Sisters recognise that in Malaysia they are dealing with a relatively liberal environment: 'There's not much cultural excess baggage associated with Islam in Malaysia. Malaysia's Islamic tradition was never like the Middle East.

Men and women participate in the public sphere here. We never had *purdah* or segregation. That's all new and most of it is from the Middle East influence.' The wearing of the veil, of a *tudong*-the traditional Muslim head-dress-is much more common now than it was 20 years ago among Muslim women, though it is still very far from universal. Norani commented: 'Veiling is part of the Islamic resurgence. There's a new definition of what it means to be a Muslim woman. Part of the motivation for the return to veiling and similar practices doesn't actually come from Islam. It's part of the need to create a distinctive, post-independence cultural identity. You use women as symbols of your culture. Veiling should be a matter of choice. It's up to you if you want to do it and that's fine, but you can't impose it on someone else.

'But people are ignorant. They do as they're told. We began our work because we asked the question, "How can Islam be so unjust to us?" We found it's not unjust after all. We do not want to give up our Islamic life, our Islamic identity. Malaysia has traditions of equality. It was once a rural society and women worked with men in the fields.' I heard views similar to Norani's from Marina Mahathir, the prime minister's daughter. Marina is a phenomenon in Malaysia and ought to be better known in the West. Her 40th birthday party, in 1997, was a rollicking event. It could not have been held for the daughter of any other South East Asian leader.

It was a surprise party, held in Chow Kit, Kuala Lumpur's notorious red-light district and was organised partly by the city's transsexual community. Streets were blocked off and guests included prostitutes and drug addicts. There were 500 people, countless balloons, stilt-walkers, professional dancers-as Marina herself put it, 'all the marginalised communities'. The party was held primarily to thank Marina for her work on AIDS. At 40, a single parent (she later remarried), feminist, social liberal and chairperson of her country's AIDS council, Marina was both an unusual Malaysian and something of an icon for social progressives. She is a celebrity in Malaysia, a kind of radical democratic princess, perhaps the most liberal, feminist and frank mainstream voice in her society. She is also at times hugely controversial.

Yet she also legitimately reflects the diversity of Malaysia. She pushes the boundaries but is in no sense a negative critic operating from outside the mainstream. In an interview, she said: 'I think Malaysia likes to think of itself as a conservative society but all kinds of things go on that aren't conservative; even Western societies would be shocked. The bureaucrats are much more conservative than the people.'

She recalled giving a talk to a group of women in a highly conservative area of rural east coast Malaysia, where PAS is strong. Many of the women wore *tudongs*. She didn't know how the talk was going over and whether the women would discuss issues of sexual health frankly. She was surprised by their openness and their determination to get the facts: 'the first question was on oral sex, whether it could cause an infection.' Marina Mahathir's story tells us a lot about modern Malaysia. Dr Mahathir was not prime minister during her childhood and she grew up in a happy and relatively normal household. (She would later describe her family as one of the 'most kissy-huggy' families she knows.) When she was about 16, Marina was sent by her father to California for a long stay with family friends. 'I think he regrets it now,' Marina recalled.

'As a 16-year-old it created a profound impression on me, on who I am.' She went to England for her A-levels and studied international relations at Sussex University. She broke into journalism in a modest way in Fleet Street and came back to Malaysia in 1980, where she worked on women's magazines and in public relations. She married a Frenchman who worked in the hotel industry and they had a daughter, Ineza. She lived with him in Japan for a year or two but the couple later divorced. Marina has custody of their daughter. This highly internationalised life is representative of thousands and thousands of modern younger Malays. 'My multiracial marriage was not an issue for my family or friends,' she said. 'If the outsider converts [Marina's husband converted to Islam on their marriage] it's no issue at all. I have two cousins, one engaged to an American and one to an Irishman. That's no problem.'

Although she is much more socially liberal than her father she has a loving relationship with him and greatly admires his historic achievements in Malaysia. Nonetheless, not only the Western press but the South East Asian media as well find her fascinating. 'In Singapore and Indonesia there's so much interest; I'm such an oddity in those countries. In Indonesia they look at me and say, "How can you possibly be like that?"' In the book, *In Liberal Doses*, a collection of her newspaper columns, Marina frequently attacks the country's religious authorities. She was particularly vexed by the beauty contest case, in which some Malay women were briefly arrested for participating in a contest. The incident led to some of Marina's most trenchant pieces. In one she wrote:

On the scale of horrendous ways to exploit women, beauty contests rank pretty low [in importance] ... what worries me most of all is this, what next? What constitutes indecency in Muslim women? Not covering our heads? Wearing skirts? Short sleeves? Will there be men patrolling swimming pools and admonishing women for wearing swim suits? Who will be targetted next? Models? Singers? Actresses? TV announcers? Sportswomen? Female public figures such as politicians? Will it end when women retreat into the home, never to emerge again?

Otherwise we are out there to tempt weak, sex-crazed men. Can all these weak men please identify themselves so we can avoid them?... Compared to incest, child abuse, wife battering, drug abuse and corruption, whether you are dressed right or wrong according to somebody's arbitrary values should rank pretty low on the scale of the concerns of our times. By the way, has anyone in the State ever issued a fatwa on corruption? By South East Asian standards Malaysia has a pretty wide range of permissible opinion but those lines are a very direct, in-your-face rejection of hard line religious interpretations.

Like Ivy's, Marina's views are shaped in part by the realities that she deals with day by day: 'People's attitudes to AIDS are changing, but not nearly fast enough. I deal a lot with desk jockeys who have no idea about the problems people really face. You learn from having to rescue people from villages and the little cruelties they face. You have to be empowered to take action and you're much unempowered when you're sick. If society would do the education work first it might not have some of these other problems.' Overall, Marina remains optimistic about Islam in her country: 'I think we've always had a pretty tolerant brand of Islam in Malaysia. There are those who want it to be stricter but it always seems to be directed against women. I thank God we have a multiracial society because we always have a basis of comparison. Our domestic violence law was held up for years because it was said to be anti-Islam. Does that mean non-Islamic men cannot beat their wives but Islamic men can? Ultimately my father had to insist that it was passed.'

Norani, from *Sisters in Islam*, acknowledges that one of the biggest factors that progressive Muslim women have had going for them has been Prime Minister Mahathir's personal liberalism and leadership on religious issues. How, then, does he come to have such a definitively negative image in the West? Partly, of course, it's his style. He talks back. He's crotchety. He's abrasive. He's verbally confrontational. But when you boil most of the rhetoric down, Mahathir has two basic complaints about the West, and both are reasonable, or at least not baseless, even if from a Western point of view they are often overstated. One is that the West is socially decadent. The other is that the Western powers bully and coerce smaller, less powerful nations like Malaysia.

Even in his frequent jousts with the Western media Mahathir is often motivated by the disparity in power between an institutions like, say, the *New York Times* and the Malaysian Government. The *New York Times* can affect the investment levels that flow into Malaysia; the Malaysian Government cannot materially affect the *New York Times*, or more broadly the economic health of the United States. Moreover, it's important to realise that Mahathir doesn't take much coercive action against the Western press. He merely argues with it.

Western journalists who deny the power, and therefore the responsibility, of their own position are being disingenuous at best. And surely it's better to have an outspoken South East Asian leader who argues with the Western media rather than one who censors or excludes it. Malaysia is totally open to foreign journalists and Mahathir himself remarkably accessible. Even if he declines to give a particular foreign journalist a one-on-one interview it is very easy to find out when his frequent press conferences are being held, to go along, sit down the front and ask the most provocative questions you like. Indeed, certain Western journalists often do this. Mahathir is infinitely more accessible to Western journalists than an American president, or even an Australian prime minister, is to a Malaysian journalist.

All the same, sometimes Mahathir's rhetoric is excessive and even damaging to Malaysia. Fitting into such a category are the convoluted remarks in which he appeared to suggest that it was at least a possibility that some of the currency speculators who, so he had it, played a role in bringing down the value of the Malaysian ringgit may have been motivated by their being Jewish and therefore hostile to a Muslim nation's success. Mahathir's actual remarks were ambiguous and he backed away from them as soon as they were uttered. Nonetheless, they were hurtful to Jews and counterproductive to both Mahathir's and Malaysia's cause. Sometimes, too, his rhetoric, while containing seeds of reasonable complaint against Western arrogance, is itself needlessly over the top. Calling the American currency trader George Soros 'a moron', while obviously plainly inaccurate, is also gratuitous and pointless.

Similarly he seems sometimes to attribute a conspiratorial malice to unseen Western powers which is either unfair or grossly overdrawn. This was particularly in evidence in his response to the East Asian economic crisis. In an address in Hong Kong in late 1997 Mahathir said:

> I don't know about the average man in the street but quite a few people who are in the media and in control of the big money seem to want to see these South East Asian countries and, in particular, Malaysia stop trying to catch up with their superiors and to know their place. If they don't they just have to be made to do so and these people have the means and the wherewithal to force their will on these upstarts. There may be no conspiracy as such but it is quite obvious that a few at least, media as well as fund managers have their own agenda which they are determined to carry out.

And on other occasions he accused Western powers of wanting to make Malaysia an economic colony. Without endorsing Mahathir's view, it must be said there is something in it, in that a lot of the Western media comment on East Asia's travails was filled with an appalling and often badly informed Schadenfreude. This was particularly true of American commentary and could lead to a resurgence of anti-Americanism in the region. And many Western media and political commentators instantly and wrongly attributed East Asia's economic problems to a lack of total Western-style democracy, so that issues of corporate governance and financial system weakness were intertwined with issues of political ideology.

But overall the conspiracy interpretation of the great financial crisis doesn't hold up. It presumes a degree of coordination and precise planning, on the part of a vast array of players, that is simply not credible. Western hedge funds were part of the problem-they were too unregulated and were irresponsible. Mainstream Western authorities recognised this eventually. But the hedge funds were not the only people selling Asian currencies; numerous Asians were doing so themselves. The failure of many Asian banks and corporations to hedge in advance their American dollar debts was hardly attributable to a Western conspiracy. Absolutely no one predicted the crisis in anything like its full dimensions-how could anyone possibly have been controlling it?

Nonetheless, Mahathir's willingness to 'talk back' to the Western powers is one of the attractive features of his personality, though in the wrong context it can be hazardous. There is also the question of how much it is motivated by domestic concerns. This should not be overstated. Mahathir has not needed to wage an anti-Western verbal war to secure his position. But he has been the master of the theatre of Malaysian politics. Lacking significant domestic opposition, at least for most of the last decade until Anwar's jailing, he has at times used bouts of anti-Westernism to unify Malaysian politics, and perhaps even to help mould an internal transethnic single identity for his state, partly defining it in contrast to the West.

Somewhat like the Thai leader, Chuan Leekpai, Mahathir has seen Asian values as a positive force that would help the region come back from the economic crisis. In an interview in 1998 he remarked: 'Asian values have their good and bad points. But Asian stoicism, diligence, family loyalty, community orientation, respect for authority, law and order and orthodoxy-these are the strong values which pulled Asians through the years of foreign oppression and helped rebuild their societies. These same values will stand them in good stead in striving for recovery from the present and future turmoil inflicted upon them. 'Are Asian values bad as compared to Western values? History provides the answer. The two world wars and the dropping of the atom bombs on Asian cities, the holocaust, the killings of Bosnians-these were not perpetuated by Asians. [And] currency trading is not an Asian invention.'

In recent years Mahathir and Anwar, though at least publicly never absolutely directly at odds before Anwar's arrest, presented the Malaysian world view in very different tones of voice. This was never more evident than in the response of the two men to the regional economic crisis. I spent January and part of February of 1998 travelling around Malaysia, mainly enjoying myself, but I did interview both Mahathir and Anwar, coincidentally on the same day. The crisis, then six months old, totally dominated the nation and the leaders' conversation. As usual, their response was a study in contrasts.

Anwar saw the crisis as offering the region a great and historic opportunity. It would end crony capitalism and in the long run lead to reformed and more soundly based modern economies, he told me. 'It will lead to a new Asia which will be more confident and more mature, and liberal and democratic. The great lesson we have learnt, which is actually a transformation and a revolution in itself, is that it has called for greater transparency, greater accountability, for greater democracy. Now people assess what the markets say, what people perceive, whether awards and grants are given to your party supporters or to friends and family. These are now openly debated, without exception.'

But he added an important rider: 'At the same time, having learned the lessons of this turmoil, we recognise that Asian identity; Asian solidarity and Asian values are not only important but will be more pronounced than ever.' Anwar was thus formulating a complex and multilayered response, designed to perform several tasks-to deal with the inescapable reality of the economic crisis, but to seek to energise the crisis for constructive reform while remaining faithful to the region's core values. Mahathir, who has certainly pushed the envelope of reform on countless occasions himself, was more lugubrious, seeing starkly the downside of the crisis not only in economic terms but in terms of loss of South East Asia's bargaining power and political strength vis-a-vis Western powers.

He told me: 'If you consider that democratically elected leaders can be displaced by outside powers there must be some loss of independence. Even if they are not democratically elected, if people have lost the power to choose their own leaders, by whatever means, then there must be a loss of power.' Mahathir was being unusually elliptical that day but

I assume he was referring to the political pressure that the International Monetary Fund, and the money markets generally, brought to bear, which effectively resulted in changes of government in Thailand, South Korea and later Indonesia would lead to regional resentment against the influence of outside powers. He replied: 'People dare not speak out now, but privately, of course, they have voiced a lot of stiff resentment.' Later Mahathir would himself speak more strongly on these themes.

Mahathir is always softly spoken in interviews. In one-on-one meetings he is solicitous, deeply courteous and answers questions slowly and quietly. In that interview he told me he was literally afraid to speak out, following savage international market reactions to his earlier harsh criticisms of the international currency trading system (he had blamed currency traders for the collapse of regional currencies): 'It's been said I've now toned down my criticisms. That is basically out of fear. It is no longer safe to speak out and give your views. If you say the wrong thing you will be brutally punished by having your currency devalued. We lack the freedom of speech now. It has been pointed out that there is a very close relation to opinions expressed or deeds done with the devaluation of currencies. The currency is devalued, jobs are lost, and people suffer. It's a very heavy punishment on the whole nation. No leader, I think, would want to say things which allow punishment, not on him personally, but on his people.'

At the time I was astonished to hear these words from the man I had come to regard as the most consistently forthright and outspoken statesman in Asia. The great paradox of Mahathir has always been that, while he championed Asian values, his personal rhetorical style, his style of leadership, was so Western, so upfront, so dialectical. That day, in a further irony almost too intricate to unravel, the power of the Western financial markets seemed to have forced on him an uncharacteristic Asian reticence. Of course, he would later recover full rhetorical self-confidence. Again Mahathir had at least half a general point.

It was acceptable for a Western economist like David Hale, or even the chairman of the US Federal Reserve, Alan Greenspan, to draw attention to the shortcomings of the international money markets, but it was, for a time in 1998 anyway, not acceptable for a South East Asian leader to do so-because the markets would interpret that as a retreat from pro-market reform and punish the currency accordingly. For his part, Anwar tried to bridge this contradiction by offering an interpretation of the crisis which accepted plenty of home-grown blame, but also gently drew attention to the power of outside forces and the unsatisfactory nature of totally unregulated currency trading and short-term capital flows. Anwar said: 'The pace of liberalisation in the region had been so fast that I don't think we had the infrastructure for a free-market operation in place.

The general public, except for a very few, have no comprehension about how a free market operates, or how the stock market operates. Secondly, of course, there's the issue that has been much discussed-the inherent weaknesses within the particular systems. You have a modern banking system but directed by those in power [as to where] to lend, as in Korea, and prior to that the Thai problem. There was the question of over lending to the property sector, a lack of prudence on the part of the banks because of political connections, and a failure of supervision. Then of course there was stock market corruption, nepotism and cronyism, which are all related. 'My reservation about that criticism is that it assumes the Western system is quite free from these excesses. Accepting all these facts, we cannot deny the role of the currency traders and short-term speculators who manipulate the market.

If it was incorrect for [regional] governments to allow these excesses I think similarly it's unacceptable for the international system to condone the excesses of these manipulators and speculators. There was thus a perfectly respectable Malaysian case that the international currency markets needed some reform. However, it was for a time a dangerous case for South East Asian leaders to make. Both Mahathir and Anwar were disappointed at the unforthcoming nature of the US response to the crisis and at Japan's lack of action. Mahathir's most radical actions, of course, were jailing Anwar and imposing currency controls. Outsiders probably overemphasise the ideological content of the struggle between Mahathir and Anwar. The specific charges laid against Anwar are obviously only part of the story.

Partly it was a struggle between two very tough and determined politicians. Partly it was a generational struggle.

Partly it had to do with longstanding factional struggles in UMNO. And partly it was ideological. Imposing currency controls was also a radical step, but one that had been suggested, after all, by the Western economist-guru, Paul Krugman. It may or may not have been good policy; it certainly was not unreasonable policy. It was an assertive attempt by the Malaysian Government to regain control of its economy. And the totally uncontrolled, extremely volatile flows of very short-term capital were widely recognised as a problem that merited serious policy attention.

Mahathir's most famous clash with a representative of American power came at the Asia-Pacific Economic Cooperation forum leaders' meeting in Kuala Lumpur in November 1998. At the last moment Bill Clinton had cancelled and his vice-president, Al Gore, had gone instead. At a speech in front of Mahathir proceeding the APEC Business Summit dinner, Gore made what might be considered a scandalous intervention in Malaysian politics. Part of his speech was a standard American call for democracy. He said, inter alia: 'And so we continue to hear calls for democracy, calls for *doi moi*, people's power, *reformasi*. We hear them today-right here, right now-among the brave people of Malaysia.'

This was a speech of bizarre, almost surreal, oddity and obnoxiousness. For a start, *Doi Moi* is the official slogan of the Vietnamese Communist Party. Since when has anybody accused the Vietnamese Communist Party of being interested in democracy? Is the Vietnamese Communist Party, a thoroughly Stalinist outfit, to be equated with Cory Aquino's People Power revolution in the Philippines in 1986? *Reformasi* is indeed a word that various groups use, both in Malaysia and in Indonesia, but Gore's using it in this way virtually equated Malaysia with Indonesia. In the context, this was grotesque. Elections in Indonesia under Suharto had been almost wholly farcical. No one could describe them as fair. In Malaysia, even the Opposition describes the elections as clean. To equate Malaysia with Indonesia in terms of *reformasi*, as Gore's speech tended to do, was both inaccurate and unfair.

The whole performance was abysmal and emblematic of the Clinton administration's general hamfistedness and perpetual concern to get a good TV grab at home no matter what havoc it might cause in US foreign policy. Gore's gauche intervention could only be contrasted with the sotto voce performance that Clinton had given a few months earlier on his visit to China, cooing and billing to the Chinese Communist Party leaders. Why so sweet in Beijing and so strident in Kuala Lumpur? Did Malaysia really deserve this? Gore also conveyed an air of pompous superiority in turning up to the dinner and delivering his insult, only to leave without waiting for the meal. Making such an inappropriate and bad-mannered intervention on behalf of Mahathir's political opponents could only reinforce every negative thing about the West that any Malaysian had ever thought. Indeed, the Malaysian Opposition felt that Gore's intervention seriously damaged their cause.

One of Malaysia's leading intellectuals, Dr Noordin Sopiee, the head of the Institute for Strategic and International Studies, an urbane internationalist and an immensely sophisticated man, took out a full-page advertisement in the Malaysian *New Straits Times* in response to Gore's speech. Its text read:

As a Malaysian, I am fed up of stupid, ignorant, 'kurang ajar' [a Malay expression meaning extremely ill-mannered] idiots insulting my country.

Mr Gore should not only have left the meeting room immediately after insulting us. He should have got on the plane and left the country, and he should not come back until he has learnt some manners. I am not a politician. I do not want to play politics. I am not anti-American. For these very strong words, I certainly apologise to my many, many American friends who are also very embarrassed. I do not even know if other Malaysians feel the same way. But enough is enough. Noordin Sopiee. A citizen of Malaysia. Noordin's sentiments were understandable, if harshly expressed. But the whole incident, which at its root was Gore's fault, can only add to the serious misperceptions that Americans and Malaysians tend to have of each other.

4

What's Different in the New Asia

In the industrial age," *Forbes* magazine publisher Rich Karlgaard wrote in summarizing the discussions at a Forbes & GartnerGroup CIO Congress, "the inputs to wealth creation were land, labor, and capital." Two speakers at the Congress, economist Paul Romer and strategist Gary Hamel, Karlgaard explained, believe that the new inputs to wealth creation are:

- Hardware-the sum of all existing tangible assets such as land, minerals, food, factories, cars, and computers
- "Wetware"-human brain power, creativity
- Software-language, math, art, culture, recipes, code.

Michael Porter, Harvard's competitiveness guru, says this way: The key to wealth creation is no longer access to inputs (or resources), but how inputs are used. Both definitions highlight the importance of creativity in the use of inputs, or what Karlgaard calls "wetware." That makes Asia's sudden concern with creativity, not just hard work, understandable. Development in Asia has primarily been a function of input mobilization, rather than input optimization. As a result, educational infrastructure, or the innovation factory, was neglected in the rush to spread prosperity. For the New Asia to prosper, both the government and the private sector must do three things. First, acknowledge that Asia's post-crisis strengths are fundamentally in contrast to its pre-crisis strengths. Second, accept the reality that those post-crisis strengths represent potential and must be developed.

(Significantly, Asia's potential still lies in its people-not the fact that they are there, but the intellectual potential they represent.)

Third, redirect resources to accomplish the task of developing new strengths. For insight into how to do this, it is useful to review what is meant by the term "Asia," consider the new role of government in post-crisis Asia, and view how the private sector is adapting. Perhaps the greatest irony of Asia is that it is looked upon as one huge, homogenous zone by just about everyone who doesn't live there. Some might argue that this is an effect of globalization; others, that it is the product of ignorance. While the economies of Asia are inextricably interdependent-and becoming more so-Asia's financial crisis illustrated the significant contrasts that exist between Asian economies, societies, and politics.

The most obvious crack in Asian unity showed up in the Indonesia riots just prior to the resignation of former president Suharto. Organized gangs attacked ethnic Chinese Indonesians, burning and ransacking their businesses, raping their women-frequently in front of their families-and taking their lives. Ethnic divisions are not the only ones obvious in Asia. There are important religious distinctions as well. As the final draft of this book was being prepared, Indonesian Muslims and the Christians were at each other's throats with consistently lethal results.

The Philippines is the only majority Christian country in the region, yet has a significant Muslim population, principally living on the southern island of Mindanao. Indonesia is the largest Muslim country in the world, yet the ethnic Chinese, the traditional targets of rioters' fury in times of economic difficulty, control the economy. Even within Chinese societies, contrasts abound. Hong Kong, Taiwan, and Singapore are each distinct societies and business centers. Hong Kong is known for go-getter speculative investors and low value added manufacturers, as well as for being a regional financial center. Taiwan is also full of entrepreneurs, but among them are those that have managed a significant and difficult transition from low value added and original equipment manufacturer (OEM) contract manufacturing to original brand development, manufacture, and distribution of world-class products. Singapore is a tiny nation of private sector bureaucrats, reflecting the interventionist policies of its well-meaning government.

The heavily American-influenced Filipinos are creative geniuses, excelling at theater and the arts as well as software development and big-company management. The Indonesians have frequently looked upon the Filipinos as their closest brothers in Asia not because of their Asianness-and certainly not because of their religion- but because they shared the unfortunate distinction of being the poorest nations in their part of the region. Meanwhile, the Filipinos and Malaysians have regularly insulted each other over the treatment of Filipino contract workers and rattled sabres over territorial jurisdictions.

Across Asia, resentment toward Japan remains surprisingly strong despite the important role Japanese investors played in support of the Asian miracle years. While Asia in a unified voice called for Japan to behave responsibly to help bring the region out of recession, many Asians chuckled that the Japanese economic invasion had ground to a prolonged and ignominious halt. Japan's financial debacle, however, should have demonstrated to the rest of Asia that basic economic fundamentals apply to high-flying Asian economies as much as they do to Western economies. During the Asian miracle years, per capita GNP ranged from approximately US$400 in Indonesia to US$31,000 in Singapore.

Hong Kong and Singapore were among the world's most competitive economies while Indonesia and the Philippines were among the most corrupt. Politically, the disorganized Philippine democracy was seen by leaders in the rest of Southeast Asia as an impediment to development although fisticuffs between Taiwan legislators failed to dent that economy's rapid growth. As Asia's financial crisis worsened, the dangers inherent in politically immature societies became evident in the overthrow of Indonesia's Suharto, destroying a damaging political dynasty but also erasing twenty years of dramatic economic development.

Other geographic regions suffer the same failure of local distinction that Asia does. But no other region is anywhere as large or populous. Practically the entire region, excluding Japan and South Korea, was an economic backwater for most of the twentieth century, and then grew faster than any other economy in history. The World Bank effectively rewrote its development handbook on the basis of the Asian miracle, praising prudent governments and highly productive, savings minded Asians. By 1998, however, one year into the Asian financial crisis, 73 percent of respondents to the Asian Leadership Survey regularly conducted by *BusinessWeek* strongly agreed with the statement that "the crisis is the fault of Asian government policies."

Enlightened government was not the only World Bank success factor under scrutiny. Economists Jeffrey G. Williamson and David E. Bloom, both of the Harvard Institute of International Development, argued that the structure of Asian populations, not work ethic and high savings rates, were the principal catalysts for the Asian miracle years. "There are two problems with the conventional wisdom. At the beginning of the miracle years, Asian investment and savings rates were about the same as other developing countries. "In other versions of the miracle story, government policy boosts savings and investment rates. But which government policy? South Korea's government-knows-best approach? Hong Kong's low-tax, laissez-faire philosophy? That's the second problem".

Williamson and Bloom say that "savings and investment rose as mortality and fertility rates fell", with the effect that eventually the percentage of the productive population-working adults-was larger than the nonproductive segments. Unfortunately, and obviously, that can't go on forever. As more baby boomers retire, there will be fewer children entering the workforce. That means slower growth because, as we said earlier, development in Asia has been based on mobilization of inputs-particularly labor, as economist Paul Krugman argued in his 1994 *Foreign Affairs* article, "The Myth of Asia's Miracle."

Not all of Asia is set for slower growth, according to the Harvard economists, just most of it. The Philippines, for instance, is just entering the "bonus phase" of the demographic transition: a majority of productive workers in the workforce. But for most of Asia, growth will depend on what Rich Karlgaard, Paul Romer, and Gary Hamel call "software, " or the capacity to replicate knowledge. Put another way, it is the capacity to boost Asian productivity and value-added. How each country in Asia does that will depend on a number of things besides population beginning with enlightened government.

The Asian financial crisis heightened the discussion of social safety nets to protect the economically challenged majority. In reality, the pain was felt principally in the middle of the social strata in most of Southeast Asia, depending on how one defines middle class. In general terms it is safe to suggest that the desperately poor never benefitted much from the Asian miracle years, especially in Indonesia, the Philippines, and Thailand. The top-level population of Southeast Asia also was in many respects immune from the effects of the Asian crisis, at least compared to the middle class. While many founders of large Asian companies lost control or were destined to lose control as the financial crisis dragged on, lifestyles were not significantly diminished. This was not true for the burgeoning new middle class, which in Indonesia lost two-thirds of its wealth. Long-term small investors in Hong Kong lost veritable real estate and stock market portfolio fortunes.

Who is the middle class? As explained in *Asia's Best: The Myth & Reality of Asia's Most Successful Companies* (Hamlin, 1998), there's a complicated answer to that question. It begins with a report in the *Asian Wall Street Journal* that illustrated the contrasts in the structure of Southeast Asian economies. For example:

- In Singapore, the 33 percent of middle-class households with the highest incomes each earn at least US$3,200 a month. In Indonesia, the middle class only has to earn US$260 a month to make the top 33 percent.
- Reflecting differences in tastes and lifestyles, the middle class is twice as likely to live in air-conditioned homes in Hong Kong as in equally affluent Singapore, where the climate is hotter.
- Despite growing affluence, Asia remains a telecommunications backwater. In Thailand, middle-class households with cars outnumber those that have telephones.

Those two hundred years of Western industrialization was accomplished in less than fifty years in Asia helps explain how such vast contrasts came about. Development has been fast but uneven within as well as without Asia's individual economies. As a result, contrasts in income are sharper and are potential sources of political instability, as demonstrated in Indonesia so dramatically in 1998. In the New Asia, the principal priority of governments should be dealing with those contrasts. The task in the New Asia is how to manage these contrasts. Management guru Peter Drucker says there is a stark choice. One is to bring everyone down to the lowest level, or to raise everyone up to the highest. That's no choice at all.

How does a country's transition from developing status to emerging status mirror the private sector transition from an entrepreneurship to a professionally managed firm? Ideally in three ways: the role of strategy is enhanced, systems and processes become critical to sustained viability, and people become the principal source of value added, or competitiveness. Let's define what is meant by emerging economy. *Emerging economy* is a convenient marketing term developed by global fund and portfolio managers to seduce investors to non-mainstream, or developing, markets. Developing economy, and certainly the term "underdeveloped," implies too much risk for jittery, inexperienced investors, often for good reason-because risk in these markets had to do with poor implementation of the rule of law, political instability and corrupt government, and inadequate private-sector management.

All those factors were still present before the crisis; as the Asian and South American markets painfully demonstrated. But the term *emerging economy* provided a good intellectual excuse to avoid reality and to take comfort in an artificial and exciting reality principally spun by American investment bankers and fund managers, but that also involved European and Japanese investors. However, for purposes here, *developing country* refers to those countries that have embraced the basic reforms necessary to get an economy growing: acknowledging the importance of foreign direct investment, developing the export sector, and gradually lowering barriers to the free flow of goods and services.

Emerging economies are those that are looking beyond these basic reforms to accelerate growth and distinguish themselves from the competition for investment and opportunity. The transition from developing to emerging country- like the transition from entrepreneurship-is not an easy one.

STRATEGY

Successful entrepreneurships frequently sacrifice profitability in favor of market share and brand awareness. Countries sacrifice value-added in order to create jobs. Both eventually find that they are generating greater revenues but with less and less impact on the bottom line: profits for entrepreneurships and budget surplus for countries. For entrepreneurships, continuing business in the same, start-up fashion results in ever decreasing returns, stagnation, and bankruptcy. Therefore, strategy is required to first achieve profitability and then to sustain it. The first step in developing strategy is determining, given competition in both the private and public sector in the new global economy, which customers are preferred in terms of profitability. For entrepreneurships, this means determining how to increase the amount of business they do with these ideal customers.

For countries, the challenge is the same: What sort of investment is needed that will create the necessary kinds of jobs? How is the inflow increased from these investors? For both entrepreneurships and countries, the central issues are 1) developing an effective strategy that distinguishes the entrepreneurship or country from the competition, 2) effectively implementing the strategy, and 3) continually updating the strategy in response to evolving conditions in order to set the rules of competition.

Coming up with a unique strategy is difficult. Take, for example, the national development strategies of Hong Kong, Malaysia, and Singapore. All are inextricably tied to technology. They had better be, because their national development strategies are all the same. Yet none of these countries is particularly well-suited for development into a technology industry cluster. During a visit to Hong Kong in

1999, Microsoft chairman Bill Gates said, "There is enough demand here that Malaysia, Singapore, and Hong Kong could all be successful in (becoming) great software centers". "It's not a zero-sum game. It isn't like one city wins and other cities lose". For example, none of these countries has the educational infrastructure to support technology development. This is something they think they can remedy. None of them have the right people- knowledge workers-in the numbers they need. They think they can import them. None of them have a tradition of value-added innovation. They think they can learn.

Does that mean the strategy is flawed? Possibly. The one thing they have going for them is fear. Fear is an important component of success, and it played an important role in the development of each of these Asian countries and other successful economies. Hong Kong developed as a lonely capitalist outpost during the Cold War; Singapore was thrown out of the Malaysian Federation with virtually no resource other than true grit; and Malaysia was faced with the specter of a race war, featuring religious and ideological unrest as well. All of these countries were scared for their futures, as they are now. Contrast this with the Philippines, where there was no sense of urgency in terms of what the future would hold as recovery began to take hold in 1999. On the contrary, there was an underwhelming sense of complacency.

While the region's strongest economies were sweating about the future, the Philippines appeared content to blithely coast along in the illusory comfort that its economy was the least impacted by the recent crisis provoked by the Asian meltdown (as the International Monetary Fund was frequently fond of noting). Even worse, there was no clearly articulated strategy for Philippine development. There was neither goal nor vision of where the Philippines were headed. There was no indication that the administration of President Joseph Estrada had a firm idea of how it intended to capitalize on the country's strengths to accelerate development and prosperity. To be fair, the government did consistently recommit itself to the principles of free trade, and it wanted to do something about agriculture. But these were tactics, not strategy.

SYSTEMS AND PROCESSES

Systems and processes have to do with how efficiently and productively resources are used. For entrepreneurships, this means acquiring the technology and professional management necessary to achieve or exceed industry standards of efficiency and productivity-while maintaining quality-in order to stay in business. Industry standards of efficiency and productivity are not sources of profitability, but rather requisites of being in the game. For emerging countries, systems and processes refer to bureaucracy and infrastructure. In the same way that entrepreneurships struggle to transition from informal and disorganized ways of conducting their business, emerging countries must struggle to professionalize the bureaucracy. In the way that entrepreneurships struggle with entrenched and uncompetitive cultures and habits to implement reengineered, technology-based business processes, emerging economies must overcome ingrained cultural hurdles and other obstacles toward more efficient and productive economic operations.

For the Philippines-even more so for Indonesia-compared to regional competition, the challenges were great. Could Philippine bureaucracy compete with that of Hong Kong, Malaysia, and Singapore? How about infrastructure? The answers seemed obviously negative. But then why is it that the Philippines were in fact effectively competing with these countries for investment, opportunity, and technology? The answer lies in people. The most difficult part of transitioning an entrepreneurship to a professionally managed firm is finding, recruiting, and retaining the best people. People are increasingly the "product" that firms sell, whether they are in manufacturing, retail, or services. People develop strategy, systems and processes, and products and services. Putting the best minds to work determines the quality in each of these areas.

For emerging countries, the task is to provide a talent pool of people with the right kind of training and effective intellectual tools. Few countries in Asia have done this well, except for Taiwan and, it seems, China. It should be noted that Singapore and Hong Kong have belatedly acknowledged this shortcoming and are working feverishly to address it. Education is the fastest growing industry in Malaysia by some reports. That's one reason they are sweating. Other Asian countries should also be worried for two reasons. First, in the case of Indonesia, the Philippines, and Thailand, many of their best people are at work in other economies.

While their dollar remittances are important, their long-term contribution to economic development would be far more profound if they were working in Asia. To get them back in Asia, governments must improve opportunities by developing effective national strategies and providing the systems and processes to make them work. Second, these countries and Malaysia have allowed their greatest competitive advantage-the productive workforce and the people's aptitude for training-to erode dangerously. Increasingly, as Asia turns to its talent pool, despite its huge population, it will find that the pool is inadequate because: 1. its development has been taken for granted, 2. national investment in education is significantly rerouted to the pockets of corrupt officials and their private-sector cohorts, and 3. the private sector itself fails to invest adequately in training and education, in part because until recently, government has not acknowledged education's strategic importance.

People are the source of competitiveness and they should be the priority consideration in the transition from developing to emerging economy. But to achieve their full potential, governments must also provide both the strategy that will focus national resources and increase returns as well as the systems and processes to ensure the nation continues to develop. Effective government in the New Asia is small government. Asia is already home to some of the world's largest privatization programs, from power generation and water supply to construction and maintenance of transportation infrastructure. Given the scale of privatization, it's not surprising that many of these initiatives have had a bumpy time coming together.

In part, that's been due to differences in valuation perspectives. In others, because competitors or consumers argued effectively that foreign ownership or management of privatized assets undermined national integrity. A Malaysian concern won the bidding, for instance, of the Manila Hotel but the Supreme Court overturned the results in the interest of something called Philippine national patrimony. Developer Gordon Woo's attempts to build infrastructure in Thailand resulted in massive losses when he failed to persuade feuding government agencies to agree with each other. Privatization of national airlines in Malaysia and the Philippines has been controversial and costly to the majority shareholders. Analysts argue that the management of the airlines are not up to the task of creating world class operations and have been slow to undertake market dictated reforms.

Many less visible projects have faired little better. In Manila, for instance, consumers have eagerly anticipated a water utility turnover to two major consortia that will rehabilitate and manage the water system for one of the world's most populated cites. But in 1997, dramatic depreciation of the peso decimated funding plans, delaying for up to half a decade plans to expand the aging network. Nevertheless, the turnover resulted in massive savings for the government. When it turned over, the system was losing 60 to 65 percent of the water it pumped to leaks and fraud.

In an *Asia Week* essay, former President Fidel Ramos said, "No mechanism can allocate resources as efficiently as the market does. Nor is there any mechanism as effective in fostering investment discipline and in rewarding creativity, intelligence, and hard work," in explaining why privatization was a priority during his administration. Despite privatization's uneven history, Asian governments will increasingly rely on market forces to supply the demands of consumers and to achieve reasonable returns on resources.

When the financial crisis hit, economists and analysts warned Asian governments that there should be no backtracking on liberalization. While that was an important message for Asian officials and private sector executives, it was not directed to the principal obstructionists: the United States and Japan. When Asia Pacific Economic Cooperation (APEC) forum ministers met to devise a liberalization timetable in mid-1998, "a United States negotiator noted that his team would need congressional authority to yield concessions", Japanese negotiators said "liberalization deadlines are at odds with APEC's tenet that member economies can implement policy changes on a voluntary basis." Meanwhile, the United States was blaming Japan for not pulling Asia out of the crisis by reflecting its economy and increasing imports from the region.

The question of steady liberalization of key sectors is clearly not a problem limited to Asia. Liberalization must be led by the world's two most important economies. It is wholly illogical to expect developing economies in Asia to set the pace for liberalization. Nevertheless, that has in fact been the case, with the Philippines leading the change to free-market economies under the Ramos administration. The danger of the Asian crisis was that it would undermine the champions of liberalization, particularly as American and Japanese reluctance to meet deadlines and otherwise contribute to easing the crisis became more apparent. In 1998, both Asian and multinational executives felt that neither country was meaningfully addressing the Asian crisis nor the danger it presented to their own economies.

Rather, liberalization was privately viewed as a license for Asia to export its way out of recession. Only when the effects of the crisis became clear in the earnings statements of Japanese and United States multinationals did the full urgency of concerted effort to resuscitate Asia begin to weigh on trade negotiators and senior government officials. Within Asia, private-sector leaders lobbied heavily for continued protection. There was great concern that the region liberalize collectively to ensure that no country gained advantage over another. This was a ridiculous argument, as there was little chance of across-the-board industry parity in the region, given the sharp contrasts between Asian economies, although basic industries such as steel and petrochemicals fretted about dumping by other Asian competitors.

Ultimately the issue for Asian business and policy makers was how long voters would remain patient while waiting for inefficient, long-protected domestic corporations to create jobs and provide value for money. Fortunately for Asian consumers, by late 1998, the tide had turned in favor of accelerated liberalization of trade in the Asia-Pacific. The sole holdout was Malaysia. Unfortunately, Japan and the United States weren't helping. By mid-1999 APEC trade ministers gave up trying to reach a consensus, and they threw the matter to the World Trade Organization

"The Asian crisis is about bad banking" Paul Krugman said in an attempt at explanation ("What Happened ..."). Bad banking practices proliferated, by implication, because government failed to provide an adequate regulatory framework. There are at least two reasons why the regulatory framework did not keep pace with development. First, governments everywhere have traditionally let bull runs get out of hand largely out of the fear of accidentally killing a vibrant economy. MIT economist Rudi Dornbusch says the United States Federal Reserve, up until the nomination of Chairman Alan Greenspan, routinely managed to clobber economies. Even if Greenspan has learned how not to do this, which increasingly seems to be the case, no one else has yet learned how to keep growth in check for much longer than a decade. So it is not unusual that Asian governments were afraid to touch the economy lest they break it. So it eventually broke itself.

Second, no developing economy in history had ever had unfettered access to cheap global funds, that, as author and consultant Kenichi Ohmae says, flow around the world beyond the reach of governments. One may ask, just how exactly does one go about regulating what management icon Peter Drucker calls virtual money in a free-market, global economy? The Asian financial crisis at first appeared to make obvious the dangers of over-reliance on volatile virtual money. But it is unlikely that governments or the private sector would-or could-choose to do without it. Instead of moaning about the evacuation of volatile portfolio investments, Asia would have been better served if its governments had worked to restore confidence and get the investments back.

Clearly, the problem was not that these funds were relied upon, but that governments and businesses thought it was a free ride. Although there was real need for government regulation in banking and equity markets, there was no way Asian governments could afford to try to control the flow of foreign capital in the digital economy. The Asian financial crisis provoked reform, but it was in the manner that banks were regulated, corporations encouraged to compete, and failed enterprise was divided up. Any attempt to exert a meaningful measure of control on the flow of virtual money would force a proportional sacrifice in the prospects for recovery and growth, as Malaysia's currency controls will demonstrate over time. Nevertheless, business, government, and Western academics were still debating the need to restructure global financial architecture in 1999. There was only one thing clear, however, and that was that no one had an acceptable remedy.

"Banthoon Lamsam is not a popular man these days. The chairman of the Thai Bankers' Association has been egging the government to close some of the country's sixteen commercial banks. 'Apparently here in this country, all financial institutions are to be funded by the (staterun) Financial Institutions Development Fund as a last resort. You can keep anything up-just pump air into it'". Banthoon believes that the marketplace should reward companies that make the investment required to be competitive. Companies that fail to make that investment to ensure competitiveness should be penalized by the market and allowed-or forced-to close shop. When government artificially protects poorly managed companies and banks from failure, it serves as a disincentive to good management. That's an argument Asian governments must take to heart.

Whether governments do or not, leaders like Banthoon say good things about the kind of corporate environment that will eventually dominate the region. From the looks of it, it is key private sector leaders, such as Banthoon, who are leading the region to international competitiveness. But they need their governments' support. That support took a backseat in the first year of Asia's financial crisis as governments rotated in and out of power or sunk into the depths of denial. And Asians were in no mood for fainthearted leadership. Developments in Hong Kong, Indonesia, Korea, the Philippines, and Thailand showed that the people of Asia have grown weary waiting for entrenched political regimes to bring about fundamental reform. These are defining acts for twenty-first century Asia, warning shots for an older generation of leaders that has found it profoundly difficult to pass on the mantle of leadership.

The message is clear: Get it right, or get out. The reasons are clearer still. As Urban C. Lehner, executive editor for Dow Jones Asia, said at a conference organized by the Asia Society, "[T]he capacity of Asia to make necessary changes is unproven. Reform has been slow and incomplete." That is, until the people get involved. In Hong Kong, Korea, the Phillipines, and Thailand, non-mainstream leaders (or, legislators in Hong Kong's case) have been elected on the basis of their promise to fundamentally reform government, level playing fields, and generate opportunity. Indonesia promises not to be left far behind. It turns out that those who proudly boasted that Asian values accounted for the region's rapid growth knew very little about changing Asian values after all.

During the very early period of national development, it was fairly easy for government to rationalize playing favorites for business persons and family members who appeared to have the talent to get things done. But it is even easier to see now why that should never have been done. Very few of the tycoons supported by corrupt regimes ever developed the capacity to fend for themselves. They robbed legitimate and talented businesspeople from capitalizing on the opportunities they monopolized. Ironically, there are Asian leaders who still refuse to heed the signs of changing times. In the same way that economic crises are cyclical (although the American economy has been trying hard to prove otherwise), so it seems that politicians in non-democratic environments invariably refuse to let go, despite the certainty of their eventual downfall and disgrace.

It would seem that a truly enlightened leader-such as Malaysia's Prime Minister Mahathir Mohamad-would seize the moment before downfall is inevitable and, in the fashion of a true statesman, display the courage to acknowledge that his people no longer need him. Indeed, that his people will do better with a leader more in tune with the times and the population. Leadership is no longer about iron-fisted control; it is about capitalizing on the dreams of a nation that knows it can do better. One thing is sure. Democratic reform is releasing the enormous energy and talent required to rebuild the Asian miracle. Leaders seeking the fast path to recovery will find it in their people.

Business Week's Asian Leadership Survey provided some other interesting insights into the future of Asian economies. Eighty-one of the fifty-eight big-name CEO respondents believed that Asia's financial crisis presented "huge opportunities for Western firms." Fully 97 percent of the respondents acknowledged that "the crisis will force significant restructuring of the affected economies. However, only 67 percent believed that changes in Asia would reduce corruption, which 86 percent of respondents believed to be a major impediment to doing business in Asia. Ninety-three percent of the managers who completed the survey believe that Southeast Asia will become more open to foreign investment, and 88 percent said that Asian companies "will move towards greater transparency in business transactions and financial reporting."

What is important here in these admittedly unscientific, but insightful, findings is that big-name private-sector executives appeared to see the future better than government leaders, regardless of the extent of their domestic financial crises or political system. Yet the private sector feels that for their vision to be realized, government must actively participate in reform by setting and enforcing new ground rules. In the New Asia, government will assume its most important role: that of leveling the playing field. That won't be enough, however; rule of law must closely follow, and that is where government credibility is at its weakest.

Fifty-three percent of the respondents to the survey said their investment plans had not been affected by the Asian financial crisis. This is opposed to 88 percent of respondents with headquarters in the United States who said in a January 1999 survey conducted by the *Asia Society/The Asian Wall Street Journal* that they had either expanded or left unchanged investment in the region. Indeed, most respondents to the *Business Week* survey felt that the region had become much more competitive. But these CEOs believed that companies in Asia should focus resources and strategy in core business areas. Information technology was seen as a key enabler, providing a critical contribution to competitiveness and productivity. While opportunities are abundant in Asia, they now have to be earned.

As Asia transitioned from the economic crisis and structural reform to recovery and enhanced competitiveness, increasing productivity and value-added became critical long-term determinants of regional economies' capacity to generate prosperity. The urgency with which business must address these issues is heightened by three factors: 1. the increasing size of the nonproductive population, 2. inadequate educational infrastructure, and 3. competition with developed economies for Asia's best minds. Like Asian business, governments as a result will be forced to prioritize national resources to achieve development objectives. And in fact, Asian governments are trying to do this. The problem is that their priorities converge and focus principally on information technology, as we earlier noted.

This is a problem for several reasons. First, there is little educational infrastructure to support a technology competence cluster or venture capital. Second, it's expensive and risky. Asia is trying to more than double the number of high-technology industrial clusters, all in the United States. Third, providing high value-added output is attained, continual heavy investment is required to sustain competitiveness and profit margins. The other end of this clash of national development priorities-and its impetus-is that Asian countries find themselves competing ever more aggressively for contextually smaller pieces of a low value-added commodity pie when they find it impossible to transition to higher value-added industry.

Asian governments are going to have to be more creative in setting strategic development plans and learn to differentiate themselves from the competition. Strategy will begin with a new development model that reflects national strengths. As obvious as this seems, the notion of distinctive competence was lost in the euphoria of the Asian miracle. This was because most people looked upon the entire region, rather than Asian nations, as a miracle of uniform development for close to two decades. Analysts spent much time and energy trying to define a model that would explain the Asian miracle, not the miracles. With the financial crisis, it became clear that there was no single Asian miracle.

In many instances, economies had managed to develop more in spite of national development plans than because of them. Japan and Korea invoked overt government support of heavy industry, and yet their most enduring companies never fell under the government's watchful eye; for example, most of Japan's electronics firms succeeded by exception, not the Japanese model, according to Harvard's Michael Porter. Taiwan relied on its entrepreneurial instincts, while Hong Kong got out of the way of business. Singapore and Malaysia tried to emulate the Japanese model of heavy government intervention and support, while Indonesia, Thailand and Malaysia, too, competed in an all-out race for job-generating foreign direct investment. Indonesia focused on a few favorites to corner industrialization and economic development investment, friends and relatives of former president Suharto.

Malaysia was somewhat more expansive in its selection of favored industrialists. The Philippines, under the administration of Fidel V. Ramos, belatedly moved to stimulate competition and encourage domestic and international investment by dismantling monopolies, a plan which was beginning to pay off when the Asian financial crisis began in earnest. As Slywotzky and Morrison demonstrated in their book *The Profit Zone*, there is no one business model that works for everyone. In the same manner, there is no one development model that works for all emerging economies. In both instances, it is imperative that development models that fit particular circumstances be defined and implemented strategically.

In revising their development strategies to fit new realities, Asian governments should establish two basic ground rules. First, development models must compete with other models in the region for foreign investment, opportunity, and jobs. Second, the development models must reflect the particular strengths of each country. It may be appropriate to add a third ground rule, and that is to communicate with a sense of urgency. If there was one connecting element in Asia's successful development strategies during the miracle years, it was a sense of urgency.

For the New Asia, the likely manifestation of the urgent need to differentiate competing regional economies is the development of what are called competency zones, reflecting the strengths of each economy. It is important to note that while Asian economies compete with each other, they also invest in and trade with each other, although the crisis greatly dented the level of intra-Asian trade. But the level of intra-Asian investment and trade is a critical element of economic growth, as well as decreasing reliance on developed economies. However, it is also indication that the regional economies should be complementary, not monolithic. But competency zones are important for other reasons: They nurture mid-market enterprises and hasten market liberalization.

"We need to go back to fundamentals" Li & Fung chairman Victor Fung advised business and government leaders attending an Asia Society conference in Manila. "Asia has been driven by entrepreneurship-by SMEs" he argued, suggesting that the Asian asset bubble bursting and the increasingly troubled fortunes of big business didn't mean that the region's competitiveness had eroded. Fung reminded listeners that Asia still had three fundamental components of competitiveness in its favor: a young, productive population, high savings rates providing domestic capital and liquidity, and a strong work ethic. The Philippine situation differed somewhat because it does not feature the high savings rates most other Asian countries do, as other speakers during the conference pointed out.

However, foreign investors usually cite the productivity and educational attainment of the Philippine workforce as a principal investment incentive. This means that while the Philippines demonstrates the capacity to attract value-added foreign investment, doing so consistently is vitally important to recovery because there is little capacity for domestic capital formation. Which makes Fung's point all the more important, but not just for the Philippines. Economic development is driven by small firms that supply multinationals and international markets, not the grandiose dreams of big business and conglomerates that rely principally on domestic consumption. "The basis of the Hong Kong economy is its 300,000 small companies. Forty percent of these companies are operating across borders in two or more locations. They are minimultinationals."

Because these dynamic firms operate across borders, Fung says that liberalization is not a threat, but an opportunity; therefore "we should hasten the process of liberalization." Fung knows what he's talking about. His successful firm excels in managing what is popularly known as an extended value chain, a virtual organization encompassing raw material suppliers, manufacturers and assemblers, printers, and shippers, aside from its own value-added processes. The success of his company is anchored on a network of relatively small firms that provide the input and services Li & Fung requires to profitably meet the demands of its European and North American customers. But the viability of that network depends on the free flow of goods and services between Asian countries.

Within Asia, mini-industrial clusters-competency zones-are already beginning to emerge. The principal features of these clusters are professionalism, quality, and innovation. While low cost remains a consideration in choosing Asian suppliers, it is not *the* consideration. The priorities are the capacity to meet commitments, produce according to international standards, and originality. Li & Fung also finds that the best yarn producer, the best textile manufacturer, and the best garment assembler are located in different Asian countries. Cost consideration then becomes not a matter of who can fulfill their part of the supply chain at the cheapest price, but how cheaply materials and finished product can be moved across borders. In other words, liberalization contributes to the capacity of small companies to increase the value-added of their products and exports because the high tariffs that confined them to low-cost manufacturing are disappearing.

As a result, they become integral components of an international value chain that consistently contributes in a meaningful way to local economies. But if we look at who dominates the business agenda in politics and media, it is not these engines of growth, but big business. That doesn't necessarily imply that the agenda big business pushes is detrimental to the interests of mid-market (or small- and medium-scale) enterprises. In fact, in most cases they are in fairly close alignment. There are exceptions, of course. The obvious ones are local, uncompetitive manufacturers who have failed to create internationally competitive organizations and the large retailers who want to keep the market to themselves to the detriment of consumers as well as the economy.

The problem with big business domination of the business agenda, however, is that it creates the perception that the robustness of the economy is tied to a few large firms. This is true everywhere, so it is not a uniquely Asian circumstance. However, it takes our eyes off the fundamentals Fung believes really account for Asian prosperity, with the result being that both government and private-sector resources are funneled toward support of big business to the detriment of mid market enterprises. The fallacy of these circumstances was expressed to us by Banthoon. Aside from recruiting fresh equity to rehabilitate his bank, Banthoon said that future profitability is closely tied to the mid-market sector.

Even without the real estate asset bubble bursting, Banthoon says that big business, "with its grandiose dreams" has not been a profitable sector for the bank. Because all banks wanted to do business with the largest firms, of which there were relatively few, these firms were able to negotiate tough terms. On top of that, the Asian crisis actually made them a worse credit risk than well-managed, mid-market firms. The lesson here is that recovery doesn't depend on how well big business does. Big business is a beneficiary of recovery. Recovery depends on mid-market enterprises, the true engines of growth.

How are Asian governments contributing to the development of competency zones? So far, government initiatives to drive competency zones have been predictable and unimaginative-if grandiose. Malaysia's well-publicized effort to spawn a high-technology super corridor-larger than Singapore in area-is likely to attract less than a quarter of the more than US$4 billion in investment originally expected from high-technology behemoths like Microsoft, Sun Microsystems, and Oracle. More than anything else, Malaysia's folly has demonstrated that competency zones should reflect strengths, not wish lists. They should boost the economy's engines of growth, rather than serve as monuments to political achievement.

As noted previously, Malaysia does not have the population or the educational infrastructure to support the development of an indigenous, leading-edge technology center. Its driving force was not resources, but one resource-the prime minister, Mahathir Mohamad. The Asian financial crisis, the imposition of controversial currency controls, political instability, and Mahathir's own erratic behavior accelerated the super corridor's demise. But it is Hong Kong's proximity to Asia's largest talent pool of highly educated professionals that ultimately will relegate Mahathir's vision to a shadow of its intended grandeur. Hong Kong will spend close to US$2 billion to build an information technology (IT) zone in its effort to reengineer its economy and lessen its reliance on speculative real estate. However, even Hong Kong's success is less than assured. It produces onethird of the scientists and engineers it needs annually, yet limits immigration from the mainland, which produces 400,000 scientists and engineers every year. And, "with tens of thousands of mainland Chinese now working in Silicon Valley and other United States high-tech centers, the potential boost for China is huge" because many of these engineers are on their way home or have founded research ventures in China.

Shanghai will compete aggressively for the honor of being Asia's Silicon Valley, and it has the intellectual resources to do so. Singapore also hopes to evolve into a high-tech mecca. Its vision of the future-called Singapore One-"envisions the networking of the entire island under an IT plan that has attracted fourteen multinational companies. The Singaporean government plans to spend nearly US$56.5 million for online education, entertainment, and information services, plus another US$1.03 billion for new computers in school labs and to wire up most of the island's offices, homes, and schools". Keep in mind that Singapore is a very small nation.

The Philippines provides some examples of how the development of competency zones and government incentives should proceed. The Philippines' chief benefit from the colonial era was its educational infrastructure, which after World War II was clearly and easily the best in Asia. But so was its economy. Both crumbled during the Ferdinand Marcos administration, and education deteriorated even more from lack of attention as well as exploitation. Still, the Philippines produce a huge number of engineers, teachers, and medical professionals. Its preoccupation with art and entertainment has also made it a creative and literary center. The problem for the Philippines is that there are not enough jobs for these highly educated, value-added, potential contributors to economic development. A look at foreign direct investment inflows quickly shows why.

The Philippines was less efficient in attracting foreign direct investment than its neighbors, and therefore has been unable to generate jobs for an under-mobilized work force with little to do.

At the same time, it is evident where the Philippines should direct its resources and provide incentives to investors:

1. Engineering-intensive export industries, including services, because of an abundance of low-cost engineers. One Japanese construction company, for instance, has established a fully-owned engineering design affiliate in Manila staffed by nearly fifty full-time engineers designing projects primarily being undertaken in Japan.
2. Publishing. The Philippines is a rich source of writers and creatives.
3. Entertainment, including production services and talent. Major animation studios, including the Walt Disney Company, have set up shop. Industry figures are trying to make the Philippines an offshore Hollywood studio.

4. Healthcare, including major surgical procedures. American healthcare organizations recruit heavily in the Philippines.
5. Software engineering. Again, United States, Asia, and European firms recruit heavily in the Philippines where contractors supply major airlines, hotels, and other service industries with core business solutions.

While allocation of resources in the strategic development of competency zones is not as well-defined in all Asian countries, it remains clear that development strategy must be designed to capitalize on national strengths and conditions. Setting up what is in effect an artificial industry without the intellectual resources required for its support and development is an exercise in folly. Worse, it is an irresponsible waste of finances and time. Asia is impatient to develop, and Asians increasingly expect their government to make the right decisions, not the easy ones. Consider the argument that Japan's best companies developed without much help from government, and that Japan's most notable industry failures featured very high levels of government intervention. We would argue that Japan's failure was its focus, the intent to build a textbook economy while the textbooks were being rewritten in the marketplace.

First, the focus should have been capitalizing on resources, not creating them. It took the electronics companies to do this by capitalizing on their expertise in miniaturization. Second, it should have focused on the markets and the customers. For all its public expenditure, Japan was building monuments, not enterprises. Its private sector took that responsibility. Instead of emulating Japan's development model as Korea and Malaysia have tried to do, they should be pouring resources into education in areas that will strengthen the distinctive competencies of their economies and people.

Structural reform will take a great deal of pressure off of Asian political leaders as government's principal task becomes levelling playing fields and enforcing the rule of law, rather than managing development. The responsibility for performance will lie with the private sector, not the government's luck at picking the champions of industry. When we speak of structural reform, however, we speak principally of two distinct elements of economic infrastructure. One is the banking system, which is *not* the heart of all economies. It is the value creators or wealth generators that are at the center of economies- mid-market enterprise. That these entities are bankrolled-or at least were before the crisis-by financial institutions does not make banks the principal source of productive national wealth. It makes them gatekeepers.

A second element of economic infrastructure is the laws regulating trade. Trade regulation prevents or encourages the emergence of monopolies by stimulating or encouraging domestic and international competition. Because the trade policies of Western developed nations, the United States in particular, have been overtly supportive of free trade, Asian governments have generally been seen as inhibitors of free trade. Indeed, many have been. But as we have already seen, so has the United States, particularly in agricultural products, for the same reason that Asian governments have sought to protect certain sectors of their economies: again, the demands of politics. Those demands are generally rooted in sectors that hold economies back, not push them forward. Japan's stubborn resistance to opening up its woefully uncompetitive agricultural sector is an excellent example.

The need to remedy bad practices and policies doesn't mean change takes place when it should. In the United States, it took the savings and loan debacle to force regulatory change in an obviously volatile sector. Calamity, as Richard Farson, author of *Management of the Absurd,* argues, really does seem to be the best catalyst of positive change. Yet in 1998, eight years after Japan's economic bubble burst, meaningful banking reform had yet to take place. One year into the Asian financial crisis, regional governments were, for the most part, benignly encouraging banks to merge and consolidate. The government was propping up poor performers in the meantime, as Banthoon complained. Indonesia was still doing this in early 1999, although it finally closed thirty-eight private banks in March that year.

Analysts believe the number should have been closer to fifty. Malaysia continued to insist that inefficient, government-connected conglomerates had to be helped in the national interest. It took Thailand until March 1999 to finally pass comprehensive bankruptcy legislation. In every instance, resistance was traced back to the interest of large industrialists and nationalists. And it held back recovery in Asia. But while reform didn't proceed at the pace it should have, Thailand, South Korea, and the Philippines, in particular, showed that reform leaders-despite much opposition-would lead the region back from the abyss. Those nations and their corporations will be at a distinct advantage to other regional governments that sought to shelter inefficient conglomerates and poorly run banks from the effects of crisis, liberalization, and globalization.

China looms large in the Asian economy as a competitor in export markets and foreign investment. Despite rocky episodes by foreign investors, recent tightening of intellectual property laws and enforcement moves to get the army out of the private sector, an effective cleanup in customs, and increasing transparency and reform in the financial sector have suggested that China's leaders understand that sustained growth is closely tied to the observation of market dictates. For the rest of Asia, these reforms make China an even more serious competitive threat. So it was not surprising that in early 1999, frazzled Asian investors reacted to what should have been light reading, sending regional stock markets into an emotion-driven tailspin.

Writing in the government sponsored *China Daily Business Weekly*, journalist Zhang Yan, quoting unnamed sources said, "As the financial markets responded positively after the Brazilian government let its currency float against the United States dollar, some analysts said the devaluation or floating of the Yuan would definitely not be a bad thing". Financial news services reported the comments on a Monday, suggesting they were a trial balloon for an impending devaluation. With the help of gleeful short sellers, jittery investors, still nervous about Asia's emerging markets in the wake of nearly nineteen months of financial crisis, blindly sent stocks and currencies across the region reeling. The Singapore and Philippines markets plummeted well over 5 percent. Jakarta dropped almost 5 percent, and Thailand was down close to 3.5 percent.

After the carnage, Zhang said, "I had no idea my article would cause such a reaction. I wouldn't worry about the Yuan; the government is quite firm about not devaluing." Because everybody knows this, Chinese government officials didn't immediately respond to the panic, apparently assuming saner minds would prevail. Wrong again. Premier Zhu Rongji finally spoke up in defense of the Yuan, denying prospects for devaluation in 1999, and probably preventing a sell-off in United States and European markets. As a result, United States markets rose strongly as prospects of instability in international markets (particularly in Asia and South America) appeared to recede.

The next day, most analysts safely and quickly suggested that there was little pressure to devalue the Yuan. J&A Securities' research manager told the *South China Morning Post,* "There's speculation that they want to devalue the renminbi, but in terms of politics they are not going to do it now". Yet other analysts kept speculation alive. CLSA Global Emerging Markets' chief economist predicted that China would devalue the Yuan by 10 percent in the second half of the year. Eddie Wong, an ABN Amro economist, suggested that devaluation would serve to enhance the competitiveness of Hong Kong's exports.

But there are a number of reasons why devaluating the Yuan would work against China's long-term interests. First among these is that although currency devaluation may provide limited, short-term benefits, as Wong suggests, it decreases pressure on local companies to increase efficiency and productivity-to become better-run companies. As a result, the "private" sector's capacity for successful participation in the global economy deteriorates further. To survive as poorly run companies, executives insist that they need state protection in the form of high tariffs and other restrictions on non-Chinese players.

With billions of dollars worth of technically bankrupt state firms still on its hands, China is not in a position to coddle inefficient companies run by poor managers. To manage the financial and social fallout of large-scale state-sponsored corporate incompetence, it is crucial that government signal managers that they are expected to live in the real world and create value instead of using up scarce resources. Recent introduction of incentive compensation seems to be intended to do this. Devaluation also removes the pressure on companies to become better value generators, perpetuating low value-added manufacturing. Likewise, it undermines the urgency of enhancing skills and technology because exports are driven by low labor costs rather than the value of labor and intellectual inputs.

This means that prosperity spreads slowly, undermining confidence in government and its commitment to its people. There is not enough generation of wealth for the nation to prosper, so a very small percentage of people-industrial titans running globally uncompetitive firms-enjoy the benefits of development exclusively. From an immediately practical perspective, devaluation would provoke chaos in China's banking and financial system just when serious reforms are beginning to take hold. The closing of state-owned Guangdong International Trust and Investment Company, or GITIC, provoked a spurt of reform that Asia's financial crisis failed to inspire. In an encouraging effort to demonstrate transparency and sound management, banks and investment houses have for the first time begun to announce earnings reports, even when the results are not entirely confidence-inspiring. Making negative but factual information available to investors is the preferred alternative to relying on investors who assume the worst.

Because of significant levels of foreign-currency-denominated debt and huge exposure to bankrupt state firms, devaluation would decimate the banking sector and bring reform to an immediate and ugly halt. Much like the rest of Asia at the onset of the regional financial crisis, investors would abruptly run for safe havens and foreign corporations run for cover as the value of their capital investments sank. Some observers believe that China has steadfastly resisted pressures to devalue out of a sense of fiscal responsibility to the rest of the region. There is certainly no argument that China's resolve has contributed in a very important way to stabilizing regional economies, providing good prospects for recovery in 1999 and growth in 2000. But any responsibility exhibited in terms of regional stability is a byproduct of China's desperate need to preserve its own development.

It does not want to see its wealth melt away overnight the way the rest of Asia's did at the onset of the crisis. Ultimately, that's the most important reason devaluation will not take place. Not that national prestige is an unimportant consideration. With the tenth anniversary of the Tiananmen atrocity in 1999-as well as the fiftieth anniversary of the state-China's generally thin-skinned government was anxious to present the public image of a nation that is competently managing its dramatic transformation into a market economy. And it wants to show that it can do this best in a non-democratic context, undistracted by the chaos associated with individual freedoms and rights.

Because devaluation is a sign of a weakening economy that cannot generate the wealth it needs to fund development, devaluation would be an admission of failure on the part of government at the worst possible moment politically, likely provoking profound change. Management icon Peter Drucker believes that China is simply too large and too diverse to survive as a single country anyway. Local governments have clearly enjoyed the degree of freedom economic development has provided by lessening dependence on central government. As a result, in the past six months, Beijing has moved to reassert its authority. But if central government undermines its moral authority to rule by an admission of flawed macroeconomic public policy, it is likely that state officials will quickly take advantage of that admission to argue that local government is efficient and attuned to local reality.

The final reason China won't devalue is that it would obliterate Hong Kong's property market, the principal source of the Special Autonomous Region's increasingly fragile wealth. China has had a hard time demonstrating that Hong Kong is doing as well under its rule as it did under the British. Part of the reason is that the British are no longer in power, and therefore no longer visible. It is easy for the United Kingdom to forget their own incongruities, especially since Chief Executive Tung Chee Hwa has so consistently demonstrated that his job is too big for him. Timing was also unfortunate, with the turnover taking place the same month Asia's miracle shattered.

The reality is that even without the problems of weak government and the regional malaise, Hong Kong is frightfully exposed. For the most part, the Special Autonomous Region's small manufacturing sector has steadfastly resisted pressure to transition to high value-added production, choosing instead to maintain reliance on cost competitiveness by shifting operations to Guangdong and other locations. Its services sector is under assault from both Shanghai and Singapore. And government has resorted to reinflating the property bubble under pressure from Hong Kong's property barons. The last thing Hong Kong needs is devaluation in the Yuan because it will serve to further undermine structural infirmities that the government doesn't know how to address.

Given all this, why all the fuss? In part, it could be that pressure for short-term respite appears increasingly attractive to a central government that, despite the lack of democratic reforms, must be much more responsive to public mood. Or, China may be tempted to put Japan on notice that failure to do its part to spur regional recovery won't be tolerated forever. But whatever the reasons for periodic panic, none of them make much sense. What does make sense is the rest of Asia's unease with China's voracious appetite for foreign investment and investors' giddy enthusiasm for this emerging megastar economy.

While the challenges before the New Asia are greater than ever, so are the potentials. Although growth is unlikely to mirror the heady rates of the past fifty years, the evolution of the New Asia over the next fifty will be at least as profound, particularly if it is successful in capitalizing on its greatest resource: the people. The three forces of change in Asia are provoking a profound transition. The effect of the Asian financial crisis is the emergence of tough, battle-tested competitors that have adapted to survive and prosper. Liberalization is not only making Asian corporations more efficient and productive, it's making them, as well as the entire region, more cosmopolitan. The confluence of interest that is focused here is creating a new society that will set the standards of social and political tolerance in the next century.

Globalisation encompasses lifestyle and values. Asia will have the most democratically elected governments serving the largest and most demanding group of consumers on earth. But for all this to happen, Asia must release the creative capacity of what economist Paul Romer and strategist Gary Hamel say are the new input to wealth creation: hardware, wetware, and software. Asia has the input. The challenge is to accelerate the New Asia's capacity to turn that input into wetware.

5

Women and Change

Understanding Social Roles

It is not a study of the emancipation of women in the feminist sense and that it is not intended to be an academic treatise but a book for the general reader. Though it is certainly not our intention to discourage professional social scientists from reading it, we have not written particularly for them. Yet this is a sociological work. Aimed at a wider public than usual, it is nonetheless concerned with matters of sociological interest, treated in a sociological framework. The general reader should therefore beware. This is not a psychological study, nor is it concerned with sexual relations in the narrow sense. No doubt a complete analysis of the changing roles of the two sexes should cover a study of the ways of making love and of mutual psychological adaptations.

It takes its stand upon social facts and discusses only sociological differences between the sexes-in other words: the division of labour, of interest and of status. What exactly we mean by these terms will appear in due course, for the final caveat we wish to enter concerns our use of words. Though intended for the common reader, the language of this book does not, is not meant to, conform entirely to common usage. This requires some explanation. It is one of the difficulties of the social sciences that they have not, in general, produced a special technical language. Unlike, say, botanists or physicists, who use terms peculiar to their own subject matter and therefore relatively easily definable, social scientists rely in the main upon the use of words already current in ordinary speech.

Hence arise many misunderstandings-and much of the layman's mistrust. For the sake of accuracy it is, of course, essential for social scientists to try to pin-point their usages, to narrow them down so that the referents are as nearly as possible clear and unambiguous. But common speech is nearer poetry than science, its tendency usually towards wider connotations and evocative rather than indicative meaning. Thus many of the words social scientists use-'family', for instance, or 'social class' (to take but two examples)-have extremely wide, if not positively vague, connotations in everyday speech. As a result, a layman's reading of a professional sociologist's article on, say, the family in the class system of Western Germany may be sadly distorted if, with the ordinary poetic overtones of everyday speech in mind, he fails to grasp the essential limitations of scientific terminology.

Faced with an article on plant genetics he may also encounter difficulties, but they will not be those of over-familiarity with the terms used. Though to non-specialists the proliferation of 'jargon' at times appears excessive, there is a sense in which social scientists may envy the natural scientists' technical vocabulary. For our present purposes, however, it is enough to let the reader be warned. Technical usages are explained in the text, and their limiting nature should not be forgotten.

THE CONCEPT OF SOCIAL ROLE

There is, however, one particular terminological warning that must be made here. In this book the term 'social role' appears in the sub-title and, frequently, elsewhere. This is a quite specific technical term referring to the expected kinds of social behaviour associated with a particular social position. Thus the position 'teacher' is associated with a role which includes all the activities of teaching and also a number of other associated items of expected social behaviour-usually a middleclass standard of living, often a certain demeanour, and so on. Similarly the position 'unmarried adult daughter' in

English society today is associated with a certain expected role which includes willingness to live within reach of her elderly parents, or with them if they are old and incapacitated, and to take over their full care and a large measure of their financial support if necessary.

These two simple examples should make it clear that the sociological concept to which the term 'social role' refers is an artificial construct. We are not talking of the social behaviour of any individual 'teacher' or 'unmarried adult daughter' (or 'businessman', 'father', 'clergyman', 'civil servant', 'teenager' or what you will). Instead, we are constructing types, and labelling them with the kinds of behaviour considered appropriate to each one. Considered appropriate, that is, by local and contemporary people. 'In Russia today the role of doctor of medicine is thus and thus'; 'In India the role of village welfare worker is to do this and this'; 'Among the Malays the role of father includes that and that'-and so on. A number of sociological writers use the term 'social status' as a correlative to 'social role'.

'Status' in this phrase refers not primarily to a placing in a graded order of power or rank or esteem, but to 'position' in the sense in which that word has been used in the preceding paragraph. Thus one can talk of the 'status' of teacher, of adult unmarried daughter, businessman, father, and the rest. Because of the almost inescapable suggestion of grading which is attached to the word 'status' in everyday speech (which most sociologists also have in mind in using the word in other contexts) this is a difficult usage to maintain. We do not, therefore, use 'status' in this way (if a word other than 'position' in this general, non-grading sense is required, the Latin locus might be more appropriate).

When, earlier, we referred to differences in the status of men and women, we used the word in its more common sense. Status in this chapter thus refers simply to placement in a graded order of access to power and legal and economic independence. This is the usage which appears, for example, in the title of the United Nations' Commission on the Status of Women. (In talking of placement in a graded order of esteem, as distinct from-though, of course, often correlated with-power, we use the term 'prestige'.) Readers who wish to follow up the concept of social role in more detail may be referred to the short bibliography at the end of this volume. For the present only three further points need to be made.

First, it is clearly possible for one individual to take several roles. The derivation from dramatic usage is obvious, and each man not only in his life, but even in each day, plays many parts. 'Father', 'farmer', 'churchman', and so on; these are not mutually exclusive roles. It is not difficult to list the various different roles in which any given individual-oneself included-appears from time to time. Nor is it difficult to see that whereas some roles are, like those just mentioned, merely mutually compatible, other roles are actually inclusive of others-whether necessarily or by custom. Think, for example, of the number of roles comprised under the label 'mother'. This is a point to which we return later on. But if some roles are compatible and others inclusive, still others are obviously incompatible or even mutually exclusive. One cannot, for instance, act as teacher and as pupil at the same time.

This would be a sheer contradiction. On the other hand, nothing in either physical necessity or social custom prevents one from switching fairly easily from one of these roles to the other. It is otherwise with, to take extreme examples, either a Roman Catholic priest or a Hinayana Buddhist monk who breaks his vows of chastity. There is no physical bar to his being both priest (or monk) and parent; but the religious bar is absolute. Thus social sanctions can, and indeed often do, make incompatible what physical possibility has not divided. This question of the compatibility of social roles is crucial to our argument below. The second point we wish to stress is closely connected with the foregoing, and equally obvious.

We express it here as a generalization: the more complex the society, the greater the number of social roles that exist, and, in general the greater the number of social roles available to each individual. In a very small-scale, simple band of primitive hunters and gatherers all men must be hunters and gatherers; for, with the exception of those of kinship and of rather rudimentary leadership, there are no other roles available. This, again, is an extreme example, but it illustrates another point to which we shall have to return below. For the new nations of the Orient are those whose social structures, for centuries already highly complex, are daily growing more and more so, through industrialization and its concomitants, and therefore those in which new social roles are daily emerging for both men and women.

SOCIAL ROLE AND SOCIAL CHANGE

This, indeed, is one of the most striking features of current social change: the proliferation of possible roles. New kinds of paid employment, new types of leadership, new opportunities for the development of new skills of all kinds- these are some of the concomitants of industrialization and urbanization, political independence and development, and technological and educational advance. For the individuals who inhabit the new nations of the world, this is one of the most significant and often exciting factors of their lives: social roles which did not exist before are now becoming available. At the same time old roles are changing. Here, too, the concept of social role can aid our understanding. We have stated that in talking of roles social scientists are talking of types, not individuals. It is more accurate to say that we are talking of norms that are matters which the consensus of reasonable opinion in any particular social group considers correct or appropriate. It is important to note that social roles are abstracted not from actual behaviour but from opinion about what behaviour ought to be.

In other words, in this instance the social scientist does not watch what one hundred teachers do and construct the social role of teacher from that, but discusses with both teachers themselves and others what teachers ought to do, watches the reactions, verbal and other, to what teachers in fact do (and say), and constructs the role from the outcome of these discussions and observations. (It would be inaccurate but not altogether misleading to say that any particular social role is compounded from all the current prejudices about the particular social position to which it is attached.) But-and here is the nub of the third point to which we wish to draw attention-prejudices are not immutable. If the actual behaviour of most teachers (to continue with our same example) begins to deviate from the hitherto accepted norm, it is likely that in time the norm too will change; similarly in certain circumstances changes in norms may lead to changes in behaviour.

Thus-as in the drama-there is room for individual interpretation of roles, and a successful new interpretation of an old role may well be the starting-point of one kind of social change. Where such new interpretations are the result of conscious planning (whether based on general principles for social betterment or personal self-interest, or a mixture of the two) they may be copied by other people or not, according to circumstances and the innovator's powers of leadership. But probably, more often than not, a new interpretation of an old role is simply the accidental outcome of ad hoc adaptations to changed circumstances. If such changes affect many people similarly and more or less simultaneously, a kind of consensus of individual adaptations is likely to emerge, and remain more or less fixed as the new norm for the time being. So-called 'static' societies are those in which the role patterns have remained relatively stable for a considerable period of time; in developing societies roles are constantly being added to and reinterpreted.

It must not be thought that we wish to contend that the phenomena of social change can be explained entirely in terms of a theory of social roles. This is very far indeed from being our standpoint. But we do wish to suggest that the concept of social role can be useful in the kind of enterprise which we are engaged in here. By making it possible to distinguish between an individual and the roles he plays it allows us to escape from the difficulties inherent in popular psychological types of explanation, and thus makes genuinely sociological comparison between personal relationships in different societies possible. In our own everyday social life we constantly find ourselves erecting stereotypes of the kinds of behaviour we consider appropriate (or 'proper') to certain kinds of persons. Indeed, as we have seen, it is largely from the consensus of such stereotypes that a social scientist constructs the social roles we have been discussing.

But there are two essential differences between the social scientists' 'roles' and our own 'stereotypes'. The scientist abstracts his roles objectively by recording the norms held by the people of the society he is studying, and having abstracted them he regards them simply as patterns, models of behaviour which individuals occupying certain social positions are expected to follow while acting in these positions. For him as sociologist they are merely roles, not moral imperatives. For us, the contemporary people under observation, it is different. Our stereotypes come from the teaching and learning which have been our constant experiences since birth in our own particular social environments. They are largely subjective: the believed-in justifications of our own attitudes. They are not merely roles, distinguishable from the individuals who play them, and valid only for particular positions in social life; instead many of them are highly charged with moral value and attached firmly in our minds to the personalities of individuals.

Thus where the social scientists speaking as such might say: 'In this society the teachers' role is thus and thus ...' we, speaking as ordinary contemporary members of that same society, would say: 'Teachers are-and ought to be-thus and thus ...' In other words, we are usually prejudiced; the concept of social roles can help us not to be so. It is probably the main justification of a symposium of this kind that it may help us to emerge a little from the cocoon of our preconceptions, including our own culturally derived stereotypes about what are truly 'masculine' and what 'feminine' social roles-and also about what are really 'Eastern' and what 'Western' patterns of living.

To make any sort of sense of the welter of information and opinion that can be collected on such a challenging topic as ours it is essential to attempt to sort out the various factors at work and analyse their differing, though interdependent, significance. As far as the sociological understanding of personal relationships is concerned we believe that analysis in terms of new and changing social roles is one of the keys. But we are still left with the questions: Whence the new roles? Why the changes? It is always easy to talk in a general way about the causes of this, that or the other example of social change. According to prevailing fashion, one can blame something called 'Westernization', or something else called 'urbanization', or 'the breakdown of religion', or 'the collapse of the traditional family system' and so on. But all these are no more than question-begging phrases. Simply calling the processes of change and their results 'Westernization' (for example) does next to nothing towards helping us understand them.

Indeed, it may be positively misleading. Historically it is, of course, a fact that recent and contemporary changes in Oriental societies have been connected with the period of Occidental economic and political dominance. But except in some strictly economic and political spheres, and where Western educational institutions have been unusually influential, it is probably true to say that comparatively little is directly and simply ascribable to Western influence or Western example. The relationship is more complicated than that. Thus to use the term 'Westernization' as an explanation is to introduce a false simplification. Orientals, if they do not resent it, may shrug their shoulders; but Occidentals, vaguely flattered, are often lulled by it into an unrealistic dream of elder-sisterly understanding-for we think we know what western patterns are, and therefore we tend to look upon ourselves as the fore-ordained guides and patrons for "Westernizing' Orientals. But patronage is always morally dangerous-especially for the patrons-and doubly so when based upon false premises.

It is not only that the peoples of the East may not want to follow Western patterns (and, as our contributors show us, they often do not), it is not only even that they are increasingly (and rightly) rejecting our self-assumed leadership: it is also that many of the changes that are taking place have very little to do with 'Westernization' in any direct sense at all. Similarly with 'urbanization': undoubtedly the rapid development of huge modern commercial and industrial towns all over the

Orient has had and is having profound effects upon almost every aspect of economic and social relationships, including political and legal relationships, family grouping and the upbringing of children; but present-day changes are various, their starting-points different, and their explanation by no means solely to be sought in the modern surge of population towards the towns. Analysis must be more subtle than this.

Again, 'religion', 'the traditional family system'-these too are blanketing terms. Religious beliefs and rituals and the effectiveness and range of application of religious sanctions are by no means uniform even within the borders of a single nation in which a single faith is officially proposed. Between different nations the differences may be manifold and profound. Christianity in Italy is not the same thing as Christianity in Sweden, nor is the Buddhism of Ceylon to be equated with the Buddhism of the Overseas Chinese; and it should go without saying that Muslims, Hindus, Buddhists and Roman Catholics-all of whom are to be found predominating in different Asian States-have very different approaches to such matters as family structure and the status of women.

As for 'the traditional family'-more nonsense is talked about this, both in the East and the West, than about almost any other subject. What was it? Who lived in it? Was it everywhere the same? How did it relate to the laws and customs governing property, marriage, the wider kinship system, politics and the economic division of labour? These and similar questions have to be answered before one can make valid pronouncements about the effect (or even the fact) of its decline. But how often are they even asked? One of our troubles is that, Easterners and Westerners alike, we are too quick to put up straw figures, stereotypes of social patterns and cultural forms (as well as social roles) which we label 'Eastern' and 'Western' respectively. We forget the enormous variety within the West, let alone the even greater variety within the much larger East. We forget, too, that most Europeans-and similarly most Asians-are ignorant of their neighbours' customs and traditions.

We generalize from our own experience of the one or two places we know something about to the very many places of which we have no experience and know nothing at all. And we all forget that social patterns and cultural forms are never simple and never develop along single-line tracks, but are always complex and always mutually interdependent in a multiplicity of different ways. (And almost incidentally, among other things they make it quite clear that the cherished Western notion of typical Oriental womanhood is an illusion.) And the effects of these things do seem to tend in the same direction, towards similar patterns of urban in place of rural living, wage- and salary-earning in place of self-subsistence, buying and selling of factory-made goods in place of home handicraft production, universal suffrage and a national bureaucracy in place of colonial administration or absolute monarchy, modern schools and universities in place of traditional religious and home education, and so on and so forth.

Not that all these tendencies are everywhere apparent at the same rate, nor that none of them has anywhere appeared before-towns are far older in Asia than in Europe, and a system of advanced competitive examination for entry into the national bureaucracy had already existed for a thousand years in China before it was taken as a model for Great Britain in the nineteenth century-but their scale, their widespread nature and the particular type of technological and economic system which underlies their present-day manifestations are new. The novelty is not least in the universality of the changes and their world-wide interconnectedness.

What in the past were largely separate civilizations though never completely isolated nor without influence upon each other, are becoming in the twentieth century ever more closely connected by the single network of economic and political relations which now enmeshes the whole world. At the same time their own economic and governmental systems are all being remade after a limited number of Western-type models. Were we then wrong to denounce explanation in terms of Westernization? In so far as the large-scale economic and governmental institutions of the present day-together with the technological features which enable them to work-are European in origin and form, the whole world may be said to have become Westernized.

But it is still true to say that the effects of the working of these large-scale Western type economic and governmental institutions (and their world-wide interconnections) upon the everyday lives of ordinary people and the personal relations of men and women can only be ascribed indirectly to Western influence. Moreover, because of such things as original difference in culture and social structure and variations in the speed and intensity of economic and political change, they are not felt everywhere in the same way. At this level, to speak of the whole world becoming westernized is to beg all the questions this book is designed to investigate. Moreover, the West, too, is changing. 'Westernization' no longer has meaning as an explanation for a general process in which the West itself is also caught up, by reason of the interconnectedness of world events which, paradoxically enough, is greater now than in the colonial era, and because Western institutions themselves are altering.

We are all in this together. Is it this, perhaps, which gives us today an opportunity for mutual understanding that has never really existed before? Be that as it may, the ground has now been cleared for the next steps in our argument. These are as follows: first, an examination of some of the ways in which the rather similar new institutional developments in South and South-East Asia are opening new roles and new opportunities, especially for women; second, an examination of some of the ways in which these new features are affecting older institutions and bringing about changes in traditional roles-particularly the family roles of women; and finally a discussion of what may be the factors which make changes in the relative role patterns of the two sexes easy or difficult, acceptable or otherwise. The argument refers in particular to South and South-East Asia, but its general applicability is much wider, and we do not hesitate to point the comparisons.

Social change is no respecter of persons. Hardly any of the profound changes which have been occurring in South and South-East Asia have in themselves discriminated between the sexes. The trend towards urban living, for example, although it usually draws in men first, nevertheless also affects women (and children) whether they follow in their turn to the towns or stay behind in the villages. Improved health services, DDT spraying, inoculation and so on are not available for one sex only, nor are lowered death rates with their results in population pressure sexually selective. Most political, economic and religious changes are similarly impartial. Only a few special measures-women's suffrage, girls' education, the provision of maternity services, for example-have been deliberately devised for a single sex, and all these, together with recent legal alterations in such matters as marriage and inheritance, inevitably have repercussions upon men as well.

Nevertheless, existing differences in roles have necessarily meant that changes affecting all equally have not affected all similarly. The rich respond differently from the poor, town dwellers differently from country people, women differently from men. Our brief is to direct attention primarily to the women's response, and in this section we concentrate upon the ways in which these general changes are opening up new roles, or the potentiality of them, for women. Obviously we cannot cover the whole canvas, but we shall select from the general changes certain aspects which appear particularly significant: modern medical measures, improved communications, increasing urbanization, new openings for paid employment, education, political emancipation and legal change. Our illustrations will be drawn primarily, though not exclusively, from the evidence provided in the articles which follow.

We have pointed out that the changes brought about in human social life by the application of modern medical measures are not limited to women's affairs only; nor, of course, are they unique to Asia. Many of the effects of postponing the age of death which are now beginning to appear in the East were first consciously experienced in Europe and the United States about a hundred to a hundred and fifty years ago. The same story appears over and over again in the history of middleclass Westerners in the last hundred years. Their families in the later nineteenth century were unusual not in the numbers who were born but in the numbers who survived. After about two generations of this, parents no longer in constant dread of bereavement started to control the number of births.

So far, as Ted Smith's article points out, only Japan in the whole of Asia shows a similar trend towards slowing the rate of population growth. Whether or not other Asian nations will follow suit is a matter of open debate; certainly, as Barbara Cadbury explains, much is being done to encourage them to do so. At the level of national (and international) policy making, control of population growth is largely a matter of economic or military calculation. For individuals, too, economic thinking is often paramount though in a different way. Small-holding farmers who depend upon heir children for increasing production naturally want large families, especially if they live under a family system which keeps adult children at home, or still more, one which maintains property (especially land) undivided for as long as possible.

Wage-earners, particularly white collared salary-earners who see a need for educating their children, do not want too many dependents. The validity of this argument is commonly borne out in the experience of family planning clinics whose clientele is predominantly from the white-collar classes and above (though standards of education, availability of clinics and degree of acceptance of Western-type medicine also play a part in determining who shall attend and where). The evidence of the articles in the body of this book points to a future development of contraception on much the same lines as that which has taken place in the West, though some of the populations concerned are larger, and the time lag may be considerable.

This is a new thing in the world. Its full effects on the role of women are not yet clear even in those countries of the West where it has been longer apparent. But undoubtedly it is one of the crucial factors. For the first time in human history there is a promise of potential freedom from the physiological and social effects of the more or less continuous period of pregnancy, parturition and lactation which, with numerous miscarriages, has been the lot of the majority of women between the ages of about 15 and about 50 in all societies.

And the babies they do have need not die. This, too, is crucial. A modern Westerner reads the pathetic inscriptions on the tiny graves which are scattered throughout the old burial grounds of Europe with pity; most modern Easterners would read them with a sympathy born of experience. One of the most striking differences between conversations with women in most parts of the West and most parts of the East today is that in the West one says: 'And how many children have you got?', in the East: 'How many have you reared?' Increasingly, as the former question becomes safer to ask in Asia as well-and this is happening-the roles of mother and wife will be affected by a new freedom from fear.

Moreover, this has been fear not of personal bereavement only, but of failure in marriage in the present and lack of support in the future. Foong Wong's article gives a telling account of a situation which is common in most extended family systems, such as exist in India and Pakistan and among the Chinese, for example: a wife must bear children (in patrilineal systems, such as these, especially sons) in order to justify her position in her husband's home. Children who die are almost as little use in this respect as children unborn, and certainly a widow without children to support her may be in a desperate plight. In countries like Burma, Thailand, the Philippines, where the true extended family does not obtain (except among some minority peoples) there is still a need for children to justify a woman's position in marriage (marriages in which there are no children are far more likely to end in divorce) and to support her in her old age. Modern medicine saves very many of the babies who formerly would have died and family-planning clinics can help restore fertility to couples who previously would have remained barren.

These are matters of peculiarly personal concern to women. Together with men they share also, of course, in the other benefits of modern preventive and curative medicine. And here the countries of South and South-East Asia are probably more greatly affected than the West, for 'the West' is on the whole a temperate zone, whereas the regions described in this volume all fall largely within the Tropics where diseases have been more lowering and more difficult to eradicate. Freedom from malaria, for instance, is one of the greatest boons that the twentieth century has brought. Cholera still strikes, but it can be controlled; leprosy can be cured; the typhoid become less and less common as sanitation improves; yaws can be easily eliminated. The list could be much longer. Dr. Smith's article describes how death rates have already been failing-often dramatically.

But Dr. Smith's article also tells us something else about current death-rates in our region, namely that they are somewhat higher for women than for men. Here is a measurable contrast with the West. In most economically developed countries the number of adult women exceeds the number of adult men, and it is well known that the actuarial figures for a woman's expectation of life are higher than those for a man's. However, it does not follow that this difference between East and West is evidence of a low valuation of females in the East. Despite some popular beliefs, there is no demographic evidence that female infanticide anywhere in the region makes a noticeable difference to the sex ratio of infants and small children. Indeed, infant mortality in India, for example, is believed to be higher for male than for female babies.

It is possible that among people whose family system shows a strong patrilineal bias girl child may not be given quite the same care as their brothers, but any such discrimination, in so far as it still exists, is likely to be of diminishing importance. It is much more likely that slowness in adopting modern methods of midwifery is to blame, whether because of their inadequate supply or from prejudice-and this is an area in which prejudice dies hard, as Begum Amna Gani points out. Compared with economically developed countries, relatively large numbers of women do still die in child-birth. But this is likely to be a temporary state of affairs. What new social roles have all these developments brought?

In the first place there are new opportunities for employment. Doctors, nurses, midwives, medical assistants of all kinds, social workers in the fields of health and nutrition, pharmacists and so on are required in increasing numbers together with the host of other technologists and administrators and the developed system of communications without which a modern medical service cannot operate. In most of these occupations women (including at least five of our own contributors) are to be found as well as men, though, except in nursing, in lesser numbers. (It is interesting to notice a recent regulation restricting the numbers of women medical students in Bangkok because they were fast outnumbering the men to the detriment, so it was thought, of the future of the Thai health services.)

The role of 'healer' is, of course, not a new one; traditionally in different countries it was performed in varying ways, often closely connected with magical and religious rituals, sometimes by men and sometimes by women. Madame Levy and Dr. Nayer both describe the high esteem in which their fathers' and grandfathers' healing powers were held. Nevertheless the full apparatus of modern medicine is a break with tradition, and the modern occupations of doctor, nurse and so on are the framework of what are essentially new roles for educated men and women in South and South-East Asia.

But those who become nurses or doctors are few. For most people the effects of modern medical measures upon their social roles are indirect. Freedom from ill-health (including the burden of continuous pregnancy and the bearing of too many children) and from fear of early death can lead to the reinterpretation of old roles in the family and the opportunity to develop other new roles outside it. Already in the West women are beginning to think in terms of a 'third period' of life in which, the tasks of motherhood completed, they still have time to re-enter the world of employment. The current campaign to draw married women in the United Kingdom back into the teaching profession is only one example. But we return to this and other aspects of what has been called 'the dual role' of women later on.

Pramuan Dickinson describes graphically how a journey which took her grandfather two months by elephant and her father a fortnight by train and on foot can now be accomplished in a few hours by fast motor-car. Eileen Arceo-Ortega and Subadra Siriwardena explain how driving their own automobiles make it possible for each of them to combine successfully the roles of housewife, mother and professional educationist. Very many of our contributors have travelled the world around in search of higher education, on professional business, or for pleasure. Like modern medicine, modern transport is a kind of enabling measure making new roles possible and forcing the reinterpretation of old ones through the freedom which it confers.

This kind of freedom-to go about easily, speedily, over long distances, and if necessary by oneself-is a new thing in the world's history; not unique to Asia. It has been well said that even Napoleon's armies could travel no faster than Julius Caesar's-or, for that matter, Akbar's or Ghengis Khan's. The writer's own grandfather was born in the first heyday of railway building in England (the first, that is, in the world); her father watched the early motor-cars proceeding, as by law they were bound to do, behind a man walking with a red flag, and later saw Bl¨riot fly the English Channel; her mother made social history in the West of England by being one of the first women to ride a motor-bicycle-in 1922. Thus the development of modern transport is almost as recent in the West as in the East. The difference is one of degree only-and anyone who has been caught in the rush hour traffic jams of Bangkok or Manila or Calcutta might be forgiven if he doubted even that!

In some of the countries of our region women have apparently always had relative freedom to travel on their own affairs; in others (notably India and Pakistan) it has not been so. It is particularly in these latter countries that Dr. Tharpar's point that modern methods of transport have been indirectly one of the most influential factors in the practical emancipation of women is well taken. Traditional customs are not always easy to maintain on modern vehicles, distance from the familiar social environment may make them seem unnecessary, even ridiculous. Dr. Sushilla Nayer describes how her mother used to keep full *purdah* while travelling by train; a complicated business, requiring among other things a large staff of servants.

There is a station on the line from Bombay to Delhi through which large numbers of the Indians resident in East

Africa pass on their way to and from that continent. The women know it as 'Anand-raise-the-veil' or 'Anand-lower-the veil' according to whether they are journeying towards their ancestral villages in India or their newer homes across the sea. It is not necessary to labour the obvious points about travel broadening the mind, helping to break down ethnocentricity, leading to new personal contacts, economic and educational opportunities, even intermarriage. Our contributors make them very clear. But travel is only one part of the modern system of communications.

Not only people, but goods and ideas too are being distributed more and more widely. Clothes which once had to be hand-made (even to the spinning of the threads, as Madame Le Kwang Kim explains) can now be bought ready-made; pots and pans can be of plastic and aluminium; soap, cosmetics, medicaments, surgical plaster, even comfortable and hygienic sanitary towels, are easily available almost everywhere; food-stuffs, once laboriously planted, weeded, harvested and processed by family hand labour, can be bought ready wrapped in the stores. There is electricity and piped water. These things are by no means true for all the people of our area, not yet; but they are for many. And their effects upon the lives and roles of men and women and the way they spend their time are profound. (Moreover, they are among the several modern developments which are making the lives of Easterners and Westerners more alike-and, therefore, presumably mutually more comprehensible.)

As for ideas-the spread of books and newspapers, and the telephone, radio, cinema, and television (already in 1961 popular television is a regular feature of life in Hong Kong, Manila, Bangkok, Singapore) marks a whole series of social revolutions. In education, the arts and entertainment their influence is obvious, producing new knowledge, new concepts, new and modified social attitudes, new ways of passing time, and new openings for employment. The husband who refused to countenance the education of women 'because my wife might learn to write and read love letters from other men' saw only a very small part of the complications that improved communications would bring.

In 1953 something quite new happened in the Chinese fishing village of Kau Sai, which lies on one of the many islands in the territory of Hong Kong: several fishermen sent their daughters to school. Previously this had been the privilege of sons only. But in the early 1950s Kau Sai was becoming prosperous. Some of the fishing junks were fitted with diesel engines; catches were larger and more regular, incomes higher. With higher incomes, wives and daughters, as well as sons and grandsons, wanted to buy things. The city had plenty of things to sell, but to find the shops you needed to be able to read-read the shop signs, the street names, the figures on the buses and their destinations. Modern communications were all laid on, travel and goods were at the women's disposal-but first they had to be able to read.

In the village literacy was not necessary; town living, even town visiting, was difficult without it. The schoolgirls of Kau Sai illustrate very neatly the interdependence of the many different factors in contemporary social change. More than that, they illustrate also the surge towards the towns. Between 1951 and 1959 four young fisher boys left the village-prosperous though their families undoubtedly were-for work in the city, and one girl was lucky enough to marry a townsman. This, which made her the envy of every other woman and the ideal of every schoolgirl in the village, meant that she went to live in a windowless cubicle about 9 feet long and 5 feet broad, whose hardboard walls reached a height of about 7 feet and which was flanked by six or seven similar cubicles with whose occupants (together with those who slept in the passageway) she now shares a common kitchen-cum-lavatory about 10 feet square.

The fourth floor of the tenement which contains this cubicle is reached by a steep, straight stairway, a yard wide, down which all refuse-including night-soil-has to be carried, and which, being no tenant's property, is no tenant's business to keep clean. The tenement is, of course, only one in a street of such buildings, and in scores of such streets. There is a standpipe for water about a hundred yards away. The good fortune of this girl, who now has two children both fewer than 3 years old, is still the talk of her old friends in the village. She has achieved their highest ambition: she lives in town. What has she gained? In the eyes of her friends and herself two precious things: freedom from the ceaselessness of toil in the village, and access to glamour and excitement. Both the 'push' from the country and the 'pull' to the towns are here reflected. There is no doubt that in most countries peasant rural life is an endless round of physically demanding work.

Chinese fishing families are perhaps an extreme example, since they live always (men, women and children) on their boats and many of them work far into the night; moreover they are driven all the time by the constant desire to make good in the material sense. By no means all the other nationalities in South and South-East Asia share this motivation, and, without it, most of them, living in a climate and environment which do not force absolutely continuous effort, do in fact lead a less strenuous life. Nevertheless, even for them, the work is usually demanding and unending; often especially so for the women who, in addition to the inescapable daily chores of child care, cooking, cleaning, collecting water and firewood, laundering, and other domestic duties, usually have the more continuous, if less arduous, tasks of agriculture laid upon them-planting out, for instance, and weeding.

In the towns those tasks disappear; water comes from a tap (what is a hundred yards or so down the street compared with a quarter of a mile or more on rough village path?); food can quite often be bought ready cooked; charcoal and firewood are in the market; there is electricity. All this and glamour too: things to see, shops to look at, the cinema, a fire engine, buses, crowded pavements, curious foreigners, rich people, perhaps processions for funerals and weddings. The fascination of town life for the imaginations of peasant women is not hard to understand. The question how far their expectations are fulfilled can hardly be answered. For the fisherman's daughter from Kau Sai they undoubtedly were. Though to middle-class Western eyes she may appear to have exchanged a healthy open-air life in some of the most beautiful scenery in the world for an overcrowded slum, she is a truly happy woman. She told me so; and I could see that it was true. But for the pavement sleepers of other parts of Hong Kong (or Calcutta, or Bombay, or elsewhere) I cannot say.

Overcrowding, unemployment, slum housing-these are common in all large Asian cities and there are probably many who wish they had never left the land. But we do not always see the alternatives. We need more information, more factual studies of the relative advantages of poor town and poor country living and the actual reasons behind the decisions to migrate. Moreover it is as misleading to think solely in terms of poverty and overcrowding as it is to ignore them. Asian towns have their well-to-do inhabitants too. Furthermore, in Asia as elsewhere it is town life that gives the greatest opportunities for recreation, cultural activities of all kinds, education, diversified employment-after all, as the derivation of the word shows, towns are the seats of civilization. And, as Professor Karim points out, as often as not they are also the places in which it is easiest for traditionally secluded women to emerge from *purdah*. None of our Asian women contributors can be described as a mere countrywoman.

In this they are atypical. Dr. Smith tells us that, apart from city-states like Singapore, the proportion of the total population living in towns containing a population of 20,000 or more nowhere in our region exceeds 22 per cent, and the average is not much above 10 per cent. In North America it is 42 per cent, in Europe 35 per cent, in the U.S.S.R. 31 per cent. One of the difficulties in the way of mutual understanding between East and West is that the overwhelming majority of Asians are villagers-or small-town dwellers-still. Nevertheless it is certain that there is a surge towards the towns in Asia, and that it is increasing. It is equally certain that the change from rural to urban living is accompanied by profound changes in social roles. What this may mean for traditional family roles we discuss below; the development of new types of role in towns is one of the topics we consider under our next heading.

When economists discuss increasing urbanization in terms of a 'pull' to the towns or a 'push' from the country they are referring to opportunities for making a living. Most of the new (that is, non-traditional) concerns are in the towns, and despite much serious urban unemployment and poverty the continuing processes of economic specialization and industrialization do mean that the towns offer a multitude of new jobs. For most men, whether 'pushed out' or 'pulled in'-or, more commonly, a bit of both-going to town and looking for work are more or less synonymous.

This is not necessarily true of women. Indeed, it seems likely that most of the migrant women who seek employment in the towns of Asia do so rather as a response to the economic necessity they find pressing upon them after they have arrived than as their intended goal on arriving. We must beware of equating the numbers of women living in towns with the numbers in employment: on the one hand, many women (and, of course, many men too) are employed in the country and, on the other hand, in both town and country many are not employed at all.

The recorded numbers of gainfully employed women are in fact always less than the total female population in any given place. This is not only because, as with men, a fairly large proportion consists of people who are either too young or too old to be included, but also because the tasks which engage most of the time and energy of most women everywhere are not included in the statistics of economic activity. Housework in one's own home is a job which has no money value put upon it; it is therefore excluded from the statistics and classed as 'uneconomic'. This fact, which complicates every discussion of the division of labour between the sexes, tends also to depreciate the social contribution of women-difficulties which could be avoided if it were possible (as surely it should be?) to set a money value upon housework at home (and, also, one might add, upon the strictly productive work of bearing and rearing children, which is likewise regarded as an uneconomic activity).

Be that as it may (and proverbial comment notwithstanding), the fact remains that most women do not 'work', including usually a large proportion of those who are of working age. In the United Kingdom, about half of the women between 15 and 59 are thus economically inactive. In India, of women aged 15 to 56, 58 per cent are inactive; in the Philippines, of women over 10, 60 per cent are inactive. Comparable information does not exist for the other countries of South and South-East Asia, which is especially unfortunate since (as will become clearer later on) the common Western assumption that women in all Oriental countries have a similar position is far indeed from the facts. In any case, we are not so much concerned here with the extent of women's employment in general as with their employment in such ways as may be expected to bring about role changes.

For some assistance with this topic we can turn to such statistics as do exist on the distribution of women workers between the three sectors of the economy: agriculture, industry, services, and on their distribution by status as employers and workers on their own account, unpaid family workers, and employees. Two points stand out: first, the high proportion of women employed in agriculture; second, the predominance of service over industrial employment. The first point reflects the preponderance of agriculture over industry in all contemporary South and South-East Asian economies. It also suggests that a large proportion of the employed women of this region have not left the countryside. The second is a feature of the industrialized West as well, but the kinds of services performed and the conditions under which they are carried out are usually different. It is perhaps worth recalling that 'services' include commerce and transport as well as domestic service.

In fully industrialized countries the proportion of women classed as employers and workers on their own account never reaches 20 per cent; in the United States, Canada and the United Kingdom, it is around 5 per cent. In other words, in those countries where industrialization has gone furthest, relatively few women are employers or workers on their own account, more than 90 per cent of the female labour force being engaged as employees. This is partly because of the greater number of women workers engaged in manufacturing, but also partly because the services in such countries tend to be organized on a larger scale. In less industrialized countries quite a large proportion of the women working in traditional ways in agriculture are employers or working on their own account, as would be expected; it is less often remembered that relatively many of the women engaged in trade or business are of this status too.

This is especially so in Thailand (and also Burma, the Philippines and Indonesia which are not on this list). But these are traditional, not new, roles in these countries. When to those facts is added the probability that a large proportion of the women who are listed as employees are in fact domestic servants (another traditional occupation, and one which has dramatically decreased in importance in the West), it will be seen that probably the great majority of the gainfully employed women in South and South-East Asia today have not entered new kinds of employment at all. But some undoubtedly have, and not only in towns.

Agriculture has its own non-traditional side, particularly in plantation work which employs very large numbers of women especially in Ceylon, Federation of Malaya, Indonesia and parts of India. This accounts for the big discrepancy between the proportion of women workers in agriculture (79 per cent) and the proportion engaged as unpaid family workers (23 per cent) in Malaya, for example. Plantation employment is rather a special case. Although certainly not part of the indigenous traditional economies, it has in most places now been going on for a fairly long time, and in any case being mainly rural and often engaging whole families at a time, it might be expected to bring about less fundamental change in the lives of the women engaged in it, and their families, than occupations which require a move to the towns.

On the other hand, many plantation workers are immigrants, or the descendants of immigrants, from overseas (like the workers of South Indian origin in Ceylon's tea and Malaya's rubber plantations). And however true it may be that rural women of the poorer classes have almost everywhere and almost always taken part in their families' agricultural work, there are important differences between being a wage-earner working for someone else, and being a co-worker in your own family enterprise. Nevertheless, it is when the wage-earning takes place in a completely non-traditional occupation in town that there are likely to be the greatest number of other differences too.

And though the proportion of Asian women so affected is small, the number is not-and it is rapidly increasing. We should be exceedingly unwise to underestimate its extent, or play down its significance. A great deal has been written about the effect of the change from subsistence agriculture in a stable village setting to wage-earning in the slum conditions of many modern towns. We have been told how the family ceases to be a unit of production, and how the bread-winner becomes for the first time a hired hand paid as an individual; how the dependants, who have hitherto been co-workers in a joint enterprise, find themselves in a new and lower status and how they may even be left behind in the villages; how when women, too, become wage-earners the disruption is even greater, children are not properly cared for, sexual morality is weakened, and the traditional family system undermined if not destroyed. This is hardly an exaggeration of a familiar line of argument.

There is some truth in it. Subsistence agriculture, which is the traditional occupation for the large majority of people in our region, is often bound up with the existence of closely integrated groups of kinsmen. It would not be surprising if, when individual wage-earning took the place of shared productive labour, some of the cement holding such groups together were removed. But it does not need an excursion into kinship theory to demonstrate that by no means all the traditional Asian family systems are in fact as fragile as some writers believe. We have already noted the traditional role of women as traders in Burma, Thailand, Indonesia and the Philippines. These women have long enjoyed an independently earned income.

And it should go without saying that all the countries of our region have had traditionally differentiated economics, such that money rewards for work have a long history for large numbers of men everywhere. Yet it is not suggested that these things have undermined the traditional family systems. (There is, however, ample evidence that the traditional family systems in the countries where women have freely engaged in trade are very different from those, of, say, India, or Pakistan; but that is just the point at issue.) Reading some of the literature on urbanization and industrialization in Asia, one cannot help feeling that it has been written by Westerners suffering from a deep-seated, possibly unconscious, romantic yearning for a rural Golden Age in which the climate is always balmy, the season always just after harvest-and electricity and running water are not far away.

It is true that the social cost of urbanization and industrialization has usually been extremely high. It is true that housing in rapidly expanding towns is often poor, insanitary and overcrowded. But we have already suggested that agricultural poverty and overcrowding may be at least as hard to bear. Experience shows that given industrialization (and only then) the extreme conditions of both rural and urban wretchedness can be mitigated. And may it not be these, rather than wage-earning, which are the significant factors in family break-up where it occurs? Where women are concerned it is probably not wage-earning as such but the necessity of working to fixed hours which is more important in bringing about changes in interpretation of roles and patterns of family living. Hours of work on family agricultural plots, in traditional small-scale trading and cottage-industry, even, to some extent, in plantation work, are flexibly adaptable to the worker.

A modern factory, big store, transport business, office, or school has a fixed time-table and pay is usually according to hours worked. People, who have prior obligations to housework, catering, cooking, and, above all, children, find this extremely difficult, and very tiring. Only those who for economic reasons must, or for domestic reasons can, are likely to seek out employment of this kind. If this is so, then it helps to explain why it is that in several countries of our region, it appears to be commoner to find gainfully employed women among the poor and the fairly well-to-do, uncommon to find them from the middle ranges, or, of course, the very rich. Where the women of the poorest classes work from necessity, those of the next higher income groups tend to stay at home, partly because domestic work demands their presence, partly because social prestige for their families may depend upon their being different in this respect from the poor.

The upper strata who can afford to give their girls both education and freedom from domestic tasks can also afford to ignore this particular badge of social prestige. (Indeed, for them prestige often comes more from having highly educated daughters or wives engaged in professional work and imbued with ideas of service to the community.) In some of the more highly industrialized countries of the West there is now a much wider scatter throughout the socio-economic scale. But this difference in social class distribution goes with another difference; in the West a very large proportion of working women are unmarried; in the East nearly all are married. And this applies not only to traditional occupations and plantation work where the flexibility of time-table might be expected to facilitate the employment of married women, but throughout. (Widows, and women deserted by their husbands, who have children to support are an important minority, of course, everywhere.)

This is not altogether surprising, for in some countries-notably, but not exclusively, India and Pakistan-girls marry young, and almost everywhere arranged marriages (usually implying the careful chaperonage of young women) are still the normal practice and spinsters hardly exist. Only among the later generations of town-dwellers in the East is there a tendency for girls to marry later and, with a higher standard of education, to seek a job as soon as they are old enough to work. We may surmise from this that more differences between Western and Eastern patterns are likely to disappear in time. For if Eastern girls are beginning to marry later and go to work earlier, Western girls are beginning to marry earlier and stay at work later, and fewer and fewer are remaining unmarried. It is now not marriage which forces a girl's retirement from paid employment in the West, but the arrival of babies.

The significance of child care in this respect is further demonstrated by the recent tendency noted widely in the West for married women to return to work after their children have grown up. We have already linked this with the increased expectancy of life and the decreased expectancy of pregnancy. We could also link it with the mobility of population which often denies a mother the support and help of nearby relatives, and with the decline in the number of domestic servants. All these are developments which are very likely to follow in Eastern countries later on. Will it also follow that there, too, the majority of the female labour force will be either pre- or post-child bearing? Or will other methods of organizing domestic work and child care-together, perhaps, with more flexible working hours, or less restricting housing programmes-be developed on a large scale? And will recognition be paid to the economic contribution of the childbearing years?

These are crucial issues in any discussion of the division of labour between the sexes and the changing roles of women. They are crucial also in any consideration of the status of women in employment. This is a many-sided subject, to which we return in the later sections of this essay. Here we simply draw attention to one practical obstacle to successful participation in the professions and to promotion which affects men and women unequally: the years during which a person of talent and ambition consolidates his knowledge and skill, builds up his reputation and makes his important contacts are just the years in which a woman with children is most fully occupied at home. It is not an accident that so many Western women in high positions and in the professions have been spinsters.

Up to now few Asian women have had seriously to face the choice between marriage and a career. Both are possible as long as domestic servants are easily available, or relatives are at hand, though even with good domestic help a professional woman with young children still has the problem of reconciling two responsibilities. Nearly all our women contributors refer to these matters. Many are beginning to wonder what their daughters and grand-daughters will decide to do, for they are well aware that given small families of father, mother and unmarried children, isolated from close relatives, unable to engage domestic servants, and with a tradition that each family lives, eats, and brings up its young children separately, there is a genuine incompatibility between the role of mother and the role of professional worker or higher grade executive.

But this cannot be the sole obstacle to women's participation in the professions and promotion or our table would not show such marked contrasts between different countries. It is clear that proportionately it is much more than ten times easier for a woman to enter these occupations in the Philippines than in Pakistan, Thailand, Singapore, India, Ceylon and Federation of Malaya-more or less in that order-lie between these two extremes. Our readers are invited to read the articles in the body of this book (especially those written by professional women) with the object of finding out why this should be so. We ourselves offer certain hypotheses in the remaining sections of this essay.

In 1960 the United Nations published a special pamphlet on equal pay for the two sexes. In almost all of them (the notable exceptions are South Africa, Australia and the Sudan) governmental and/or trade union policies endorse the principle of equal pay and seek to extend its application. Up to 15 October 1960, thirty-four governments had ratified this ILO convention, among them India, Indonesia and the Philippines. No other South Asian countries appear on the list of ratifications, but neither does over a dozen Western countries, including the United Kingdom and the United States. It is, however, only fair to point out that ratification implies accepting the principle of equal pay, application of the principle does not automatically follow; moreover, failure to ratify does not imply rejection of either the principle or its application.

The practice of paying equal reward for equal work regardless of sex is, in fact, more common in some of the non-ratifying than in some of the ratifying countries. From our present point of view, however, the significant facts are that all South and South-East Asian governments endorse the principle of equal pay, and nearly all of them apply it in the public administrative and other services while at the same time endeavouring to promote its application in the private sectors of employment. Two further points should be noted: first that sex-linked pay differences are common for unskilled and semi-skilled work in all countries where they exist at all; and second, that a relatively larger majority of women than of men workers are in unskilled and semiskilled occupations. This also is true everywhere.

If there is any single point on which our contributors are all agreed, it is the immense significance of education. This is not surprising. Although our region has been the seat and cultural domain of all the classical civilizations of India, and the sphere also of Chinese and Arabian influences (both long ante-dating the contacts with Europe, which themselves began as many as 400 years ago), most of the ordinary people have remained illiterate. Education in the formal sense was the privilege of a limited proportion of the population, to which, though with quite numerous and often notable exceptions, women did not usually belong.

There was, of course, nothing peculiarly Oriental about this. Universal education was nowhere even envisaged much before the twentieth century. Only advancing industrialism, ready to take virtually whole populations into its employ and depending for its further development upon vast numbers of relatively educated consumers, has begun to make general literacy (and numeracy) an economic necessity. This has been a recent occurrence even in the West, which was the cradle of industrialism. And even there the education of women has everywhere lagged behind.

There are certain rather obvious difficulties in the way of estimating a country's degree of literacy, but even if we allow for these we still have to admit that there are large variations not only between the industrialized and the non-industrialized nations of the world but also within each of these two categories. The report published in 1959 by the International Institute of Differing Civilizations, which we have already quoted, gives the following proportions of non-literate women in the total female population: Ceylon 46 per cent, Thailand 64, Federation of Malaya 84, and India 92. In Vietnam, we are told, 30 per cent of those who have received at least primary education are female; in the Philippines, more than 40 per cent. The statistics for Indonesia are less definite, but it is reported that no more than 35 per cent of the total population were illiterate in 1958.

From evidence that girls are less freely given access to education in Indonesia than boys, we have to assume that the ratio of females in this 35 per cent is high. The figures for Pakistan appear in a different form; in 1956 enrolments in all

Pakistani places of education taken together were: males, 4,893,265; females, 566,834 (rather less than 11 per cent). Although Pakistan's is the extreme case, it is clear that women are everywhere at an educational disadvantage. The Philippines goes nearest to affording equality in this, as in most other, respects. Our other countries lie at successive points along a continuum of which these two represent the respective poles..

It omits, however, several important features which are particularly relevant to education: for example, governmental policy (and in the case of colonial governments the influence of contemporary metropolitan views on the education of girls) and the demands made by the economy for large numbers of literate female workers and consumers. Broadly speaking, the economic demand for female education is only now beginning to become apparent in South and South-East Asia. Furthermore, it is not to be expected that industrial development will occur evenly, or that existing differences will be quickly eliminated. In the Philippines women already and traditionally do most of the shopping; in traditional Pakistan they do virtually none. It is noteworthy, too, that India, which is without doubt industrially the most advanced of our countries, still has one of the highest rates of female illiteracy.

What have already told about the fisher-girls and boys of Hong Kong shows well enough the desire for literacy. Some of its potential effects upon traditional roles are also discussed elsewhere. The demand for it creates the new roles of primary school teachers, mass education workers and so on, and beyond these it acts as a kind of lubricant for almost all the other changes we discuss. It is probably fair to describe it as the enabling measure par excellence. But industrialized countries have already found that literacy is not enough.

The achievement of universal primary schooling (which we are, for brevity's sake, equating with the achievement of general literacy) has been followed by the development of universal secondary education. Here, too, the Orient is beginning to follow suit, but as yet there is everywhere a much smaller proportion of pupils in secondary than in primary schools and a still smaller proportion of these are girls. Once again there are national differences, the Philippines, where 44 per cent of the secondary school pupils are females, being well ahead of the rest. In so far as we are considering the approach towards universal education-whether primary or secondary-we are considering something which is in a substantial sense much less of a novelty for boys in the East than in the West.

In Ceylon, Burma, Thailand, Cambodia, Laos and indeed anywhere where Theravâda (Hinayana) Buddhism is practiced, all boys traditionally enter the monasteries for a shorter or longer period before attaining manhood. This novitiate includes training in the scriptures, with the result that in these countries all boys have long had the opportunity of becoming literate. Girls, however, had to depend upon such teaching as their brothers, fathers, husbands or other male relatives were willing to give, for no monk is permitted any personal relationship with a female. In Muslim areas (and in addition to the predominantly Muslim populations in Pakistan, the Federation of Malaya and Indonesia there are quite large Muslim minorities in every country of our region) a somewhat similar custom obtains for scriptural training in the Holy Koran, which is often given to girls as well as boys.

It would therefore be quite untrue to say that universal education is in every sense a new thing in the East. Nevertheless, in content and aims and in its ideal extension to both sexes equally modern education is certainly very different. Literacy is no longer sought mainly for the sake of reading holy texts; and going to school nowadays is an important step towards personal advantage in this world as well as the next. Even if widespread formal education is not the new idea to South and South-East Asia that it is to the West, its modern manifestations are quite unlike the traditional ones. Much the same can be said about higher education. In so far as this is thought of as the training of élites rather than an extension of general education it-or something like it-has long been familiar in our region.

What is peculiar to the modern situation is not that such training exists but that its content is vastly changed and its scope vastly extended both as regards more and new subject of study and as regards a greatly enlarged student body. And for the first time this now includes women-again only a little later in the East than in the West. This is something really new. Here, indeed, is one of the crucial points for studying the emergence of new roles for women. To what extent are they now being trained intellectually to enter the élite? It is common knowledge that there is no country anywhere in which the number of women receiving postsecondary education is as great as the number of men.

It is worth pointing out, too, that the highest proportions of women students are not always found in the West, for Burma, the Philippines and Thailand, in each of which women make up about 36 per cent of the total number of post-secondary students, are among the most progressive in this respect in the world. It is clear that the expansion in numbers of post-secondary students is fairly general, and that this has included in many countries an expansion not only of numbers but actually of proportions of women students. (It is noteworthy that this has not always been true in the West.) Nevertheless women are still in a minority, usually very much so. Most of the several reasons for this are discussed elsewhere.

The strictly educational factors include the late entry of women into the field of formal education of any kind, the still very much smaller number of girls than boys in primary and secondary schools, and the various special curricula for girls which are often directed mainly towards preparing them for their traditional roles in the home at the expense of their intellectual advancement. This is not the place to pursue these and the other educational arguments further. They are well known. It may, however, be worth suggesting the probable value of a controlled inquiry into the question of whether the segregation of the sexes in education is compatible with equality.

In the countries of our region the proportion of women receiving degrees is higher than the contemporary proportion of women to men students. The answer to our former question is, then, that women are now being given élite training, but almost everywhere in small numbers. If education alone was the criterion for entry, we should expect to find many fewer women than men in the professions and in executive and managerial positions in general. But we should not expect the discrepancy to be as great as it is. Even in the Philippines where girls have very nearly equal educational advantages and there are, as we have seen, remarkably large numbers of women in the professions, administration, and relatively high posts in commerce and industry, the really leading positions are almost all held by men.

The fact that the differences between the countries of our region on this list follow much the same kind of graduation - with the Philippines, Burma and Thailand standing at the opposite pole to India and Ceylon-makes it seem likely that these other processes are fairly constant. We discuss this further below. It is often forgotten how recent the achievement of political equality between the sexes is. Fifty years ago only one country in Europe (Finland) had granted women the vote, and certainly no Western woman could hold political office except for those very few who in certain exceptional circumstances happened to inherit royal positions. Today no country in South or South-East Asia discriminates between the sexes in this respect.

Where the right to vote exists at all (and that is almost everywhere) it is held equally by women and by men, and in almost every State all political offices are similarly open to both sexes. Whereas in European Portugal and Switzerland women are still in 1961 denied the right to vote in national elections, Ceylon in 1960 elected the world's first woman Prime Minister. This is a revolution indeed. There are many questions one could ask about it. For our present purposes we will confine ourselves to two: How has it come about? What does it mean in practice? For the first question, the most striking thing for a Western observer is the relative ease of the revolution.

Not for the East, it seems the rigours of a militant campaign, but simply a quiet and quick advance. Indeed, one can often hear ladies in South Asia decrying what they regard as the hysterical excesses of the Western (particularly the British) feminist movements, whose small and short-lived (but spectacular and long-remembered) militant branches are so often wrongly assumed to have been representative of the whole, and whose historical and sociological backgrounds were very different from their own; whose success, moreover, undoubtedly influenced theirs. Despite quite considerable national variations in background, and in the speed and effectiveness of advance, it seems likely that the relative smoothness and rapidity of the political emancipation of women in Asia may be largely ascribed to the immediately prior (in some cases contemporary) success of the feminist movements in the West.

What we are concerned with here is sociological analysis. So, of course, to a considerable extent is she. She mentions the relevance of types of family structure and religion, both of which we examine again here, and points to the connections between the movements for women's education and women's emancipation both in the West and the East which we have also mentioned. She shows, too, how to some extent Western experience was paralleled in the East, for much as the two world wars in Europe, so the anti-colonial struggles in southern Asia provided opportunities for women to play roles which had not been open to them before, and thus to demonstrate their capabilities and prove themselves actively welcome as fellow fighters with men. It is not surprising that in such circumstances national emancipation and female emancipation went hand in hand or that in those places where political rights had already been given to women by the colonial powers they should not be rescinded but rather enlarged.

It would not be surprising, either; if once national independence had been gained there should have appeared some reaction against the new political status of women, at least in countries where their previous subordination had been most marked. Dr. Vreede de Stuers has drawn attention to just such a reaction in Indonesia. But time has been too short to tell whether it will have much success there, or whether something similar may appear elsewhere too. On the whole, it would seem rather unlikely. Though women may well have to overcome great difficulties in winning office or promotion, perhaps more so in some countries than in others, the general trends of world opinion-and, much more important than that, of world economic development which more and more requires the contribution of women both as workers and as consumers-makes it unlikely that there will be a general return to second-class citizenship for women as a category.

This opinion of ours implies an important distinction between actually holding political office, on the one hand, and simply exercising the full rights of ordinary citizenship, on the other. It is obvious that for the majority of both men and women office is in any case unattainable, but as long as the number of girls at school remains markedly less than the number of boys, as long as they continue to leave school earlier, attend less regularly, or receive a different quality of education, so long will there be proportionately fewer women likely to enter office than men. The exercise of the franchise is quite another matter. Nowhere in our region are educational qualifications required for this, and, in any case, 'wisdom' in voting cannot be measured except by untestable opinion. The only valid measurement is the number of people taking the trouble to cast their votes, and such figures as exist for the countries in our region so far show a marked consistency between men and women in this respect.

There are other differences. Whereas voting is an individual's personal concern, holding political office is a matter of exercising power over others, and the necessary qualifications for that cannot be inculcated in schools alone. People who are expected from earliest youth to submit to the demands of others and not to assert domination, given few or no opportunities to build up personal followings or practice the exercise of authority, may be expected to find it difficult to develop the traits required for active political life-the more so if they have to compete in a world populated mainly by those to whom they have been taught to defer and who, at the same time, expect their deference and have not suffered the same disabilities.

This, which is the common situation of any politically subordinate people, is aggravated if the individuals concerned live largely separated from one another in such a way that they meet too seldom to make their common organization possible, or if the roles they play are so limited that they get little practice in wielding power even amongst themselves. All these disadvantages-and others which we will leave aside for the present-apply in a greater or lesser degree to women in different countries; but the franchise having been granted they are relevant much more to the holding of office than the casting of votes. We shall return to this distinction, and mention others, a little later. Now, in some parts of our region the roles traditionally open to a woman were very few in number, and almost all incompatible with the assertion of power.

As 'daughter', 'daughter-in-law', 'wife', even 'mother', a girl living in a patrilocal extended family household, with few or no property rights of her own, has virtually no power. Such would have been the situation in the traditional three-generation family households of Hindu India, Muslim Pakistan and Confucian China. And for a respectable girl there were no other roles available. The limitations implicit in this situation were narrowed still further by the conventions which insisted-still insist, in many cases-upon *purdah,* backed by religious sanctions, as in Pakistan and parts of India, or at least upon careful seclusion backed by the full force of moral disapproval (not to mention foot binding) as in the gentry families of pre1911China.

Granted seniority, sons, long life and a strong personality, a woman might expect to reach a position of authority in her husband's household later on. She might even come to exercise almost complete control-within the home. Outside it her traditional power was always officially nil, though indirectly by working upon the men who came under her domination at home (or, if she was not of the respectable class, elsewhere) she could possibly exercise considerable influence. Only in the most exceptional circumstances, however, could exceptional characters have any decisive effect upon political life. Information, contacts, experience, all were lacking; neither training nor opportunity was present. Today opportunity (in the shape of formally granted rights) is open, but where schooling is still inadequate and the traditional attitudes pertaining to the type of family we have just described are changing only slowly, training often lags behind.

It is probably not an accident that out of all the South and South-East Asian peoples for whom the patrilocal extended family was traditional the women who have so far shown themselves most politically advanced come from the upper middle and middle classes of India, and, in rather lesser numbers, Pakistan. These are the classes in which modern education has made most headway, and where family structure has been much modified, as we shall see; they are also those where women took an active, often leading, part in the struggles for national independence. Dr. Nayer and Dr. Dube both underline the significance of this practical training.

By contrast, political consciousness is apparently less highly developed among Overseas Chinese women. Both Ann Wee and Foong Wong mention the modifications of traditional Chinese family structure brought about in Singapore by the effects of migration, urbanization and the influence of British colonial law, and it is well known that schooling there is widespread, even for girls; but these things alone have clearly not been enough, or Ann Wee could not have described Chinese women in Singapore as being uninterested in politics as she did in an article published in 1954 in the book, *The Status of Women in South-East Asia*, edited by Dr. A. Appadorai. At least until more recently than that they have had little practice in active political campaigning.

Where the traditional kinship structure did not produce patrilocal extended family households, where there is no tradition of *purdah* or close seclusion, or where recent political history has followed different lines, the situation is different. In Burma or Thailand, for example, women have long held property in their own right, and often managed it, and have been accustomed to handling business of many kinds on their own behalf outside the family circle. Our figures of women retail traders in these two countries make this quite clear. Members of small, simple (or 'nuclear') two-generation family households usually with near relatives living close at hand, these Asian women have been subjected neither to the overriding rule of mother-in-law as in India or China, nor to the overriding demands of domesticity, as in the West.

The number of roles opens to them having long been relatively large, 'the vote' is not regarded as the necessary precondition and guarantee of other kinds of freedom, which it undoubtedly was (and probably still is) in most countries of the West. Moreover Burma's attainment of national independence was not preceded by a long country-wide campaign of anti-colonial resistance in which women could learn the practices of political activity, and Thailand is the one country of our whole region which never came under colonial rule at all. In each of these countries, too, the franchise was granted fairly freely (and early). Considerations such as these probably go far towards explaining the relative 'apathy' towards political affairs which our contributors report.

If our diagnosis so far has been correct, we are now in a position to suggest a number of hypotheses to explain how it came about that out of the very various conditions prevailing in the different countries of our region have issued apparently very similar, smooth and rapid revolutions in the political status of women. However, before doing so we must clarify our use of terms a little further. We earlier drew a distinction between holding the franchise and holding political office, both of which are comprised in the idea of emancipation. We now draw attention to two further usages: the first refers to a general level of freedom to engage in social and economic as well as political activity without restriction or supervision; this is the most generalized usage.

The second refers to a degree of active political awareness, such as would be implied if one heard it said: 'Of course, only the women who have actually joined in [such and such political organization or activity] can be said to be truly emancipated.' There are thus at least four quite separate notions included under the one label 'emancipation of women'; it is not useful to confuse them. In the following analysis, which has relevance for all four, they are distinguished as: the holding of the franchise, the holding of office, ability to engage in activities outside the home, and level of political awareness, respectively. With the exception of the last, all are easily measurable in terms of the numbers of women taking part. The level of political awareness can only be gauged by opinion, though the extent of women's membership in organized political associations could perhaps be used as a more objective measure were full data on the subject available.

Let us now consider the countries we have already discussed briefly. If we set aside the common modern factors (such as Western-type education) which differ mainly only in degree throughout, we can isolate three other main sets of conditions which appear to have relevance for all four kinds of emancipation. First, there are sociological conditions: in Burma and Thailand the social structure of family households, their location and the division of labour between the sexes have traditionally tolerated the relative mobility of women and their engaging in occupations outside the home. In these countries we found a minimum of opposition to their being granted the franchise at the same time as men, but very few women are in political office and there is a generally rather low degree of political awareness.

On the other hand, the present-day level of ability to engage in activities outside the home is still high-as witness the figures we have already quoted. In India, Pakistan and the homeland of the Overseas Chinese, by contrast, family structure and the traditional division of labour and responsibility between the sexes largely immobilized women except in the lower economic ranges. Equal franchise was not granted early in these societies, nor is the general freedom to engage in occupations outside the home even yet very marked. Among the Overseas Chinese the political apathy we might expect from such conditions does appear, but in India and Pakistan this is not so. There, albeit overwhelmingly among the upper-middle and middle classes in the towns, there is a relatively high level of political awareness and India at least can even show a relatively large number of women holding political office.

To explain this apparent contradiction we must turn to our second set of conditions: namely, historical. The active part that Indian and Pakistani women, especially-but not exclusively-of these social classes, took in anti-colonial struggles is sufficient to account for their political awareness. It is also probably the explanation for the relatively high number of women in office in India, and the ease with which the franchise was granted after Independence in both countries. A cynic might suggest that it was a series of lucky chances which brought the hardships and opportunities of anti-colonial struggle to just those countries whose women most needed them. He would have to add, however, that they appear to have been less successful agents of change in Pakistan than in India. To explain this difference we refer to a third set of factors: religion.

We do not follow the lead of most previous writers on the position of women in the Orient who has, almost without exception, emphasized the paramount significance of religion. We find this un*satis*factory partly because the differences in this respect between the major religions of the region are often not clearly explained, and partly because it tends to mask other factors which we consider sociologically more significant. It is always sociologically unsound to argue as if social facts were derived from religious beliefs and rituals and did not exist in their own right. There is enough evidence from other parts of the world to show that the two basically different types of traditional family structure we have just mentioned as pertaining respectively to India, Pakistan and China, on the one hand, and Burma and Thailand, on the other, would have had their own characteristic effects upon the status of women in these countries quite irrespective of the prevailing religious systems.

The various divisions of Hinduism and Islam and the mixture of Confucianism, Taoism and Buddhism, which was the religious background of traditional China, deeply influenced the social systems in which they have flourished, but they did not produce them. Perhaps we should add that we do not argue the other way (namely, that religious beliefs and rituals are simply a product of social structure) either. The relationship is one of subtle mutual influence, differing with different religious and social systems, and at different historical periods. These differences are important. Although it is always to be expected that traditional religious attitudes will reflect and support traditional social practices and will probably be rather slow to change, the degree and effectiveness of their conservative influence differ considerably with differences in dogma and ecclesiastical organization.

This is not the place, nor has we the space, to develop this argument fully, but very briefly stated it is that of the four major religions found in South and South-East Asia, only one, Islam, is inevitably resistant to change in general, and change in the position of women in particular. Hinduism, despite its close hold over family and marriage, its special ideals of womanhood, its theories of caste and pollution, comprises an essentially flexible system of dogma, inclusive rather than exclusive, in which there is room for a huge variety of interpretations and many sects. Its long perspective, with its cyclical view of history as an endless rhythm of good and evil and its doctrine of reincarnation, teaches a sovereign non-attachment which is ultimately incompatible with too close a concern with the details of secular life.

Moreover, its organization is far indeed from the monolithic, theocratic ideal which is Islam's, and gives no scope for enforcing an over-all supervision of secular matters. India today is a secular State. Very similar remarks can be made about the Buddhism of Burma, Cambodia, Ceylon, Laos and Thailand. Philosophically and doctrinally it shares the ideal of non-attachment to the things of this world which an unendingly long view of history and a firm belief in reincarnation render essentially illusory. For Hinayana Buddhists the true religious life is lived apart from the world, in the monasteries; the details of secular social organization are therefore of secondary importance, and change in them is not necessarily intolerable. Daw Mi Mi Khaing's article below adds practical evidence of this state of affairs.

For Christianity and Islam the situation is otherwise. Both monotheisms, both based upon revealed scriptures, they are both also exclusive religions with histories of the persecution and fighting of heretics and unbelievers. Unlike Hindus and

Buddhists, neither Christians nor Muslims regard the experience of earthly life as an illusion, both (in most of their forms) maintaining that a truly religious life can be lived in the world. For each this necessarily argues a very close concern indeed with even the smallest details of everyday secular life. But Christianity is both more flexible in its interpretation of scripture (many forms of Christianity allowing also for new revelation through the Church) and less all-embracing in its organization than Islam.

Christian doctrine, even at the height of the temporal power of the Church, has always looked upon the State as a separate entity, a necessary concession to human sinfulness, not as a means to attain the other-worldly purposes of life which are the business of the Church. Thus change is allowed for, and a separation between secular and sacred maintained. But this is not so in Islam. There, in theory at least, there can be no distinction between sacred and secular, with the result that not only the life of the individual but the whole of society, the State, the army, all things are subject to specific prescriptions issued by the Lord, and issued once for all, through His Prophet. In such a system any social change is necessarily difficult to accommodate. And the roles and statuses of women, being laid down in the Holy Koran, are at least as immutable as anything else. We have no need to feel surprised at the greater conservatism of Pakistan.

Our hypothesis is, then, that the general freedom of women to engage in activities outside their homes, their holding the franchise, their holding public office, and their political consciousness are connected with (among other things) one or more of the following sets of factors: first, a non-restricting traditional family structure and division of labour; second, a history of prolonged anti-colonial (or possibly other) political struggle in which women played a full part; third, a religious system which can accommodate at least a fair degree of social change. Some of the variations are fairly clearly concomitant. Experience of political struggle and degree of political awareness appear to vary together; so, too, it seems do family structure and the relative ability of women to engage in activities outside their homes; Pakistan differs from all the rest in type of religion, and from those with similar kinds of family structure in the relative slowness of her women to enter employment.

None of these correlations occasions any surprise, but setting them out side by side does help to make them clearer. Let us now tabulate what we know of the other countries of our region in a similar way. We confine our detailed discussion of these tables to the data from Ceylon, Indonesia (Java), and the Philippines. It might have been expected that the women of Ceylon would have been granted the vote only after the attainment of national independence, but in fact it came in 1931-the first in Asia. Just under thirty years later Ceylon produced the world's first woman Prime Minister. Neither of these two 'firsts' could have been predicted from the facts nor, indeed, from Mrs. Siriwardena's picture of the life of Ceylon women. But they are somewhat misleading.

Great though Mrs. Bandaranaike's achievement is, her position is partly a legacy from her deceased husband; and the early granting of the franchise was due to the then British Colonial Government's decision to take advantage of the 1931 revision of the constitution in an attempt to draw in women's personal interest in such matters as the incidence of maternal mortality, at that time very high. The fact remains that there is a very big disparity between the very few who have achieved highest position or do show political awareness and the general many in Ceylon. It should go without saying that this kind of disparity exists everywhere, and by no means only in the East (or only among women).

Our discussion of India and Pakistan, for example, has been seriously lopsided because we have concentrated upon the upper and middle classes. It remains our general impression, however, those even comparing similar social classes, Ceylon's politically advanced women are proportionately fewer than India's. We connect this with the fact that they have not had to struggle either for national independence or the franchise. What of Indonesia? For the sake of simplicity (and for no other reason) we have confined our tabulation to those parts of Indonesia (Java, for example) in which simple (nuclear) family households (father, mother, unmarried children) are the usual type, and women's property rights are guaranteed not only by Islamic law but also by traditional local custom.

About 85 per cent of the people of Indonesia are Muslims, but even so Javanese family structure has not been fundamentally altered, and Javanese women retain a great deal of the traditional freedom to engage in activities outside the home which we have come to expect from the previous examples of Burma and Thailand. The difference between Java and Pakistan in this respect is extreme. (Incidentally, it provides an excellent demonstration of our earlier argument in favour of the greater sociological significance of family structure than religion, while underlining also the astonishing durability of family structure in the face even of Islam.) Family structure and recent political history being what they have been in Java-the Dutch withdrawal in 1949 having been preceded by a long and bitten anti-colonial struggle in which women played a full part with men-the present situation follows our expectations.

The Philippines gives us the most striking example of rapid advance for women on all fronts. Here is a country where the traditional equality between the sexes that we have learnt to expect from the simple family system (and which Robert Fox also reports) was partially removed, though only for the upper classes, by 300 years of Spanish rule, only to emerge with great vigour in the last half-century under the United States Government's policy of equality of opportunity and free education. This last, which does not appear in our tables, was as we have seen, more widespread earlier than in any other country in our region, and there is no doubt it was crucial. Certainly the achievement of Filipino women in education, business, social welfare and the professions has been remarkable; they are in general well organized and politically aware-so much so that at the lower levels of political life, particularly during election campaigns, their voice is said to affect substantially the political climate of the whole nation.

If both recent government policy and traditional family structure have been favourable to women's emancipation in the Philippines, religion has been a conservative influence which probably most Filipino women have welcomed, at least as regards its refusal to countenance divorce. In the last resort, too, all forms of Christianity are committed to accepting the full equality of women with men. As for the training ground of long anti-colonial struggle, that too has not been lacking, for Filipino women took an active part in helping to overthrow Spanish rule, as well as against the United States occupation in its early days and in the resistance to the Japanese in the Second World War. Thus from our present point of view women in the Philippines may be said to have had everything on their side-the only ones in our tables to have three 'plus' signs in the first series.

Perhaps we have already spent too long on what at this stage can only be a preliminary discussion of some of the factors which may have contributed towards the apparent ease and rapidity of the general political emancipation of women in South and South-East Asia over the last thirty years or so. If we have concentrated particularly upon family structure upon the history of national independence and, though less strongly, upon religion, it is not because we believe that these are the only matters of significance, but because we do think them peculiarly important. This applies most especially to the first set of factors, family structure, and our readers are asked to look upon the analysis we have just been making as a kind of preliminary sketch for the fuller treatment of this subject.

What are the practical results of women's participation in political life-we do not mean their 'success' or otherwise in the usual feminist sense, but the results in everyday life? What are the effects of their being in office, of exercising the right to vote? As for women in office, or even in any kind of full-time or policymaking role in political life, it is frequently and correctly remarked how few they are in any country in the world. Even in the Philippines, since 1941 when the first woman entered the House of Representatives there has been but one woman chosen every election, and only one in the Senate. Even the situation in India may not be long-lived; indeed there is a curious set of facts from the analysis of the last general election in India which shows that those areas and constituencies in which the standard of women's education was highest returned fewest women members, even produced fewest women candidates-but we need more study and much more comparative material to make sense of this phenomenon.

The fact is that nowhere in the world are there many women in high political position. This is, of course, in one sense nothing more than a reflection of the general paucity of women in the upper ranks of most other kinds of employment. It is probably to be explained largely in a similar way-that is, by the lack of equal educational opportunity, the inhibition of appropriate experience and inculcation of inappropriate attitudes, the practical difficulties of combining both domestic and outside responsibilities, and so on. But where posts which entail policy-making and the exercise of power are concerned, that is not all. Women do in fact remain at a disadvantage in appointment to leading and managing positions in almost all kinds of occupation (except those which employ solely female labour, and sometimes even there)-and in politics. As we have said, politics is in the last resort a matter of power, and, by and large, power remains a male prerogative.

Despite the very great variations which undoubtedly exist between individual countries, we would expect Eastern and Western women to be in much the same predicament here. It is not for nothing, that Mrs. Pandit -and she must know-has written of herself as a woman in a man's world. In countries where the seclusion of women has been traditional, life is often exceedingly difficult for those few women who have emerged into this man's world. Even in those (rather few) Western countries where the free mingling of the sexes in social life is common, one often hears a woman of ambition and talent complaining of the difficulty of keeping abreast with her male colleagues into whose informal social life she cannot easily enter.

And it is through informal social contacts that much significant professional and political business is conducted. An Indian or Pakistani woman may find this same situation far more difficult, the separation of the sexes having been traditionally so marked that there may at the outset appear to be virtually no respectable social patterns available for her and her male colleagues to model their professional relationships upon. Professional women and women politicians in Asian countries without the tradition of seclusion are likely to find themselves in much the same situation as Western women, or perhaps rather more so, owing to the rather greater separation of the sexes in ordinary social intercourse. In many cases, as Daw Mi Mi Khaing and Daw Ni Ni make us understand so warmly, this is a situation which is accepted with grace even welcomed. But it does not make for the advancement of women in new political roles.

But we must remember the distinction we drew at the beginning between holding political offices and exercising the franchise. All the available evidence goes to show that enthusiasm for the role of voter is at present a characteristic of South and South-East Asian women in general. It would obviously be as unwise to assume that every illiterate village woman who casts her vote does so with complete understanding of all the issues at stake as to assume the same thing for every illiterate village man. Descriptions of the first national elections in India tell of some women who appeared to pay exactly the same reverences to the ballot boxes as to the Hindu altars in their own homes. But they voted. Indeed they flocked to the polls. Yet there was no compulsion. And in the towns at least there is evidence that their votes were often cast quite independently: women did not necessarily vote as their husbands did. They discharged their duties as citizens in their own right.

What are we to make of these things? First, it is again obvious but necessary to point out that voting is not a full-time job. Occurring once and then not again for a matter of years, and taking the minimum of time to perform, voting in a national election creates no problems for domestic organization. Polling day can be, usually is, and regarded as a holiday, a welcome break in daily routine, not an interruption. Reciprocally, the actual casting of the vote has virtually no effect upon traditional roles.

But what about its implications? We know already that wives do not always vote the same way as husbands even in the most conservative areas of our region, and even where patrilocal extended families with a 'patriarchal' type of organization have long been traditional. A vote is an individual matter. It cannot be doubted that this must have some effect-long term in most cases no doubt, and additional to many other modern influences, but nevertheless significant-upon the structure of families and the traditional roles of women in them.

6

Family Roles and their Modification

Only two social tasks are everywhere inescapably sex-linked: the begetting and the bearing of children. Apart from this infinite variety is possible, though as far as we know all social systems do in fact make other sex linkages more or less rigidly. Men can make excellent child minders, but in the absence of artificial feeding babies have to be suckled, so it is more convenient for child care to be a female occupation; cooking, cleaning and other domestic jobs can be done by people of either sex, but it is more economical to give them to those who are already anchored to the home by the small children.

It is probable that such simple principles as these underlie the almost universal practice of handing over child care and household work to women. Further than this, as the well-known studies by Margaret Mead have demonstrated, generalizations about what are the 'right' or 'proper' or 'universal' or 'natural' roles of men and women simply will not take us. Variations exist even between the different social groups and classes of a single country, still more from one country to another. No matter how much it conflicts with popular belief, we have to agree that there was not a single traditional 'Oriental' conception of women's role and status any more than there was a single 'Western' one.

THE SIGNIFICANCE OF TRADITIONAL KINSHIP SYSTEMS

We have several times referred to the significance of family structure, but we have not yet set out what we understand by this term. At the same time, it should have been quite clear that there are several different types of family structure to be found (and traditionally) in South and South-East Asia. In order to relate these differences to their sociological contexts, and to understand their significance for our subject matter, we must make a brief foray into the general theory of kin relationships. Under 'kin relationships' or 'kinship' we include all social relationships which can be plotted on a family tree (genealogy, pedigree). These obviously include family relationships, relationships by marriage (affinal relationships), by descent, and so forth. Within the general category of kinsmen so defined there are nearly always certain particular groupings which are known in English as 'families'.

We use this word to refer to a group of people related by marriage and descent (including adoption) who customarily live together and share a common household budget. The family, then, in our present usage, is simply the domestic unit of relatives, and we do not use the word in any other sense. Thus it refers to a hybrid concept, defined partly by genealogical relationship, partly by residence and partly by the economic criterion of shared consumption. All three criteria are essential. The first, however, is elastic. Although groups of this general nature exist practically everywhere in the world, it is well known that the genealogical ties between their members are by no means always the same. So we can distinguish formally between the simple family (also known as the 'nuclear' family, the 'biological' family, etc.), which comprises father, mother and unmarried children, and various types of compound family.

Compound families consist in effect of a number of simple families linked together either by the further marriages of (usually only one of) the spouses (polygamy), or by bringing in the spouses of adult children, or both. The first method gives rise to the polygynous family (father, mothers, unmarried children) or the polyandrous family (fathers, mother, unmarried children), which is rare; the second to various types of extended family (a three- (or more) generation family) of which the patrilocal version is the most common in our region.

In the patrilocal extended family married sons stay with their fathers and bring their brides home to join them with the result that the group comes to include father, mother, unmarried daughters, sons, sons' wives, sons' children. Such a family may also be polygynous. Matrilocal extended families, in which brides stay with their mothers, though predominating locally in parts of Malaya and Indonesia (and elsewhere), are not widespread in our region.

The term 'joint family' does not appear in this classification. We find it more useful to restrict this to legal rather than sociological use. As a term which has special connotations wherever Indian legal codes apply, it is not strictly relevant elsewhere. It seems likely that other things being equal the traditional status of women has often been rather higher and their roles often less restricted in simple than in compound forms of family structure. Within a simple family the wife is subordinate to no other woman, and because of the sexual division of labour her occupational status vis-à-vis her husband is likely to be complementary rather than inferior. Moreover, the hands to do all the necessary work being few, a wife are likely to have to take a part in management and policy-making for the group as a whole. This is especially probable in a subsistence economy, or among small-holding agriculturalists, or in cottage industries, where the family itself is the unit of production, or in small-scale family trading business.

All our contributors are agreed that the traditional status of women within the family has been relatively higher, and their activity less restricted, in the lower socio-economic classes in, say, India, Pakistan, Ceylon or among the Chinese, than in the upper classes. People with lower incomes could not usually afford to build up large extended families or to maintain several wives, and their families were, therefore, usually of the simple type; at the same time they were likely to be gaining their livelihood in ways which required the wives' as well as the husbands' economic contribution. The traditional ideal of the extended patrilocal family (often polygynous) which existed in these countries was, generally speaking, realized only by the relatively well-to-do.

Among them virtually no adult married woman could avoid a period of subordination to her mother-in-law, and very many women (young widows, wives of younger sons, for example) could hardly have been able to look forward to attaining any sort of position of real authority in the home. At the same time the economic contribution which women made to the family's livelihood in the upper economic classes was negligible. The sharing of tasks and interests between the sexes was likely to be at a minimum. When to this was joined, as in all these countries it was, a set of values which required the more or less complete seclusion of a respectable man's female relatives, and their very early arranged marriage, it is obvious that these traditional extended family systems set narrow limits to the number and scope of the roles available to women, and often denied them power even at home.

The traditional family structures of India, Pakistan, Ceylon and China thus present us with a paradox in that in certain senses women whose fortune it was to be poor enjoyed higher status than those who were rich. In Burma, Thailand, the Philippines and most parts of Malaya and Indonesia this did not apply. There traditional families' at all socioeconomic levels were simple families. We have already noticed that these-especially the first three-are the countries in which proportionately more women have entered paid employment and received higher education. Can we assume that this is because of their simple family structure? We think that there is a close connection, but that the argument is not quite so simple as that.

We earlier used the phrase 'other things being equal'. They seldom are. Family systems are subject to non-family pressures which may well be strong enough to modify their influence. We have already put forward some of our arguments against those writers on the position of women in Asia who have emphasized only the religious pressures, but we do not deny that the influence of religious and ideological systems can be very great. So, too, we must consider the influence of occupational systems and systems of stratification, of political and legal systems, and of the wider kinship systems in which families themselves are embedded. As we have already discussed religion and politics-and will have to mention them again-we will deal here mainly with socio-economic, kinship and legal matters.

We have just mentioned the significance of a family's means of livelihood. In simple families which are themselves units of production, a wife's (mother's) position is inevitably fairly strong. But this may be reversed if the source of livelihood is one which employs the husband separately and takes him away from home, as has been the tradition now for a long time in most parts of the West. If, further, as in the contemporary and nineteenth-century West, prestige is derived largely or even partly from economic achievement as such, there may be a tendency to denigrate domestic work at home-i.e., 'women's work'-which is not economically priced. At the same time domestic work, being a form of manual labour, has little prestige on its own account.

The abundance of domestic servants which existed in nineteenth-century Europe made possible the emergence of the 'lady' whose freedom from domestic chores was regarded as an index of her husband's social and economic success, and not at all as an opportunity to gain education and enter the world of occupations outside the home, from which indeed the prevailing sexual division of labour long continued to exclude her. In such circumstances the situation of middle- and upper-class women in Europe (the Americas and other areas of European settlement overseas had their special differences) was remarkably similar to that of their sisters in the patrilocal extended family systems of India, Pakistan, Ceylon and China.

Legally, too, their position was similar. A hundred years ago the status of a married woman in England was as stated by Blackstone: '... the very being and legal existence of the wife is suspended during marriage, or at least is incorporated in that of her husband... . But though our law in general considers man and wife as one person, yet there are some instances in which she is considered inferior to him and acting by his compulsion.' Only in 1882 were married English women given the full right to the enjoyment, management and disposition of their own property. In 1923 they were allowed to claim divorce on the same grounds as men, and in 1925 permitted equality at law with their husbands in the guardianship of their children and the doctrine that a man and his wife are one person and that person the husband is not dead even in the England of today.

There is an interesting study waiting to be made of the comparative influence of differing economic systems and legal codes upon family structure in the West, but this one example will have to suffice here to show the effect occupational and legal factors may have. By the nineteenth century-and for a considerable period previously-the simple family system of England was almost as strongly biased in favour of male dominance as any patrilocal extended family system. We have already seen that this latter system where it existed in India, Pakistan, Ceylon or China, went with a division of occupation which kept family women at home.

The legal status of wives, too, though not identical in each place, was compatible with their social inferiority. In all four countries women were traditionally regarded as perpetual legal minors, whose affairs must be conducted for them by others; divorce, if permitted at all, was harder for women to obtain than men; guardianship of children (except when they were very young) rested with the father and his male kinsmen; inheritance rights of daughters were either limited or non-existent. Our contributors from these countries give ample illustration of the practical effect of these limitations, and tell us as much again about the modern changes that are being made. To these we shall return. What of the legal position in the simple family areas of Burma, Thailand, the Philippines, Malaya and Indonesia?

Here daughters traditionally inherited equally with sons; guardianship of children was usually a matter for mutual convenience; divorce-though certainly easier for men in Muslim Malaya and Indonesia-could be initiated by either party; adult women-though with disabilities in Muslim areas-were not regarded as minors. The differences are striking indeed. To try to explain them solely in terms of family structure, however, would be to beg the question. This is where we must look to the wider kinship system in which family structure itself is enmeshed, and with which local customary law is always closely connected. Setting aside the somewhat special case of Ceylon for the moment, we can state formally that the difference between the predominating kinship systems of India, Pakistan, Vietnam, China on the one hand, and Burma, Thailand, the Philippines, Laos, Cambodia, Malaya and the simple family areas of Indonesia (we have in mind mainly the Javanese) on the other, is that whereas the former are patrilineal the latter are what we shall call radial systems.

In the next few paragraphs we explain what we mean by this difference and the ways in which we believe it to be crucial for our subject. When an English-speaking person talks of 'my relatives' he has in mind all those who could be placed anywhere on his own family tree. Each kinsman and kinswoman in the total aggregate of relatives can be imagined as occupying a point on one of the circumferences of a series of concentric circles centred upon the speaker (to whom anthropological jargon usually gives the nickname 'Ego'. The only thing such points necessarily have in common is some kind of radial relationship with the centre of the circles-Ego. This radically reckoned collection of relatives on both sides and in all lines is usually termed Ego's kindred.

His kindred include, of course, his family, but whereas a family is by definition a corporate group (sharing at least residence and a common budget) a kindred is not. Membership of a kindred does not, therefore, entail responsibilities towards all the other members jointly, but simply connects one in a particular way (the way of kinship) with a series of individuals. Whether or not one uses these connections is usually a matter for personal choice, but it is commonly found that people do make use of them for support in illness or other trouble, on ceremonial occasions (such as a family wedding or funeral), and for raising loans, making business contacts and so on.

Every people we know of reckon kinship radically like this. A very large number of peoples, including most Western and South-East Asian peoples, use no other method. The result is that for them families and kindreds, as we have defined them, are the only recognized aggregates of kinsfolk. Such kinship systems are usually termed 'bilateral' or 'non-unilineal'; in some ways the term 'radial' which we have used here is more useful. A pure type of radial system would give equal weighting to males and females, with the result that the monogamous simple family, living separately, would be usual and such kin-linked matters as rights of inheritance would be equally held by both sexes.

Equal balance of this kind does appear to exist in our region among the Iban and the Land Dayak peoples of Borneo, for example, aboriginal peoples whom we have not mentioned before. It is less in evidence among more sophisticated peoples, but very nearly exists among the Burmese, the Filipinos and some others. The kind of upper- and middle-class English system we have just discussed is today approaching the pure type of radial system after a prolonged period of weighting on the male side (probably to be ascribed partly to ecclesiastical and legal influences derived from the patrilineal systems of Judea and ancient Rome); there is some evidence that some lower-class English systems are, or have been, slightly biased towards the female side.

The connection between these differences on the one hand, and differences and changes in the distribution of various kinds of property and in mobility, occupational status, and political, legal and religious pressures on the other, requires much more detailed discussion than we can give it here. But it certainly has a bearing on our subject matter; for it is obvious that the more nearly a radial system of kinship approaches to the pure type, the more equally balanced are the rights and duties, and with them the roles and statuses, of men and women. The countries of our region in which radial systems predominate are Burma, Thailand, Cambodia, Laos, the Philippines, Borneo (which we have not mentioned previously), Malaya and parts of Indonesia. These are, as we should now expect, the simple family areas, and we have already argued some of the consequences for women of this. We can now see that they are also likely to be the areas in which women have equal rights to inherit and own property. And this is so.

But not all these radial systems are of the pure type. The effect of Islam in Malaya and Indonesia, for example, has been to introduce a certain male bias; Robert Fox argues that more than three hundred years of Spanish rule had a somewhat similar effect upon the upper-class systems in the Philippines, now thrown off in so far as legal status is conceived, but lingering still in attitudes; where polygyny exists outside Islam, too, as to some extent, though decreasingly, among the Thais and, still less, the Burmese, an element of male bias is inevitable. (In Laos, on the other hand, the custom of living with or near the wife's parents may impart some female bias, such as has been suggested also for certain areas of working-class England; but a tendency to live nearer the wife's rather than the husband's kin if both are not equally nearby is also reported from Java and elsewhere. It seems likely to be more a matter of practical convenience than of basic family structure. But we shall return to this point again.)

A detailed working out of the various differences between these several radial kinship systems of South-East Asia and their influence upon the reciprocal status and respective roles of men and women in the family and beyond is outside the scope of this essay, but enough has been said to demonstrate their significance. The chapters which follow-particularly Daw Mi Mi Khaing's on Burma, the Hanks' on Thailand and Robert Fox's on the Philippines-provide ample illustration. A glance at the contrast presented by the predominantly patrilineal systems traditional in India, Pakistan and China will make the point even clearer. In these countries, as in many others, the predominant kinship systems are somewhat more complicated. In addition to the radial reckoning of all relatives, there is the custom of emphasizing certain kinds of relatives-those linked by common descent in the male line-more than others. In most Western countries, there is a custom-historically fairly recent-of using surnames.

Though there are variations in their employment, Western surnames are usually handed on from fathers to their sons and unmarried daughters. Women do not transmit surnames to their children. In other words, in so far as the surname in the West is inherited, it is inherited unilineally (i.e., through one parent only)-and indeed patrilineally (i.e., through fathers). It is likely that this fact has helped to introduce some of the male bias we have noted in Western radial systems. (It is noteworthy that there were no surnames in traditional Burma or Thailand, that the Filipino ones were introduced by the Spanish, and that the method of naming after the father used in Malaya and Indonesia is strictly Islamic.) But Western surnames, though they do mark off patrilineally related kin from others, are not in fact much more than useful identification marks. In traditional India, Pakistan, China, the principle of patrilineal descent was taken much further.

Above all, it was a framework for the formation of kin groups of a kind unknown to purely radial kin systems. This may be seen in its clearest form in traditional China. The Chinese use surnames patrilineally inherited by both sons and daughters (traditionally a Chinese woman did not take her husband's surname on marriage). But these were more than mere identification labels. Strictly speaking, it was held that all bearers of the same surname were ultimately descendants of the same distant common ancestor, and as such they were forbidden to marry one another. In its widest extension (stretching over more than 2,000 miles of territory and possibly several mutually unintelligible dialects) a Chinese surname group could contain many hundreds of thousands of individuals.

They could clearly never form a fully corporate group, and indeed their only shared activity was the general interdiction on intermarriage; but even this goes far beyond the requirements of a 'surname group' in radial reckoning Europe. Locally, however, those who bore the same Chinese surname could recognize and trace the details of their common ancestry, and did in fact often form a close-knit corporate unit. In south-east China (the original homeland of most of the Overseas Chinese in our region) it was common to find a whole village occupied solely by members of one such local surname group (and their wives) who organized local surname temples, schools and so on, and regarded themselves as a largely self-contained unit against all the world.

To such groups as these, gaining their membership by shared and traced unilineal descent from a single common known ancestor; social anthropologists give the name 'lineage'. (If, as in this case, descent is derived from fathers, the group is a patrilineage.) Unilineal reckoning does not supersede radial reckoning; it is merely additional to it; so a unilineal kinship system is also radial and can, therefore, form at least three different kinds of kin grouping: families (which may be of varying composition), kindreds and lineages. (The word 'clan' is usually reserved for wider unilineal groupings in which common descent is not actually traced but merely believed in. The widest Chinese surname groups we have just described would be examples.)

Now, in such a system as this, one overriding interest of the lineage is to perpetuate the male line. Daughters are inevitably less valued (though not necessarily less loved) than sons because they cannot help in this-worse; they leave on marriage to become active contributors to the growth of other lineages. Women in the local group are therefore either young unmarried girls or outsiders brought in as wives, essential for the production of new recruits for the lineage, but not themselves birthright members. It is not surprising that they should be regarded as of lower status than adult males who alone are full members. Obviously compatible with this state of affairs is the institution of polygyny-making the higher production of sons per father possible, but necessarily subordinating some women.

Closely connected, too, is the ideal of building up a patrilocal extended family so that property, inherited by sons alone-daughters get a marriage portion which does not break up the estate, but no more-may be held together as long as possible. Again, it is only to be expected that in such a system divorce should be very difficult, if not impossible, and widows and their children should be under the control of the deceased husband's brothers or other male kin. All these things, which we have already noted, are documented in the articles by Ann Wee and Foong Wong below.

In traditional India (we are now writing of the days before the partition of the subcontinent between two separate States) the predominant types of kinship system were not altogether dissimilar from the Chinese. Without either the concept of the surname or the local single lineage villages of South China, most kinship reckoning in India nevertheless emphasized the male line and used it as the framework of family groupings. Like any other patrilocal extended family, the usual Indian 'joint family' (to give it its commonly used legal appellation) comprised in effect a small patrilineal core of males (which could be called a small patrilineage) together with their wives and children.

On marriage the sons (full members) remained, the daughters moved out to make their contribution to the continuation of a different patriline. Property, especially if it consisted of real estate, was ideally kept undivided, being held jointly (not severally) by all male members of the group, relinquished rather than transmitted by those who died and entered into rather than inherited by those who were born. Women held fights to maintenance only. Again it is obvious that such a system sets a premium on polygyny, and against divorce and the remarriage of widows, controlling women in the interests of the group-in effect, of the men-and denying them full property rights or the guardianship of children. In other words it necessarily places them in the position of minors.

It is interesting to note that whereas in the radial system of the Javanese (Indonesia) Islam appears to have imparted a male bias, in the patrilineal system of India it worked to some extent the other way. For under Islam a daughter is entitled to inherit property (though a lesser share than a son), polygyny is limited and divorce and the remarriage of widows are permitted. Thus it was that upper-class Hindu women, who in many parts of India experienced the full influence of patrilineal kinship institutions backed, as Romila Tharpar shows us, by religious sanctions, were in several respects more restricted than their Muslim counterparts. (But, as we have already argued, Islam can impose a stronger control than Hinduism, and when modern changes began to flood in upon

India, Hindu women often profited by them earlier than Muslims.)

As for the radial systems of Java, the relatively slight male bias introduced by Islam seems to have been far less than the male dominance which existed in eighteenth- and nineteenth-century Europe, let alone in the patrilineal systems of India. Islam itself, of course, like *Judaism*, arose in a predominantly patrilineal area where the subordinate status of women was taken for granted. We have now enough material to try to classify traditional (by which we mean, say, the eighteenth- and nineteenth-century) kinship systems of our area. We can place them in a graded series, stretching from the almost pure radial systems of aboriginal Borneo and traditional Burma through the slightly more male-biased radial systems of Laos, Cambodia, Thailand and the Philippines, and the Muslim influenced radial systems of Malaya and Java to the more or less strictly male-dominated patrilineal systems of Muslim India, Hindu India, Vietnam and China. Ceylon, which we have so far omitted, occupies a kind of intermediate position.

Traditional Ceylonese kinship was complex, but in general it appears to have been reckoned radically and to have allowed the inheritance of property by women. However, at least in areas where irrigated land was in short supply, a strong effort was made to meet the difficulties of land division which this would entail by restricting it in practice and building up extended patrilocal families, or, it seems, developing polyandry. Our readers are invited to compare this graded list with the tables we have presented earlier, and to bear it in mind when reading the articles which follow. We believe that the facts recorded in our tables and the articles of our contributors together support our present hypothesis, which is, simply, that the reciprocal statuses of men and women are likely to be more nearly equal, and their respective roles less rigidly demarcated, among people who emphasize the radial rather than the unilineal reckoning of kin relationships.

Matrilineal reckoning requires fuller treatment than we can give it here. It occurs sporadically in our region, notably in Minangkabau (Sumatra, Indonesia) and Negri Sembilan

(Malaya) and elsewhere, but is predominant in none of our countries. Briefly our argument would be that whereas a woman is likely to have a higher lineage status in a matrilineal system than in a patrilineal one, it does not follow that she has a higher status than a man. The point about matriliny is not that women are the recipients of inherited rights and positions (they often are not), but that these things can be transferred only through mothers. The analogy is with the genetic transmission of certain kinds of haemophilia (bleeding disease) which are found only in males but inherited only through females. Although the fact that her children are members of her own lineage group and not his may give a woman a certain measure of independence of her husband in a matrilineal system, her lineage status vis-à-vis her brothers may well be low and her roles relatively circumscribed. Our hypothesis is not affected.

What of modern changes in traditional kinship? In general we see them tending in the direction of pure type radial systems. We have already remarked this tendency in the West, where, it is important to remember, eighteenth- and nineteenth-century systems of kinship, radial though they were, were much more male-biased than most South-East Asian ones. There is every reason to suppose that the essentially similar influences which are at work in the East will have similar effects. One set of influences which we have not so far considered is the legal.

Legal changes are discussed by many of our contributors. The ending of polygamy, the raising of the ages of consent and marriage, the granting of inheritance rights to widows and daughters, and so on-these and similar provisions are aimed directly at raising the status of women. They will have an indirect influence in the same direction too, for they are in effect attacks upon the principle of patrilineal descent and the patrilocal extended family. The degree to which legal changes are effective in practice is said to be small as yet. It is likely to grow.

It will grow because other changes are tending the same way. Anything which gives women the status of full adults in their own right before the law, allows them to own and manage property, gives them access to occupations and contacts outside the home is an attack on strict patriliny. Our contributors show us more than enough examples, and mention in their turn nearly all the innovations we have discussed earlier. We shall dwell upon only one: urbanization. Professor Karim's is the most decided of our contributions on this subject. Women, he tells us, are much freer in the towns than in the villages of Pakistan. Why?

The reasons usually given are many. They include the contrast between the greater conservatism of villages, where everybody knows everybody else and no-one dares to break customary conventions, and the relative anonymity of city life; the break-up of extended family living which the shortage of housing often brings about; the greater opportunities for employment, education, 'Westernization' and so on. Most of these points are valid though their weighting must vary greatly from place to place. It is unfortunate that detailed studies of what really happens when, for example, the members of a strictly patrilineal type of family and kinship unit come to town are so few.

One of the fullest is Maurice Freedman's book on Chinese Family and Marriage in Singapore. This makes it quite clear that one of the most significant concomitants of living in Singapore has been the virtually complete loss of the southern Chinese lineage system and the almost complete disappearance of polygynous extended families of the traditional type. Stephen Morris (in an article in the British Journal of Sociology, 1958) has recorded the somewhat similar disappearance of the legal joint family organization among the Indian and Pakistani immigrants in the towns of East Africa. Can we take it that this kind of thing is typical not only of immigrant communities overseas-obviously cut off from their home ties-but also of modern urbanization in general? It is our suggestion that we can-and that the evidence of our contributors supports us.

We must first distinguish between two conceptually different things: the custom of stressing the patrilineal line in reckoning kinship on the one hand, and the existence of exclusive corporate groups of patrilineal kinsmen on the other. What we wish to draw attention to is the effect upon these two things (in practice usually closely connected) of two particular aspects of modern urban life: first, economic relationships, and second, the legal and administrative framework in which they operate. What a person in a modern town wants is a job, or a commercial or professional contact of some kind. To rely solely on one's patrikin for this would be as obviously foolish as to ignore them if they could be useful. One exploits any and every connection, or better still series of connections: one's acquaintances, friends, friends' friends, co-members in any and all sorts of organization, and, of course, all possible kinsmen. Neither in India nor China was it usual for people to rely on their relatives alone, even traditionally or even in the rural areas, and certainly not on their patrilineal relatives alone; but where matters of essential livelihood were concerned and income was derived from land they were usually more important.

Where income is derived from employment in non-traditional occupations, from commerce, and the professions, as it is in a modern town, this is no longer so. There, radial linkages-in addition to non-kin ties, of course-are more valuable because they are more numerous and wide-spreading. It is probable that commercial businesses and indeed any undertakings that require wide personal contacts (politics, for example) have always had this kind of effect for those who practice them. Be that as it may, we suggest here that in so far as the reckoning of kinship is concerned an economic system such as we find in most modern towns adds weight to radial rather than merely unilineal methods.

This might not necessarily weaken the use of patriliny for group formation, however, as the long continued existence of patrilocal extended families in many trading communities' shows. A more direct attack upon patrilineal groupings appears to come from the legal and administration and the provision of certain social services-especially Ann Wee both have something to say on this topic, in addition to the points we have already raised. Our present comments are confined to economic matters. The traditional South Chinese patrilineage never had much economic importance. Its practical *raison d'étre* was closely bound up with the management of relationships with a particular form of local administration and the provision of certain social services-especially education-for its members.

Neither of these tasks is necessary in the modern city of Singapore, or, indeed, in any well-run modern city. Even the substitutes for local lineage organization which developed in the early days among Singapore Chinese are now largely redundant. Different factors can lead to somewhat similar results for the traditional patrilocal joint family of India and Pakistan. It should be obvious that in writing of this we do not have in mind the poorer sections of the population but the rather better-off who in traditional times would have built up extended families based solidly on joint property. Their modern counterparts are the people who now go ahead in business, the professions and the higher salaried positions. But it is hardly possible for any of these occupations to be run as a joint family enterprise today.

It is true that a pair of brothers may be partners, or a father and his sons form a company, and that various forms of so-called 'nepotism' may be discerned in the allocation of salaried posts; but none of these things is necessarily an indication of the persistence of the joint family in the strict legal sense, or even of the custom of living together in extended families. After all, similar 'familial' links can be found in similar concerns throughout the world, including many places where there is no tradition of extended family living or joint family property at all. Moreover-and this is the point-the legal and administrative framework of modern economic institutions is a modern innovation, developed originally in the West, different in principle from that of the joint family. This is obvious for institutions employing salaried workers, but is no less true for partnerships or companies whose members hold shares (for shares are owned severally not jointly), and they can be withdrawn.

Thus, to use the distinction drawn by Maine, the modern relationship between partners is contractual; the traditional relationship between members of a joint family was one of status. Once this change has been made, and property is no longer jointly held, the peculiar legal structure of the joint family-which we insisted earlier was its distinguishing mark-is destroyed. What is left may well be some kind of extended family dwelling group, bound by strong ties of affection and feelings of mutual dependence and obligation, which find expression in mutual assistance of all kinds and also in continued co-participation in family ritual observances. But these things alone do not constitute a 'joint family' in the strict (i.e., legal) sense.

Furthermore, as our contributors show us, once the element of legal jointness has been removed, the component units of an extended family often set up separate households, though, of course, there is continued visiting, mutual assistance, and sharing in family rituals and ceremonies (as, indeed, there is between related families in radial kinship systems which have never developed extended family organization at all). It is interesting to note too-as Morris did in East Africa-how often at the present time business partners are in fact not patrilineal kinsmen at all. We conclude, then, that the economic, administrative, and legal systems of modern towns are such that while they lend weight to radial (and non-kin) linkages they also undermine the importance of patriliny as a principle in the formation of corporate groups.

The full working out of these tendencies is likely to be a slow process; at present all stages of the change are still to be seen. Moreover, by no means all towns are 'modern' in the respects we have picked out, and even in truly modern towns traditional occupations continue to be organized along largely traditional lines. Nevertheless, we claim that the trend away from patriliny is plainly built in to modern urbanization. Indeed we go further and suggest that it is built in to modern economic systems in general. It is only because in our region towns are in effect still the only centers of modern economic organization that this appears to be an urban phenomenon. It will spread.

It is likely, of course, that however rapid economic development proves to be pockets of traditional economic structure will linger for a very long time, much as small-holding ('peasant') farming and family trades businesses still continue in the modern West. As far as kinship organization is concerned, however, this will make little difference to our prediction, for, as we have already seen, such small-scale enterprises as these were not usually organized in extended family units anyway, nor did their members pay much attention to lineage organization where this existed, either. In any event, the majority of the population is likely to be caught up in the developing modern systems, and as these will also be those of the well-to-do they will set the standard.

What will this standard be? We have argued a general tendency in the direction of a pure type radial system of kinship. Our earlier argument leads us to expect two interrelated concomitants of this: first, the general appearance of simple ('nuclear') family units, and second, the more equal balance of status and role between the sexes. But other modern developments are working in the same direction. Urban housing, the need for mobility of labour, 'Westernization'-all require the simple family; modern world opinion demands the raising of the status of women. So, too, does modern economic growth which probably depends, even more than on the increasing employment of women as well as men, upon an increasingly numerous and discriminating set of consumers.

Because of their special position in the family, wives and mothers are potentially society's most active buyers; but as long as the status of women is relatively low, and their role relatively restricted, the full effect of this particular spur to economic growth will not be felt. Our previous hypothesis was that the relative statuses of men and women were likely to be more equal and their respective roles less rigidly demarcated in societies which emphasized radial rather than unilineal methods of reckoning kinship. If we have now established that one of the particular effects of modern change in general is the strengthening of radial and the undermining of unilineal relationships, we can put forward the further hypothesis that modern socioeconomic development favours the greater equality of the sexes-and not only in South and South-East Asia.

THE QUESTION OF COMPATIBILITY

It will appear to many of our readers that we have left the most obviously important aspects of modern changes until last. If it is a fact that women everywhere spend most of their time on domestic tasks, then surely the things that really matter to them as individuals are the layout of their houses, their access to water supplies, their furnishings, pots and pans, and methods of cooking, the kinds of clothes they and their families wear and how these are made and mended and washed? And surely when a family moves to town or a village improvement scheme gets under way or imported cloth and processed foods replace the home-made varieties, these are just the matters that change most quickly and easily?

Of course this is largely true. We have touched upon it in our discussion of modern communications. If we do not describe it further here it is because we do not feel it necessary to anticipate what our contributors can and do tell us so much more expertly from their own first-hand experience. In any case, the extent to which such strictly technological changes, vitally important though they may be in affecting almost every aspect of daily life, lead actually to changes in the respective roles of men and women is problematical. Is the division of labour between the sexes affected by, say, the fact that cloth is now imported and no longer woven at home, or cooking done on a gas stove instead of a charcoal *chatti*?

Potentially much more important for role change than changes in the techniques of domestic work are changes in its organization. We have frequently referred to the indirect contribution to these which the 'enabling' nature of some technical innovations makes. Sometimes there is a direct connection; the design of living accommodation in a tenement block in, say, Singapore, which makes impossible the traditional separation between the men's and the women's quarters of a Malay house is an example. Sometimes role changes are connected with the adoption of new medical or hygienic measures; for instance, Javanese husbands who traditionally played a responsible and important part at the birth of their babies are now shooed out of the way by modern medically trained midwives. More often, however, role changes within the family seem to stem from such changes in the family's own structure and organization.

A simple family is a very different work group from an extended family. Because only one adult of each sex is present, even the most rigid traditional sexual division of labour cannot always be maintained. We have argued that this fact helps to raise the status of a wife and extend her activities; but there is another set of factors we have not considered. Experience of the 'isolated' simple family in the West-removed from all kin, unable to rely on neighbours for help, and without domestic servants-shows it to be only barely a viable unit, especially if (as is usual) the husband is employed away from home. As long as all goes well, no-one is ill or incapacitated, and the children are fairly widely spaced out, this domestic unit can be self-contained-given hard work and sensible management on the part of the wife; but sickness, too many children too close to one another, the additional work caused by the presence of, say, an invalid mother or an elderly father-in-law, any of these things can make it impossible to manage.

The development of social services, the custom of putting old people into institutions, and the determination to control birth spacing and numbers in the West should be seen in the light of this organizational fact at least as much as in purely economic or psychological terms. Moreover-and this is a point we wish to stress-there can be no doubt that one of the factors which today make further change in the respective roles of Western men and women difficult is the relative isolation of the simple family, for this necessarily creates a practical incompatibility between the role of wife-mother and the role of worker outside the home-at least during the years of child bearing and child rearing. Are we therefore faced with the paradox that the predictable spread of the simple family, which we have argued augers a less restricted set of social roles for women and their improved status, carries within itself also the denial of these things?

There are, in fact, various possible solutions. They include the widespread development of specialized domestic services, whether commercially or through governmental agencies, the employment of household servants and, of course, the removal of 'isolation'. The first has hardly been fully worked out anywhere in the world as yet, though the social services in certain European countries go a long way towards it. It seems likely that if increasing economic growth makes increasing demands for women workers such services will be widely extended. At present they barely exist anywhere in the Orient.

In most parts of South and South-East Asia, however, household servants are still easily available, and the isolation of the simple family is also far from complete. In the traditional simple family areas of Burma, the Philippines, Indonesia and so on, it is usual for a couple to set up house after marriage near one or other (often both) of their parental homes, with the result that practical assistance is always at hand-as it is also for the so-called 'matrifocal' clusters of families found in many settled areas of, for example, working-class England. But we do not need to dwell on these matters. Our middleclass contributors are all well aware that in this respect change of role are easier for them than for their Western counterparts today; they are also much concerned for the future of their daughters and grand-daughters in the coming years, when household servants may well be hard to find and families may well be both simple and scattered.

Mrs. Subandrio's article is of particular interest in this connection. A woman of great achievement outside the home, she is also the wife of Indonesia's Foreign Minister and a mother in a Javanese simple family. She has several ways of dealing with the practical business of organizing this apparently rather complicated series of roles. There are household servants; there are commercial suppliers of excellent cooked meals; there are close relatives nearby on whom she can rely but to whom she is not at all subordinate in the running of her own home. The result is that in fact her several roles are not incompatible.

She herself makes another point. Nowadays, she tells us, sons as well as daughters are being taught to take their share in domestic work. If this means that a Javanese man can, without loss of dignity, perform what are usually considered women's tasks it is of more than practical significance, for it implies a flexibility of attitude towards the sexual division of labour which is not found everywhere in our region-or in many parts of the West-and which where it exists must help to make some modern changes relatively easy. By contrast, a rigid sex-typing of occupations can make change difficult, for it may lead to such a close identification of occupation with sex that it becomes impossible for a man to perform 'women's work' without loss of 'manliness', or for a woman to perform 'men's work' without diminution of 'femininity'. These are usually not strictly practical but what we have earlier called ideological incompatibilities.

Our previous argument might lead us to expect greater flexibility in this respect in the traditionally more purely radial- and simple family-kinship systems, of which Java's is certainly one. But there are other factors too. It is sometimes suggested that it is relatively easier for women to enter paid occupations in the new nations of the world than in the West simply because most occupations there are too new to have been given any rigid sex-typing as yet. If there is no tradition of, for example, modern medicine at all, so the argument runs, then there can be no traditional sexual allocation of the role of doctor. Similarly, if women are prominent in pharmacy, for instance, as they are in Vietnam, this is because pharmacy is a new occupation without any traditional sex linkage.

There may be something in this argument, but it ignores the possible carry-over from traditional occupations which were similar if not identical with modern ones (after all, healing is not a new art), and fails to notice that the sexual division of labour in many a new nation often follows that current in the Western nation which has most influenced it. Pharmacy is popular among women in France as well as Vietnam; employees in textiles are predominantly female all over the world; transport and communications work is strikingly masculine in most parts of both East and West; the majority of pre-university teachers are women in the United States of America as well as in the Philippines. On the other hand there are important divergences from this pattern. Typists and secretaries, in the West so often female, are in our region predominantly male, and most countries of South and South-East Asia can show large numbers of women working in unskilled tasks on construction and road building which in the West are performed either by machines or exclusively by men.

These last two examples, however different from modern Western practices, are closely similar to those of the nineteenth century when, as in the modern East, secondary schooling-essential for office work -was still primarily for boys, and the harder manual work had not yet been legislated out of the hands of the poorer women. Fashions as to the belief in compatibility between certain occupations and the 'natural' physiological and personality characteristics of the two sexes vary historically as well as geographically. There is one further problem of compatibility which is crucial to our subject matter. It arises from the family role of men, which despite our earlier protestations we have so far almost entirely neglected. In most of the countries of our region-probably most in the world-the chief nurturing role within the family is a female one.

Men may take part in it, or not. But there are other roles equally necessary which are predominantly male. Two in particular, the roles of chief breadwinner and of holder of authority and power, are discussed very fully by our contributors below. Closely allied with them is a third: the role of status giver. Almost everywhere in the world a family's prestige and status are judged according to the prestige and status of its senior male members. This is probably because in most societies-and our region is no exception, as we have seen-men take a larger part-in the occupational, political, religious and legal systems of society at large, and thus have the main responsibility for their families' relationship to it, and are seen as their representatives.

It appears to follow that a woman-certainly a married woman-is allotted the prestige and status of her husband (in a simple family; her father-in-law in an extended family). A social system which permits married women to participate in occupational, political, religious and legal roles outside the home may thus create considerable difficulties if such women are then allocated prestige and status in their own right. What if the status of husband and wife are incompatible? What if the wife stands higher than the husband-to whose status shall the family be allocated? Social systems which do not permit women to compete with men at all certainly avoid this problem. In other words they obviate any possible incompatibility between the status of husband and wife (father-in-law and daughters-in-law) by postulating an absolute incompatibility between the roles of men and women. We have already argued that such rigid sex-typing as this makes change particularly difficult.

We suggest that the social system traditional to Pakistan was of this kind. Other systems allow women to compete in certain occupations only-as actresses, for example, or in other kinds of entertainment in which they can have a prestige ranking in their own right, but at the expense of being altogether déclassées in the 'respectable' world of the regular (male) stratification system. Several Western countries have fallen into this category at certain periods of their history; so also, we suggest, did traditional China, Japan and probably India at certain periods. Change in such countries will not be easy, for women must face the charge of being not only unfeminine but also disreputable. (The example of Florence Nightingale comes to mind immediately.) Once fairly launched, however, women may well find change less difficult in such a system, for at least the walls have been partially breached.

A third method of dealing with the problem is to allow women to enter freely into most occupations, leaving questions of status and prestige to be settled in a different sphere altogether-as in Burma, for example, where men have prestige built in to their manhood and recognized in their superior religious status with which women by definition cannot compete. A rather similar system seems to obtain in Thailand, and probably also in Cambodia and Laos. Most occupational changes here are likely to be relatively painless, at least as long as the religious system holds its prestige. But there is one exception. Because status (in our usage) is necessarily associated with power it can never in fact be a purely spiritual attribute. It is not an accident that, despite their long tradition of relatively unrestricted access to occupations outside the home, Burmese, Thai, Cambodian and Laotian women have not entered political life in any numbers or really competed for authority in any sphere.

Our contributors make it perfectly clear that this situation is gladly accepted along with the religion which entails it; it is a religion which also holds out prospects of future rebirth in masculine form and does nothing to limit the very wide choice of secular occupations in this life which the kinship systems of these countries permit. By contrast, the Republic of the Philippines, with a similar kinship system and a similarly wide choice of occupations outside the home, but with Roman Catholic Christianity instead of Theravâda Buddhism, is one of the few countries of our region which has produced a strong feminist movement. It is not suggested that these three ways of trying to meet the problem of avoiding ambiguities in allocating family status exhaust the sociological possibilities, but they do illustrate the main differences in our region.

A complication enters the picture when a man's prestige (if not his status), and therefore the children's, depends in part upon his wife's assisting him in his career, especially in its public social aspects. Hitherto this has been largely a Western phenomenon. Dr. and Mrs. Hanks have interesting things to say about its adoption in Thailand, where women have up till now played roles in the secular and nonpolitical world in their own right, and left questions of status largely to their husbands. The Hanks see this piece of 'Westernization' as a threat to women's personal independence, and predict revulsion from it once Thai women fully appreciate what is happening. In other words, they see Western women as being considerably less independent than their Thai sisters.

The arguments we have put forward above prepare us not only to agree with this view, but to maintain that it holds good for several other aspects of the mutual roles and relationships of men and women and for several other parts of South and South-East Asia as well. We shall not recapitulate the various points this essay has tried to raise. We have made some tentative sociological analyses in general terms, using mainly the concepts of role and status. We should, however, be the first to insist that role analysis alone cannot be exhaustive, and further, that even the fullest sociological analysis alone cannot give complete explanation. It is for our readers to decide, from the detailed studies of particular countries and the personal documents which follow, how far our present essay goes towards this desirable ideal.

Bibliography

Adburgham, Alison. *Women in Print. Writing Women and Women's Magazines from Restoration to the Accession of Victoria.* London: Allen & Unwin, 1972.

Arnold, Ethel M. *Literature for Ladies, 1830-1930.* Manhattan: K.S.A.C. Press, 1930.

Barrell, Joan. *The Business of Women's Magazines.* 2nd ed. London: Kogan Page, 1988.

Beetham, Margaret. *Victorian Women's Magazines : An Anthology.* Manchester: Manchester University Press, 2001.

Boston Women's Health Book Collective. *Our Bodies Ourselves.* New York: Simon & Schuster, 1976.

Braithwaite, Brian. *The Business of Women's Magazines: The Agonies and the Ecstasies.* London: Associated Business Press, 1979.

Braithwaite, Brian. *Women's Magazines: The First 300 Years.* London: Peter Owen, 1995.

Brody, Michal, ed. *Are We There Yet? A Continuing History of Lavender Woman.* Iowa City; Aunt Lute Company, 1985.

Burman, Barbara, ed. *The Culture of Sewing: Gender, Consumption and Homedressmaking (Dress, Body, Culture).* Oxford: Berg, 1999.

Coakley, Mary Lewis. *1907-Sex, Sisterhood, and Self-Delusion: What Happened to Women's Magazines?* New Rochelle: Arlington House, c. 1979.

Dancyger, Irene. *A World of Women. An Illustrated History of Women's Magazines.* Dublin: Gill and Macmillian, 1978.

Danky, James P., ed. *Women's Periodicals and Newspapers from the 18th Century to 1981: A Union List of the Holdings of Madison, Wisconsin Libraries.* Boston: GK Hall, 1982.

Doughan, David, and Denise Sanchez. *Feminist Periodicals, 1855-1984: An Annotated Critical Bibliography of British, Irish, Commonwealth and International Titles.* Brighton: Harvester, 1987.

Eskridge, Melissa J. *How the Psychology of Women Is Presented in Women's Magazines,* 1986.

Ferguson, Marjorie. *Forever Feminine: Women's Magazines and the Cult of Femininity.* London: Heinemann, 1983.

Friedan, Betty. *The Feminine Mystique.* New York: Dell Publishing Co., Inc., 1963.

Gough-Yates, Ann. *Understanding Women's Magazines: Publishing, Markets and Readership.* London: Routledge, 2003.

Grimstad, Kirsten and Susan Rennie, eds. *The New Woman's Survival Catalog.* New York: Berkley Publishing Corporation, 1973.

Hermes, Joke. *Reading Women's Magazines: An Analysis of Everyday Media Use.* Cambridge: Polity Press, 1995.

Hoffmann, Phyllis P. *Women's Magazines.* 1983.

Incantalupo, Patricia. *The Portrayal of Women in Sport Advertising in Two Women's Fitness Magazines,* 1992.

Johnson, Judy M, ed. *Spot Illustrations from Women's Magazines of the Teens and Twenties: 828 Cuts of Women, Family, Home, Garden, Etc.* New York: Dover Publications, 1989.

Mann, Robert S. "Women and the Newspaper." *The University of Missouri Bulletin,* no. 2640.

Millum, Trevor. *Images of Woman: Advertising in Women's Magazines.* London: Chatto & Windus, 1975.

Ramet, Adèle. *Creating a Twist in the Tale: How to Write Winning Short Stories for Women's Magazines.* Plymouth: How To Books, 1996.

Shevelow, Kathryn. *Women and Print Culture: The Construction of Femininity in the Early Periodical.* London: Routledge, 1989.

Sievers, Sharon L. *Flowers in Salt: The Beginnings of Feminist Consciousness in Modern Japan.* Stanford: Stanford University Press, 1983.

Waller, Jane, and Michael Vaughan-Rees. *Women in Wartime; the Role of Women's Magazines 1939-1945.* London: Macdonald Optima, 1987.

White, Cynthia L. "Growth between the Wars: 1920-1938." In *Women's Magazines 1693-1968.* London: Michael Joseph Ltd, 1970.

White, Cynthia L. *Women's Magazines 1693-1968.* London: Michael Joseph Ltd, 1970.

Winship, Janice. *Advertising in Women's Magazines, 1956-74.* Birmingham: Centre for Contemporary Cultural Studies, University of Birmingham, 1980.

Winship, Janice. *Inside Women's Magazines.* New York: Pandora, 1987.

Yackey, Lena Millicent. *Contributions of Women's Magazines to Homemaking Problems on Food.* New York, 1930.

INDEX

A

Abolition, 98.
Anthropological Works, 7.
Archaic Patriarchal, 7.
Asian babe, 19.
Audio-visual Education, 51.

B

Benevolence of Charity, 3.
Bidri Ware, 87.
Bread-winner, 187.

C

Capitalism, 13.
Child-bearers, 29.
Colonial Masculinity, 5.
Conformist, 4.
Cross Section-men, 73.
Crotchety, 123.

D

Development Studies, 11.
Dogma, 3.
Dollar Remittances, 140.
Doubt Gaining Ground, 46.

E

Entrepreneurship, 137.
Extreme Case, 193.

F

Financial Debacle, 133.
Front-line State, 103.

G

Globalisation Encompasses, 161.
Grandiose Dreams, 151.

H

Hand Pounding Rice, 87.
Health Frankly, 120.
Heteronomous - ethnology, 1
Home Economics Wings, 65
Homogeneous Country, 86
Hot Topic,16

I

Imperial Ladies, 6.
Implement Reengineered, 139
Interstitial Ways, 5
Interventionist Policies, 133

K

Khaki Cloth, 87

L

Long-term Interests, 157

M

Managerial Categories, 7
Melodramatic Constructions, 1, 20
Metropolis, 6
Mid-market, 151
Migrant Cartographies, 17
Mill-made Yarn, 87
Multiracial Marriage, 121
Multiracial Society, 122

O

Occult, 17

P

Paranoia-ethnic Division, 103
Patriarchal, 13
Pedagogy, 1
Politburo, 91
Political Emancipation, 174
Politically Immature Societies, 133
Polling Clerks, 90
Post-crisis Streng, 131
Post-romanticism, 3
Poultry Raising, 66
Prolonged Struggle, 93

R

Race, 13
Race-resistant, 11
Racial Contract, 6
Rehabilitation Periods, 72
Rescue Paradigm, 5

S

Sophistication, 17
Spur Regional Recovery, 160
Subaltern Female, 1
Subaltern Women, 11

T

Tailspin, 156
Thin-skinned Government, 159
Time-consuming Process, 97
Tongas, 47
Town-dwellers, 189
Transferential Relationship, 3
Trenchant Pieces, 121
Typical Oriental Womanhood, 172

V

Vast Archipelago, 104
Vested Interests, 89
Voluntary Workers, 98
Volunteer Social Workers, 77
Voyeuristic Pleasure, 6

W

Wage-earner Working, 187

Y

Yardstick, 8